Hiking Alone

HIKING ALONE
Trails Out, Trails Home

TEXT AND ILLUSTRATIONS BY

Mary Beath

UNIVERSITY OF NEW MEXICO PRESS

ALBUQUERQUE

© 2008 by the University of New Mexico Press
All rights reserved. Published 2008
Printed in the United States of America

13 12 11 10 09 08   1 2 3 4 5 6

Library of Congress Cataloging-in-Publication Data

Beath, Mary, 1950–
Hiking alone : trails out, trails home /
        text and illustrations by Mary Beath.
        p. cm.
ISBN 978-0-8263-4329-1 (pbk. : alk. paper)
1. Beath, Mary, 1950–
2. Poets, American—21st century—Biography.
I. Title.
        PS3602.E263Z46 2008
        811'.6—dc22
        [B]
                        2007046304

Barry Lopez quote from *Arctic Dreams* reprinted by permission of Charles Scribner's Sons,
an imprint of Macmillan Publishing Company. Copyright © 1986 Barry Holstun Lopez.

"Dancing In the Dark" by Bruce Springsteen. Copyright © 1984 Bruce Springsteen
(ASCAP). Reprinted by permission. International copyright secured. All rights reserved.

"Zuni Maize" originally appeared in *Canyon Gardens*. Copyright © 2006 V. B. Price and
Baker H. Morrow.

This is a work of nonfiction, but the author has changed the names and specific details of
some people in the book to protect their privacy.

Drawing on page 190-91 from photo reference of Mimbres black-on-white bowl
ca AD 950–1150 from *Within the Underworld Sky, Mimbres Ceramic Art in Context*
by Barbara L. Moulard (Twelvetrees Press, 1984).

for my father

Paul Robert Beath

1905–1982

Contents

Open Ground

An Introduction

Twenty-two years ago I stepped out of the Phoenix airport into a blowing April afternoon: dry, not hot, the air hissing with constant wind sounds. I'd never been in the Southwest—I lived in New York City then—and no one but Andy, the person I'd come to visit, knew where I was. Immediately I paused in some confusion and looked around. An unfamiliar inner voice said clearly, "I belong here." We drove back roads to Andy's place in Tucson, and the feeling only grew stronger as we passed open desert scrub, more and more saguaros, the lonesome monument marking the death of silent film's original cowboy Tom Mix, finally the foothills of the looming Catalinas. That became the first of many visits. Eventually I spent two years alternating two weeks in New York, two weeks in Tucson, in a semibicoastal romance—partly with Andy, partly with the desert itself. My attachment to the land has proven to be the stronger and more enduring love.

In recent years many writers have explored the tensions between the myths of the West and the realities of the New West. For almost twenty years I've lived in New Mexico, an embarrassingly short time compared with those whose roots extend back generations. But I've been here long enough to learn about an unending list of controversies, from water issues to toxic-waste disposal to development pressures to immigration conundrums to tribal sovereignty. I know much has been lost and how much more is threatened. I understand the difference between the

1

West as a symbol of freedom and the ground truth of the heartbreaking destruction of places and ways of life.

But despite many changes, the West still exists: vast space, clear light, astonishing landforms, violent and extreme weather, isolated ranches, extravagant gestures, people looking for a new start. It still works its magic, not only with imagined possibilities, but with its literal presence.

In many ways my story is an old one, so familiar it almost seems iconic. Go west. Unbind. Connect to the land. Link your inner journey with your outer one. As a woman, unblock your voice and speak your experience. But within those broad outlines, any individual life unfolds in a complex way, despite threats from the modern impulse toward over-simplification. I've largely lived outside this culture's expectations for women, always giving my own direction—creative work, curiosity, exploration—equal weight with the desire for love, connection, and career. Even when that direction seemed unclear, I've persisted, traveling multiple paths: in science and natural history, in the visual arts, and more recently as a somewhat astonished award-winning poet. My life has been happily zigzaggy.

This story also acknowledges the tenacity of knots tied in childhood—even knots that were collateral damage in a loving and well-meaning family—and the unexpected ways they can loosen.

For ten years in New York City, I lived the way many people in the arts live, cobbling together jobs that paid the bills while I also did my own work, or tried to. In my case I hired out as a graphic designer, mostly for *Artforum* magazine and for a successful design studio half-owned by an art school friend, whose clients came from the financial industry. Periodically, windfall book-illustration projects appeared, projects that required my science background in addition to my drawing skills. "My own work" presented more problems. I believed it should be abstract and visual, an extension of the work I'd made in art school, informed by current cultural ideas. But no coherent body of work emerged; my efforts were swamped by the difficulties of New York life and by the endless and addictive adventures the City offered. Tucson's attractions included not only Andy and the desert but also unencumbered time to explore what "my own work" meant.

Since *Artforum* took off two months for vacation, I headed out for six weeks alone during the second Tucson summer, planning to drive from trailhead to trailhead, hike the backcountry, and see what I might find. By that time Andy had begun to chafe under my constant goings and comings and welcomed my absence. I returned with a photo project chronicling that trip. A small arts press published it later that year as a book called *LAND*: black-and-white photographs, many of blown-up details of stones or water or grasses, human-free except for the eye behind the camera. On each large photo, four small close-ups of my own body parts—taken with a cable release back in Tucson—form a square: a knee, or a bent thumb, or the hollow at the base of my throat where collar bones meet, or the swell of a breast under a white T-shirt. Along the bottom of each page, a strip of contact prints of the same location as the larger image provides a clearer context. The book contains almost no words, only a list of locations and an introductory quote from *Arctic Dreams* by Barry Lopez: "The differing landscapes of the earth are hard to know individually. They are as difficult to engage in conversation as wild animals."

Over time that quote has changed for me. Then, I understood it to mean I *had* engaged in some sort of conversation with the landscape, however mute and tentative. The images and their juxtapositions are frankly sensual, suggesting the often wordless physical contact of sex. The conversation of body with body. Now, in addition to those echoes between flesh and stone, between human presence and wildness, the quote seems freighted with the enormous effort involved in bridging separations. In the words I chose then, the hope of real, reciprocal "conversation" remains faint, the sense of isolation and distance much stronger.

I meant the book to be a modest record of my deepening physical identification with the land. An old idea, woman = nature, but grounded in my own experience, intensified by my solitude—I rarely spoke to anyone and only ventured indoors to pay for gas or to buy food—it became a touchstone for the release I felt in the West, an inkling of what else might be possible beyond what I'd so far found.

I *didn't* understand then that though the trip seemed short on revelations, it had made possible a crucial shift. Not only did I leave New York and move to Albuquerque the next summer, but in the openness of the high desert, I began to reclaim words.

My relationship with language had long been ambivalent: from childhood on I'd read widely, loving abstract ideas as well as complex stories, but I also had a deep shyness about speaking myself. My low voice sounded odd to my ears, for one thing. But more to the point, my quiet served to keep my sweet veneer intact. Self-exposure seemed dangerous, a way that I might become vulnerable to others' definitions of me. Especially when I was growing up, those definitions seemed to lead to culture's narrow expectations for women. One cultural message: "Don't do it alone, whatever it is, or you'll end up a victim, or at the very least, a lonely, regretful outcast." And I wanted no part of that restrictive world. Yet I didn't have the power or self-confidence to be vocal about my opposition, so I conformed externally with my silence and shyness.

Only in the relative safety of home would I chance any disobedience. "You're just so contrary," my grandmother would growl in her mild Appalachian accent whenever I resisted her control, whether overtly or passively. I grew up as an only child in a household with my parents and grandparents, and she attributed my temperamental defiance to the Devil's mischief. That worried me for some years until I finally recognized my objection to authority, stereotypes, and conventional dogma might be healthy.

But those prescribed behaviors from my childhood seemed like traps, efforts to fix me in formaldehyde. And that early need for camouflage, necessary for me to maintain what mattered most of my self, translated into a long-standing way of perceiving the world—as a series of traps I needed to avoid or to wiggle out of, as honorably as I could manage. A quick list will suffice: I've never been married, though I've had several long-term loving (but rarely monogamous) relationships; I have no children; for years I owed no money and resisted taking on a mortgage; since college I've always supported myself; except for three years early on, I've been my own boss.

Visual art—especially abstraction—seemed a safe sort of expression. I could *imply* many things without getting down to any self-revealing details. Words, however, required me to be more specific and to figure out what I meant in order to say it. As I relaxed into my New Mexico life, first I found I could speak more and more easily; then I began to write, finding the process much more satisfying than anything I'd ever done. My inner world seemed to loosen and expand to reflect the land around me.

These essays relate to each other in several ways. They all involve the natural world. They're about an independent woman pursuing adventures that include self-exploration. And they're about the tensions and synergies between mind and nature, the rational and the nonrational.

But when I began to link these pieces together into a loose narrative, I recognized a deeper thread. I saw that each piece traced a variation on the most tenacious of my realities: my deep unease with constriction—fear of traps—and my efforts to unbind from that gripping, in whatever guise it appeared. These essays explore the territory between limitation, with its threat of suffocation, and a greater openness combined with trust. They're about learning to inhabit my own life in a less self-conscious and self-protecting way. They're about hiking alone. They're about hiking with others without losing my self. They're about abandoning my attachment to traps.

The book itself follows a similar trajectory. New York City is a wild place of mostly *human* nature, filled with unending options. Despite the City's richness, it became for me increasingly tight, geographically and emotionally. After my summer wandering alone in the West, I packed my books and my hopes and crossed the hundredth meridian. Together, the essays relate a tale of unfolding and of claiming a deeper involvement in my own experience as I've worked to break down the barriers between inner awareness and the outer flux. The surprising inner voice that spoke to me when I first felt desert wind didn't mark the start of that craving, but it did signal an indispensable change. *I belong here.* As I've become more familiar with my new place on the map, I've found I can use my capacities and increasing knowledge to help protect it. And my growing joy and comfort in the land has been accompanied by the opening any deep love engenders.

These pieces also trace an unexpected path from one sort of daily life to another. For years I militantly maintained my self-reliance and independence, spending much of my time happily alone without loneliness, the pleasures of solitude frequently interrupted with the joys of connection without domestication. I felt like a feral creature, even though I lived in the city. Now I've come to a life that seems to impinge little on my need to choose my own direction, but has expanded to include another human, with our constant dances together, and a small grey dog named Gunther, whose unabashed insistence on being just who he is, with no camouflage, continues to be a delight-filled example of a healthy way to live in the world.

When I began working on these pieces about a decade ago, every morning for several years—without fail—I would get up, make tea, and write one page in a green six-by-nine-inch notebook. I meant only to prime the pump for my other writing, with no expectation, or even wish, that the words would ever become public; therefore my internal censor—the one orchestrating my camouflage—left me alone as I filled page after page. But as I began reading them to friends, it became clear a selection might make a book. In 2005 *Refuge of Whirling Light* was published, and I had to swallow my terror—not too strong a word—at the impending self-exposure. To my surprise, the book has either won or been a finalist for three poetry awards. I can't ignore the lesson, well-known, but often hard to remember in the presence of fear: only if you open your heart, reveal intimate (and sometimes embarrassing) truths, and make yourself vulnerable, can you touch others in a meaningful way. I hope in these essays I've continued along that trail.

A snow last winter, huge by the Rio Grande Valley's standards, snapped off a large branch from the gnarly Mexican elder that guards my weathered back gate. In the last few days new leaves have covered the remaining stump of the broken branch, and I expect the tree to grow back the green curtains that make a shadowy bower near its main trunk. On my list of warm-weather tasks, I note that I need to replace the irrigation valve just beyond the four-year-old cottonwoods and clean up dried wildflower stalks from last fall. The path through the native-grass meadow has gotten overgrown and needs attention. I hope that if I fertilize the grape vines soon, they'll produce more fruit in July. On the part of the barn that used to be a goat shed, the roof would leak less if I slathered some more black gunk on its long-standing cracks. Already I've spotted the roadrunners that nest at the far edge of the back half acre; in the summer they lurk by the garden to hunt striped whiptails, those quick lizards with long blue tails. This afternoon, before the sandhill cranes begin their migration north, I'll take Gunther for a run in the wide alfalfa fields just down the road. In the next few days, I'll begin plans for a trip at the end of April to Paradox Valley in southwestern Colorado. Not minding the occasional misguided bee, I leave the kitchen door open to the warm, dry spring wind.

The Brilliant Air

When I found myself in Houston with a few hours to spare, I made a pilgrimage to the Rothko Chapel. I knew nothing about it, except that many had praised its quiet transcendence: art critics, Presbyterians, the Mevlani Whirling Dervishes, the Dalai Lama. I knew Rothko's luminous paintings, the way they floated off the canvas, hovered in consciousness. I thought I was prepared. But when I walked into the chapel, his enormous black canvases stopped me cold. They hung on the walls of a harmoniously proportioned octagonal space. They surrounded clean-lined central benches. The room pulsed with quiet. *Très élégante*. But at once my chest tightened and my eyes began to tear.

I'm in the presence of the oppressor.

This high-art heresy made me squirm, but I can't deny what I felt. Suffocation by the static. Equilibrium not as dynamic balance, but as extinguished movement. I recalled Rothko had killed himself. He'd been trying to come to terms with the Ultimate as Abstraction. Or the Abstract as Ultimate. I doubted he wandered much. I stayed an hour, working to breathe deeply, trying not to panic. Then I walked across the carefully kept lawn to The Menil Collection. There I unexpectedly found myself in galleries filled with the antithesis of the abstract: Oceanic art, African sculpture, innumerable Cycladic figures from early Greece. Every piece throbbed with life, with the specific, with the multiplicity of this world, despite its glassed-in, guarded state. I felt waves of relief.

My tent sits at the upstream end of a small island, on an exposed crescent of smooth, cliff-colored stones: rust-red, dun, ash-grey, ivory, black. The dawn river glows and shimmers. Across the pale peach sky, a peregrine streaks toward the brightening canyon wall, her long pointed wings beating hard. In a breath she vanishes behind a blunt sandstone fin, then as abruptly reappears in unbounded air above the rock and rushing water.

Periodically I'm gripped by a black fury. It always arrives hard upon the same grim mire: I'm wrapped with invisible sticky threads; every part of my life has sprouted hooks and an anchor. The hooks hooked in me. No anesthetic. What I crave to calm that fury is also always the same: I want to wander.

Wandering catalyzes a transparency beyond the realm of light. It generates a barrierlessness to movement, *of* movement; the membrane of self becomes more permeable.

I am on a river trip with twelve others, monitoring peregrine falcons. In orange inflatables, we float Ruby and Horsethief canyons, seventy-five miles upstream from Moab on the brown Colorado.

Although many claim *peregrine* means *wanderer*, the dictionary lists instead derivations from words that mean *foreigner* and *through the land*. Like a pilgrim, the peregrine travels through foreign lands, speeding on her erratic path, in constant, roving search. At the proper season, peregrines migrate in patterns that have their own mysterious order. A peregrine doesn't wander aimlessly at all, no more than I do, however ambiguous our destinations.

I can never engineer my own transparency for very long, never quite wander to lands so foreign I recognize nothing. My roaming zigzags. Its indirection allows space for what's beyond my skin. And whatever's scrambled and tight inside unscrambles at its own speed, in unpredictable flow.

The canyons we raft down aren't wilderness; train tracks run along one bank, a holdover from roadless days, and passing engines blast air horns at us. We know conductors alert Amtrak passengers in advance that they might spot rafters out their safety-glass windows and just maybe get mooned. At night Freud has nothing to do with my dreams of long freights tearing through camp, preceded by their powerful head lamps raking the canyon walls. I doubt this trip could be called a wilderness experience when we eat curry for dinner, French toast for breakfast, smoked oysters and ripe brie for hors d'oeuvres, carrot cake for dessert.

The life we encounter recalls peculiar neighbors, deadlines, traffic noises. A feral Chinese goose has escaped from her pet yard and with her pale exaggerated forehead bump waddles and paddles from camp to camp, noisily begging food. Weighed down with water and spotting scopes for a view across the channel to a bald eagle nest, we trek along the train tracks. In the huge stick nest, a pair of nearly fledged chicks bob and jostle like awkward hand puppets. When we hear the train, we scramble down the cinder slope and watch graffiti-washed cars clatter by.

🌿

Wandering has long been an impulse of humans, long a problem for established order. Think only of Cain and Abel. Abel's wandering seems blank, unproductive, irresponsible; Cain's wandering is punishment for murdering his wandering brother. It's an unspeakable burden. Abel's wandering, I remember, also reflects the movement of everything that lives.

🌿

Water rush mixes with willow swish punctuated by staccato calls from hidden yellow-breasted chats and melodious songs from blue grosbeaks. Upriver a storm has darkened the sky, and a new fresh wind blows the smell of rain past us. From the shore a loud crack explodes from a dead cottonwood, and we look over in time to see half its branches tumble to the ground.

Phenomenologists say consciousness is always consciousness *of something*. Wander is always wander *in some place*.

My raptor-spotting abilities have improved after days on the river, and I've become proficient at distinguishing new peregrine whitewash from old golden eagle whitewash. Golden eagles engage in projectile evacuation from their ledges, making distinctive messy splashes. Newer whitewash shines whiter.

Turkey vulture vees dot the sky. Swallows loop in bogus Brownian motion along the cliffs. A canyon wren rings the air with clear cascades. Water swirls into an eddy behind a polished black boulder, its dark smooth surface puckered into unlikely wave forms by the constant river. Two billion years ago during the Precambrian, when life hadn't evolved much beyond single cells, the boulder's molecules had solidified into *rock*.

Those black boulders. Rothko's black paintings. How sad he must have been. How hard he worked to solve his life. How much he thought about it all. How badly he failed. Why hadn't he at least tried to wander?

The water races past all the rocks. The river follows the canyon. The peregrines never guess we're here to watch their wings beat and beat against the brilliant air.

*Deer mice have adapted to every possible
North American habitat.*

—The Audubon Society Field Guide
to North American Mammals

Mice

Mice had colonized my truck. In a land where oversized pickups regularly hauled several tons of working horseflesh, I was embarrassed to be concerned about several ounces of rodent.

"No, no, no," said the hardware store matron. "You have to get rid of them. In the winter they get into our garage and love our truck. The engine's warm and toasty, you know. They haul dog food into their nests, and when we turn the heater on, it spews puppy chow all over us. You've got to trap them."

With a knowing nod she sold me two Havahart traps. At least I could deal with the mice in my engine. I couldn't so easily banish the scurrying mice in my brain. And with two grey contraptions designed to preserve tiny mammals, I drove out of Pinedale, Wyoming, in my little white VW pickup. I had owned it for a month. Three weeks before, its shell had been built with a violin-maker's skill and windows from the junkyard, by my honey Andy. For some years he and I had carried on a sporadic romance long on lust, short on continuity. Predictably, he had snorted in disapproval when I'd painted the shell white and covered it with black thumbprint dots. I didn't tell him that twice I'd fended off gifts of Dalmatian puppies.

Off the leash. On the road for my own reprise of the American wide-eyed roam. I considered mine part quest, part art expedition, part a great emptying. New York, where I still lived half time, had fed and nurtured my brain mice, and I believed they deserved credit for this trip. With some obscure mechanism, New York *required* brain mice in order to get along, plus an invisible Gardol Shield so you could negotiate the sense barrage and still remember your name. I liked living there but couldn't stand feeling both fizzingly full *and* achingly empty all the time, as if I constantly ate twelve-course meals but still missed out on some major food group. Logic and deep annoyance made me want to quell that internal, nibbling excess. And round out my psyche's diet, too. With what? I didn't exactly know.

The week before, the flesh-and-blood mice had jumped aboard my diesel motel in Echo Park, where it had rested long enough—three days—for the little fur balls to imagine it would never move. Short lives meant quick decisions with no perspective.

Dimly, slowly and dimly, my picture of the West, with its distances and details and the complex maneuverings of its humans, had begun to materialize. I'd fed it with books and trips with Andy and with more books. I'd discovered in the annals of western environmental fights that Echo Park had the distinction of being The Place Some of Us Knew. Therefore it had been rescued from "damification" in exchange for drowning Glen Canyon under Lake Powell. A poignant detail, but I wasn't clued in enough to tell what it meant beyond the urgency of checking ground truth and remembering what you found.

If my image of this territory so far remained woefully spotty, I hoped at least it wasn't total mirage, since it had begun to draw me like grav-ity pulls water. I needed to check ground truth, all right, but I could also tick off my agenda as if I were a librarian arranging a display of travel books. My reasons were hardly original, but probably honorable, and at least I'd find out if this solitary meander was any better than staying home and behaving.

And maybe I'd also find out if I could begin to settle down my unruly, disorderly, ever-present brain mice.

🐁

While I camped under Echo Park's cottonwoods beside the river's smooth power, the mouse couple, just reaching puberty, must already have found my engine with its mouse-scale architecture. But I hadn't noticed them, since I'd been concentrating hard on my justification for being on the loose. My justification was work. That meant painting watercolors *en plein air*, in the manner of most of art history's icons. For an activity that seemed as mellow and bucolic as they come—sitting down quietly with little palettes filled with luscious colors, brushes, and small sheets of Whatman's watercolor paper in dramatic landscapes—that work felt alarmingly hard.

I didn't have trouble once I'd humped myself over into alpha state and entrained my nerve impulses with agitated cottonwood light. I only had trouble getting to that state. But even then, blowing dust drifted into my paints, and whenever I slapped mosquitoes, blobs of color splashed across the paper.

I wasn't an art rookie: for years I'd been "artist," professionally, legally (IRS category 8888, "Other"), perceptually, and in my parents' Xmas letters. Except I'd never mixed painting with camping. But whenever I needed to explain six weeks wandering around alone to my nibbling jury mice, creatures always chorusing in a frenzy of shrill doubt, I had the answer. Not only would watercolors get produced (I promised them with grave seriousness), but I would also take black-and-white photos that might, like an add-a-pearl necklace, grow to be something, someday.

Upstream from the picnic table, where I alternated painting water-colors with attempts to gather hints to transcendence by reading the only book I'd brought along, *Pathways Through To Space*, the clear Green River flowed out of the Canyons of Lodore. It had already dropped its share of Wyoming behind Flaming Gorge Dam. At the upper edge of the park, the Green's translucent flow merged with the muddy Yampa, one of the few undammed rivers left in the West. They rolled along side by side for three hundred yards, unmixed, then slowly mingled. Every day, in this dry year, the river dropped half a foot.

Across from the campground with its solar-powered privies, Steamboat Rock rose sheer from the Green, eight hundred feet to its captain's bridge on the mesa top. The campsites arced up to a wide gentle bowl—Echo Park itself—so the kids yelling insults to each other were so satisfied with the earsplitting echoes and receding re-echoes, they had to sample the effect again and again.

After three days in Echo Park, I hadn't succeeded in catching any of the elegant channel cat, which looked like golden carp, but brown. They eyed me from the bottom of a clear side stream and ignored my worms and hunks of cheddar cheese. And I couldn't endure another campfire talk by a ranger changing from funny hat to funny hat, slightly nervous because her boss—who was staying the week in the campground with his family—sat puffing his pipe in the audience. Time to move on.

At 8 a.m. I popped the hood to make sure the engine hadn't self-destructed and discovered my mice chasing each other around the spark plugs, air filter, distributor, and various hoses. No problem, I thought. As soon as I start moving, they'll jump to the ground and be gone. They couldn't possibly *like* engine noise and heat and violent lurching over washboarded roads.

This qualified as one of my generic opinions, applicable to many situations. If you moved, the mice would leave. Brain mice, four-footed mice. That it had never worked before, except temporarily, didn't stop me from believing it might in the future. Random variation in conditions, after all. Perhaps that explained why I had such trouble sitting still to paint. Deep in somewhere, my muscle bundles twitched, and I always wanted to get on with it, whatever it was.

The mice in my brain, and along every winding nerve fiber, weren't nearly as cute as the speedy critters playing tag on my transmission. In fact, I didn't know what my brain mice looked like, only that they felt like Mexican jumping beans given self-determination. Not that they were unique to me. Conceivably, they inhabited all New Yorkers, thriving on subway rumblings and the availability of bike messengers. And once well established, they seemed destined to stay for good, even out of their original habitat of midnight sushi, siren concerts, opposite-side-of-the-street parking, caffeine jitters, and heavy sidewalk traffic.

Maybe nothing at all could be done about my gossiping, yammering, rattling, cackling, fidgeting brain mice.

Some twenty river miles above Echo Park, but many more miles along dirt roads skirting the rocks cut deeply by the river, the Green meandered slowly through huge open wetlands. Porcupines sauntered along the paths, and I caught sight of a single grey streak disappearing into the grasses. The mice, I hoped, would be happier with their own kind and jump ship, if they hadn't already.

In the late spring, advertising for sex and claiming rights to open-air tract houses mattered most in the marsh, and the cacophony surpassed any New Year's Eve in Times Square. Frogs peeped high and low, dense, insistent, and nonstop, their chorus layered with birds whistling, buzzing, and wailing like clarinets and soprano saxes following limited scores. Musicology has a term to describe how Andean Quechua natives sing through the night at their festivals: heterophony. They each intone the same traditional song over and over, all at once, but not in any organized or even tuneful way. Dozens of wordless heterophonies exploded

in the marsh, and any sociobiologist clued in to Quechua festival singing would have been pleased. Most obviously, hundreds of red-winged
and yellow-headed blackbirds, clinging high up on dried cattails, belted
their short ballads toward some distant galaxy. Though the wall of sound
thwarted any attempt to make patterns, it still couldn't obscure the clam-
oring individual voices.

At dusk, nighthawks swept past in courtship dives, their wings
booming in strange, hollow reverberations.

I strained, unsuccessfully, to catch the small squeaks of mice.

The winter had been exceptionally dry, and I wondered if mice liked
internal combustion engines better in snow-free years. Or maybe I'd
simply won the adopt-a-rodent sweepstakes. I didn't know if they still
frolicked under the hood, but if they did, I left them behind with most of
my supplies when I struggled up into the Wind River Range some days
later under a pack so heavy that I didn't at first know if I could carry it
across the road, much less twenty-five hundred feet up and ten miles in.
I managed. But, distracted by the danger of keeling over, I didn't notice
until the second day that only one other pair of boot prints marked the
ground. The backcountry trails had opened early because of a dry winter, but only rare (and ignorant) stragglers like me seemed to be taking
advantage of it. I wondered if the dryness also somehow accounted for
the orange and blue surveyor's tape flagging branches along the way.

Along the western side of the high, glaciated peaks, a wide plateau
sheltered scores of lakes brimming with trout. The cold, clear waters
offered perfect trout conditions, but most of the lakes had been fishless
until the Depression. Finis Mitchell and his wife—a couple struggling
as fishing outfitters—had figured that more fishing business might come
their way if more lakes had fish. With the invention that can germinate
from difficulties, they'd packed in horses loaded with five-gallon milk
cans filled with water and trout. The sloshing of the ride kept the fish in

oxygen; burlap across the tops kept them in the cans. Today the lakes can still be mapped according to their trout. Blue Lake—brookies; Black Joe Lake—cutthroats; Temple Lake—brookies and German browns; and on and on, into and past fisherman's heaven.

Too bad I hadn't been bitten by the fishing bug.

In late morning, rounding a licheny, sun-dappled boulder, I nearly collided with the owner of the other boot prints.

"Oh, hi," he smiled, as if he'd been expecting me. "Where're you headed?"

"Raid Lake, if I get there."

"Great spot. You didn't happen to see a little red Toyota at the trail-head, did you?"

"Nope."

"My friends' car overheated on the way here, and they were going in to town to fix it and then join me; but I've been out here five days, and I haven't seen them. I haven't seen anybody. That's why I marked the trees. So they could find me."

Instead, I'd found him, and we stood midtrail with our packs on, feeding our mutual talk-hunger for half an hour. He lived in Englewood, New Jersey, just over the George Washington Bridge from Manhattan, and studied French horn at Julliard. With some difficulty, he'd talked his friends into driving west with him so they'd understand why he loved Wyoming. But, not experienced in mountains, they had neglected to fix their thermostat first. They'd promised to join him once their car had been returned to health.

"Really, you're from the City, too?" he shook his head again in mild surprise, but seemed to find it less curious than I did. Then we slid into the most important topic: other places to backpack. He'd hiked far more than I had and seemed to have successfully melded his New York life with regular doses of walking in rugged, isolated mountains. Along the way, he must have learned some French horn Pied Piper tricks for brain mice. I didn't ask him.

Finally he headed on out, eventually returning, I guessed, back to the City. Like a homing pigeon. I continued up. When I finally walked out of the shadowy forest into blinding sun on the open, rolling plateau, a lone raven high above broadcast her raucous laugh across the stillness.

❧

When I returned to my truck after four days in the Wind Rivers, the mice had taken over. Their tiny torpedo droppings covered everything, and corners of boxes and Ziploc bags had been gnawed open. Half the map of Colorado had been shredded, though they hadn't touched Wyoming or Montana.

And they'd made dramatic inroads on the back cover and index of *Pathways Through To Space*. I'd brought *Pathways* along as prompt, or maybe recipe book, for the altered-state part of the agenda. I'd admitted this New Age indulgence to no one. During two months in 1936, *Pathways*'s author, Franklin Merrill-Wolff, had broken through a Barrier of Consciousness to experience Ambrosia, a sensation that Transcended the senses. Or, that's what I'd gleaned so far from his journals in *Pathways*. He'd managed to get beyond the physicality of the world and tap into a greater Current that crackled all around, but that required special perceptual apparatus to Recognize. I imagined the sensation might be like turning on a radio and suddenly understanding that easy listening, country rock, heavy metal, Jimmy Swaggart, and *All Things Considered* had been coursing through your stomach and pancreas all along.

A little unnerving ("All Enlightenment, All the Time" if you had the right call numbers), but it sure fit the vague, poorly formed notion of what I hoped to find in the realm of transcendence (or in finally discovering the right aisle in the spiritual Dean and Deluca's): potential escape from those pesky urban brain mice and access to some abstract, but palpable, Mellow All. I knew enough to confess such Aspirations only with many caveats, but I still had to cop.

No disrespect to Franklin Merrill-Wolff, but I had a terrible time reading his serpentine prose—littered with capitalizations—that discussed the relative paltriness of physical Manifestations while I nearly swooned in sage-saturated air after a bone-shaking thunderstorm, the low sun catching rabbit brush and a handful of attentive antelopes so that a bright nimbus surrounded each narrow leaf and hair.

Ambrosia, indeed.

How could I ever keep up my interest in Transcending while I basked in the thick of Manifestation twenty-four hours a day? Better to ask a painter not to think about color. Possible—and we have paintings to prove it—but not easy. A rube from the city, I'd gotten more and more intoxicated by this *earthly* space and what filled it. Slowly, I'd also begun to realize I hadn't arrived on a stage set to play out my preconceived, though lightly detailed, story. The props weren't props, but the story itself. Maybe I'd forget Transcendence and concentrate on Manifestation.

Even if Manifestation included tiny wildlife in my truck.

In gratifying order, my trip dreams had begun erotically with Andy's warm, smooth skin, smelling of lemons and coffee, then had progressed back in time until they'd stopped altogether. Not even any dream companions kept me company, only nimble-footed, half-hidden mice. I hadn't been prepared for any loneliness, and the day it arrived, I stopped at the first phone I passed. As I called Canada, Boston, New York, cold wind whistled around the booth. No one had been willing to fly to Cody at the last minute for a short cruise in the Dalmatian VW. Even Andy, back in Tucson, had found himself stewing in some unarticulated tar pit, which he promised had nothing to do with me, but meant he wanted to stay close to home. Hmm, I thought, even if the gooiness had no link to me, Andy's stewing did. Now and then I chewed on our complicated dance between New York and Tucson but tried not to let those love concerns take over, concentrating instead on problems that seemed more soluble. Or at least more immediate. Like the mice.

In the Pinedale hardware store, I welcomed the tiny bit of human contact, barely admitting it to myself.

"These should do it. Bait them with cheese or a glob of peanut butter. Then let the mice out a ways off. They'll work," instructed my partner in mouse destruction.

My smelly diesel chugged up toward the triple divide of Union Pass. The 4WD road had been bladed and graveled for lumber trucks, so it resembled the Merritt Parkway. Not to worry about oil pan clearance, only head-on collisions with eight tons of Douglas fir.

I had enough sense not to camp by Mosquito Lake, but stopped up the road at Buffalo Meadow. No buffalo, plenty of mosquitoes. Ignoring my ear rash from days of 100 percent deet in Jungle Plus, I slathered more on to get through dinner. I nestled cheese *and* peanut butter in the backs of the grey plastic traps, then balanced them open next to my clutch pedal. The spaghetti had only half cooked when I heard the faint, hollow click of one door tripping shut. Before I finished eating, the other one had also closed decisively. I figured the mice would be OK imprisoned for the night, and I zipped myself into my tent away from the voracious muskies. I woke some hours later to an enormous cracking sound that I thought meant the rock wall next to my tent would crush me before my next breath, until I realized it must have been thunder. Soon after, I reminded myself the coyote pack howling inches away from my head probably had no interest in me at all.

In the morning, after I'd gotten ready for a quick getaway, I carried the closed grey traps off into the forest and set them on a rotting trunk. Slowly I pulled back both doors at once, expecting drama. From the left one, a mouse snout tentatively emerged, matted with moisture from ten enclosed hours. After a dozen blinks, he understood his freedom and hopped out and away, in no great hurry. Nothing in the other trap. One down. Was that it? Were there more?

No matter what you do, there are, of course, always more mice.

🐭

Long before I'd set off in my little white truck, even pre–New York, I'd recognized some nearly foolproof antidotes to brain mice, but not any that could be called upon at will. Both fight and flight were sure-fire, but they required legitimate threats. With similar adrenaline rushes, injury fit the same category. Be here now or risk destruction. Not subtle. And I knew that brain mice masqueraded as other animals: Buddhism called them collectively "monkey mind"; and one of my dance teachers had declared, "Your mind is a wild elephant, you have to harness that power in your body."

I'd moved to new territory. Across the meadow the trail overflowed with blooming pale lavender violets that bruised underfoot. Dense growth and mucky ground on the trail's sides required I step on the blossoms, but I regretted it. Visions of King Arthur's court flitted through my mind: spring in sylvan glades with delicate, long-haired maidens singing madrigals and dancing, of course, on violets. Distinctly unmedieval and undancerly, I crept along, trying not to limp.

Half an hour before, I'd crashed sideways, a top-heavy, mobile pole suddenly unbalanced by stepping wrong on a root. And something had snapped in my left ankle.

Now I've really done it, I thought. In an out-of-the-way corner of backcountry, I'd lost the trail and followed a game path into shoulder-high brush where my feet disappeared beneath young leaves. No one from the trail, wherever it had gone, could see me, even if someone happened to pass by. And I didn't know if I could manage to get from lying down to standing up with my pack on, even if I could put weight on my foot. And without a boulder or log as platform, I couldn't wiggle out of my pack, stand up, and then get it back on. It was too heavy and too unwieldy. I remembered all those warnings about not hiking alone.

For ten minutes I lay on my side, cradled in broken bearberry branches, staring into a green thicket, pissed at my vulnerable ankle.

I'd first sprained it when I'd been mugged on Ninth Street and Second Avenue one drizzly New York evening. Since I'd been working in midtown that day, I wore my good black coat with polished heeled boots, and must have looked like a good target. I'd hung on to my bag stuffed with sweaty dance clothes and ten bucks while I'd cursed my mugger, screaming at the top of my lungs. Very cathartic. No brain mice then. People had rushed from everywhere and chased off the poor guy, who couldn't figure out a better way to make a living. And I'd lost none of my city-confidence. But ever after my ankle had been weak.

In the backcountry, only one of my alternatives had any appeal. If I could stand up, my boot's ankle support might let me walk gingerly to my campsite, about a half mile farther, much closer than the trailhead. Using tricks of balance and activating odd combinations of muscles, I managed to get up. I found I could walk, but slowly. Retracing the game path out of the shrubbery, I regained the trail that meandered through thigh-high grasses and sedge. Watered by runoff from the surrounding plateaus and leveled by underlying geology, the meadow stretched across many miles, broken here and there by pockets of bearberry and buckbrush, like the one I'd strayed into, and small stands of dark conifers. Where the meadow met the trees, the spring bloom held nothing back, liberally scattering scarlet paintbrush, maroon and white shooting stars, bluebells, and bright violet penstemons among the grasses. Like the Wind Rivers, like the rest of the West, this area had begun to dry early because of the light snowpack during the winter, and few people had been out hiking yet. I did pass two exuberant guys returning from a day hike, in just boots and shorts. I nodded to them and didn't mention my ankle.

When the trail entered the forest, it crossed narrow creeks spanned with lattices of downed lodgepole pines. Clear, ice-cold streams alternated with steaming warm flows that were crusted with delicate, crystallized white rims like elongated margaritas. The meadow drained a higher caldera where recent volcanoes still warmed subsurface water.

A creek only degrees away from snow curved around my campsite. Perfect for ankle therapy. Without my boot, my foot responded to any weight at all with loud pain messages to my brain. I planted myself for several hours on the stream bank and circled my immersed foot in the ice bath until it cooled to numbness. Then I lifted it out and continued to work it until it thawed enough to begin hurting again. Then back in the water. Sprained-ankle drill as meditation. The instructions, minus the scenery, came straight from a book called *Listen to Your Pain*, and I meditated on that unmeditative (and unstoic) directive.

The brain mice had disappeared.

I had begun to notice that something about making art, about looking for Transcendence (even with sidelong glances), about contemplating my love life fostered brain mice and took me away from concentrating on Manifestation. Even worry about what to do with my ankle and my hike could be a version of their disruptive buzz. That scheming for self-preservation still required an inner focus that brain mice needed to keep up their chattering commotion. Franklin Merrill-Wolff might have included my ankle in Manifestation—it couldn't be Ambrosia—but to me Manifestation referred not so much to inner phenomena, even physical ones like sprained ankles, but to what existed outside my skin, especially what went beyond my capacity to invent.

Like quaking bogs.

The ranger had warned, "We don't know if there's a bottom." No *bottom?* "We've never lost a person," he said, then cleared his throat, "but we did have a horse break through once."

With my ankle wrapped in an Ace bandage, I gingerly continued on my hike the morning after my crash. I could go a mile before I would need to decide whether to take a cutoff back to the trailhead. At the crossroads, I knew I couldn't possibly pass up such an oddity as the bog. It floated a thick skin of matted vegetation and debris over its hidden deep lake. Across the bog's center, the trail had a reassuring worn look with no suspicious seeps; but as I followed it, the entire surface gave way like a trampoline, or more exactly, a water bed. With each step, the ground sank six inches under my foot and vibrated slightly, rippling as I moved along. Each foot formed the center of a ten-foot-diameter disk of bog plants that offered a springy resistance. Suddenly no longer predictably solid, the earth had become reliably responsive. And, to my relief, my ankle took it.

Other unexpected water behaviors met me after I'd climbed for several hours beside the rushing river that splashed down stair-stepped rock benches so noisily I kept startling cow moose and their calves lounging in ferns by the trailside.

In an extensive rocky basin, icy tributaries tumbled into the main river from the edge of the higher plateau. The cliffs on three sides dropped to a broad open area, filled with not only cold creeks and warm creeks, but also tiny hot rivulets steaming in flowering expanses, warm pools clogged with orange algae that looked like slimy sewage effluent, and bubbling hot pools whose temperatures supported deep turquoise algae grading paler away from the central boil. In the cool air, mists rose through the vertical maze of trunks. Sulfur whiffs drifted by. Waddling, oblivious porcupines negotiated the pathways and, in the quiet afternoon, I felt vaguely silly singing and whistling and jingling my large bear bell just in case any grizzlies chanced by.

Hot spring as an abstract concept didn't encompass the way a bubbling funnel in rock could nuzzle up to a cold stream, mixing the hot and cold flows to various perfect hot tub temperatures. Nor had any of my expectations included the yellow monkey flower blossoms floating past or the sweet, pungent breeze.

All the next morning, I lay in a pool with braided cool and hot currents, my body supported by boulders and fine gravel on the bottom, my senses in full relaxed alert. But decidedly, and paradoxically, *un*grounded. Reality became unreality. Or vice versa. Andy would have loved to lounge away some hours with me in the sensual soak, and I missed him, but my solitude added to the hallucinatory buzz. I remembered I might be blitzed from hiking and from picking myself up from crunchdom. An altered state? Or simply the luscious world? I tried to fix the place and the sensation in my memory.

Two days later I returned to the meadow where distant sandhill crane pairs bobbed their heads just above the high waving green, their large, four-toed tracks everywhere on the trails. Real "wilderness," I'd been warned, no longer existed in the West. Well, OK. The quaking bog had signs, the trails were mapped and maintained, the ranger might worry if I didn't reappear, but still something powerful and engrossing and beyond my capacity to imagine breathed around me. It had throbbed in the Wind Rivers, and it pulsed here. And, I'd been alone with it again for most of five days. I'd kept no record except in my *being*. By the time I reached my truck, my ankle seemed mostly healed, and my brain mice resembled benevolent, purring tabbies.

"Choose carefully who you tell about this spot," said the ranger, his eyes focused ten degrees off mine, after he'd quizzed me about fresh grizzly scat, the hot pools' conditions, and the downed trees, since I'd been first on the trail for the year. I only mentioned my injured ankle in passing, and I suspected *he* was never afflicted with brain mice. "It's been saved, so far, by being so out-of-the-way and unknown." He waved warmly as I drove off.

In my gut, I didn't grasp his request until I got to Yellowstone, where touring hordes took in sights as if they gobbled Whopper burgers. I should have been prepared, but I wasn't. Even when I reminded myself I qualified equally as tourist, with my own list of thermal features to check off, the massive suburbia on wheels made my stomach clench. I could handle Fifth Avenue and Fifty-seventh Street at rush hour, but not Mammoth Hot Springs at noon. I tried to outwit the crowds by being abroad during mealtimes. At dawn I visited geyser basins that looked like the outskirts of the London blitz. At dusk I toured bubbling mud pots that resembled demonstrations of digestion. Marvels, yes, but after three days, I'd had enough. The cranky-family context outdistanced everything. I understood. The magnet of Destination. Then the crowd control, management plans, parking lots, interpretation. Loving it to death, organizing it to death, sanitizing the jolt of the unexpected, obscuring the irrational bonds in favor of picnic mode. The wide-eyed roam become raucous recess with video camera.

No signs of mice in my truck, but my brain mice performed circus tricks with an enthusiasm that matched the park's carnival frenzy. I had to get away.

🪶

Full up with adventures and physically spent, I had three more weeks of utter freedom. But the freedom had begun to feel like banishment. Still, I couldn't squander my time. I *wouldn't* squander my time. But, abruptly, a different level of my psyche grabbed the controls.

At ten thousand feet, I woke in an alpine meadow filled with low purple gentian and larkspur spikes and the white ear-swab blossoms of bistort, my sleeping bag between my truck and a clear, small lake that supplied the foreground to the granite peaks of the Beartooths. More torture by spectacular scenery. I felt puffy and nauseated, with a pounding headache and a strong urge for sagebrush and nonrecreating people doing real things in a bug-free zone.

I shook with restlessness, gripped by an irresistible desire to drive, drive, drive. I sped over Beartooth Pass, "one of the three greats," hardly glancing at the views; through Red Lodge, where I stopped for homemade blueberry pie with ice cream; into Belfry ("Home of the Bats") where the only moving object at three o'clock on a Wednesday afternoon seemed to be the postmistress; past the turnoff to Sunlight Basin (but it's all sunlight!); east across the seared badlands between

the Beartooths and the Bighorns. Storms raged in five directions, all so
far away their lightning flashed in silence. Few other cars traveled the
roads. Whatever had been assailing me slowly drained out. Maybe the
blueberry pie had kicked in. Maybe the space calmed me. The light. The
sage. I drove.

Quieted by hiking, revived by Yellowstone's sightseeing fungus, the
brain mice transformed into road glaze—a magical stupor filled with
vision after vision woven together with my trail of burning fossil beds.

Some days I got so mesmerized by speeding across vast distances
while I aimed at a far mountain range or a name on the map or a cash
machine in Cody, or nowhere at all, that it seemed spookily like watching TV. I became dazed, disconnected, and exhausted. But not always.

Some days the space blew into me with the hot air through the truck
windows, and as I crisscrossed the land, more and more of it became
incorporated into my cells. I still made art stops, but my need for justification had become raging curiosity.

My dreams had returned, but I only worried over and over I'd fail
my geography exam. In my waking hours, Shell and Ten Sleep and Lost
Cabin and Lysite and Hoodoo Ranch and Meeteetse abandoned their
abstractness and became solid. My pile of watercolors remained pitifully
small, my revelation list nonexistent. I couldn't tell whether it should
disturb me or not.

I understood that such jackrabbit travels added up to a surface
view, a thin slice off the top, but they whetted my appetite for more.
Instead of shuttling from trailhead to trailhead, I inhaled towns and
ranches and tiny rodeos, red dirt roads skirting high red mesas, and
air above eroded green clay hills, lubricating itself with oil and gas.
Ground truth followed more ground truth, however fragmented.
Evidence of unending trade-offs appeared around every wide curve,
beyond every exposed, folded mountainside. Hard winters, living rivers
trapped in immobile reservoirs, and flimflams visible in retrospect all
furnished an essential vocabulary for considering human tenacity, both

wise and unwise. Without a recipe, the rough details of "civilization" mingled with backcountry Nirvana and the huge sky into an unfathomable stew that grew more and more irresistible as I drove. All my rational explanations reeked of cliché and sent my remaining non-road-glaze brain mice into cackling derision.

"Shut up and drive," they snapped. And it occurred to me they might be allies in disguise. Regardless of what I did, I couldn't escape my century, my decade, my background, maybe not even my brain mice, except temporarily. But, the mice reminded me, I wasn't then, nor need I ever be, stuck with rational explanations.

🍃

With little warning, I suddenly reached my limit. I felt like a failure and bone tired, brain mice or no brain mice. A few watercolors, countless rolls of exposed, undeveloped film, *Pathways Through To Space* unread, no clear Directives from the Universe. No matter. Time to go home.

In Laramie, the university town, the cold I'd picked up at the public hot springs in Thermopolis had me sniffling and dragging. When I wandered the aisles in all three bookstores, distractedly fingering the paperbacks, not quite up to anything more, I knew I must really be winding down.

I pointed my little truck south, back toward Tucson. Immense relief flooded me. And with that decisive shift, I could turn on the radio again. It had stayed silent the whole trip. *All Things Considered* immediately Manifested itself with a long, audio letter that could have been sent from Franklin Merrill-Wolff's Ether, direct to me.

"Dear Friend," it began in a gentle male voice. "When I got the money, first I fixed my roof, then I fixed my teeth, then I went hiking for a month in Wyoming. I ran up and down mountains. Then I returned to the City because I thought I should work. I decided instead to go to Nepal." As I drove between the Rockies and the Medicine Bow Mountains, past high fields of hay harvested into huge flaxen rolls gilded by late light, the tink-tink of Nepalese goat bells and the lush Katmandu hubbub threaded together the narrator's misadventures and kept me spellbound. I'd left behind Wyoming skies that had already hazed over from that summer's Yellowstone fires, but I thought I could smell burning yak dung. Twenty minutes later, the letter ended, "I had spent all the money. I had done none of the work." But, I protested to myself, of course he had. We'd just heard some of the work. What could he be thinking? It was only a question of definitions.

I slowed enough through Arapaho National Wildlife Refuge to watch a low-slung cinnamon duck bobbing in prenuptial anticipation, his bill bright blue, then crested the Divide to sleep beside yet another burbling creek thick with mosquitoes. The next morning, the truck wouldn't even burp.

I popped the hood. And there, in infuriating cuteness, quivered the forgotten mouse family, full-blown. Mother had grown large, sleek, beautifully golden: a deer mouse. Her three grey babies hid ineffectively in the hood insulation. Did mice eat wires? Brain mice only jiggled the neural network—these guys might do literal damage to my roam-mobile. With the help of passing strangers and an expensive tow, I found a puzzled mechanic who sent me on my way with a can of ether (Ether?). He hadn't thought to check the seventy-nine-cent glow plug fuse, notorious for sabotaging diesel engines.

Road glaze possessed me on through Colorado, through New Mexico. Flower-strewn aspen groves graded into coal mines and orchards around Paonia, where I stopped for fresh sweet cherries. The dramatic mountains and sheer drop-offs on the road from Telluride to Dolores disappeared in a series of violent storms, hidden by fog and downpours and wet snow. South of Cortez, War of the Worlds towers kept someone's distant food processor juiced up with enough hydropower to pulverize entire supermarkets.

And the radio added a surreal soundtrack. Near Gallup, the public radio station broadcast country music interspersed with the announcer's

Navajo, that language of mystical incantation. Then unaccountably, at 2 p.m., it switched to a program—complete with British accents—about nineteenth-century French high and low art. Later, while I sped to El Morro in New Mexico's desert for a dry, bugless night in sage, the Ether serenaded me with Iron Butterfly's "In-A-Gadda-Da-Vida," then Beethoven's *Missa Solemnis*.

Every night I baited the traps. Every night mother mouse squirmed into the plastic contraptions, her bulk big enough to keep the doors from clicking shut, and stole the hunks of cheese. Every night the quartet pilfered more gorp, dribbling nut bits across my front seat. Every night while I ate dinner and wrote in my journal, they peeked around the tires at me, then scampered off, but never far enough.

A day and a half away, in Tucson, I would leave the truck sitting undriven for weeks while I tended my job back in New York. I had to find a more drastic strategy.

"I need some mousetraps. The spring-loaded kind." I'd lost all hints of my earlier sheepishness. "I have mice living in my engine." This purveyor of nails, plumbing pipe, enamel coffee pots, and shotgun shells looked surprised. Maybe only Wyoming mice had evolved truck nesting behavior.

Reserve, New Mexico, as isolated and as beautifully situated as any town in Wyoming, had kept its claim to land in the middle of the Gila National Forest. Its funky single street looked like a cross between Dodge City and a disorganized flea market. Fly-specked windows lit the dim and cavernous hardware store that seemed filled with stuff that had been on its dusty dark shelves since Coronado.

As I left the store with four sure-to-kill traps, a blond-haired boy about twelve followed me out and asked, "Do you really have mice in your engine?"

"Sure do."

"Can I see them?"

"Maybe. They might be hiding." I opened the hood, and one small grey shape disappeared beside the crankcase.

"Do they have a nest?"

"Yes, but I haven't looked for it." It had never occurred to me. We both began to inspect the engine and quickly found the grass matted with shredded tissue, maps, and *Pathways Through To Space* (the telltale blue of the back cover). The mice had crammed their bungalow onto the plastic shelf that sits just under a VW's windshield to catch debris. A perfect spot for mouse housekeeping. This seemed to satisfy him about the mice, but then he turned his attention to me.

"Where're you going?"

"Back to Tucson."

"Do you live there?"

"Sometimes."

He considered this, but moved on. "Where're you going now?"

"Down toward Pleasanton."

"And what're you gonna do there?"

"Find someplace to camp for the night."

"And then where?"

"In the morning I'm going to San Francisco Hot Springs."

"But hippies go there!" He seemed genuinely alarmed for me.

"What's wrong with hippies?" I thought hippies had left office with Richard Nixon.

"They take drugs and they're dirty and they live in buses and they steal."

Despite my knee-jerk solidarity with the maligned footloose, I couldn't take on this kid's reeducation.

"Maybe I'm a hippie, too."

"Naw. You're not."

"How do you know?"

"You're nice."

What could have happened to hippies once I'd stopped being one? What would happen to this curious, straightforward child in such a remote, limited town, embraced by these waves of gorgeous land? What had happened to me on this ramble? Anything at all?

"You're nice, too." I smiled. It was the most personal conversation I'd had since I'd left Tucson. "Do you always talk to people who stop here?"

"Yup," he nodded. "Mostly. I like to know where they're going. I'm gonna be a writer when I grow up."

Five months later, back in my all-purpose one-room apartment in New York, I read through my journals and came across the day I'd felt I could withstand the radio-Ether again.

"Dear Friend," my notes from the broadcast began. I put down my notebook, looked across the room to sun patterns filtering past the fire escape to my bookshelves, and finished with my own story.

"When I had some extra time and some extra money, I bought a truck and went nosing around the West for six weeks. In Wyoming I heard ravens and coyotes and smelled sulfur hot springs and distant forest fires. After weeks in the mountains, I craved dryness but saw that water made all the difference. I saw that trade-offs were everywhere. I didn't figure out my love life. I painted some watercolors. I didn't see God. I trapped some mice. Then I returned to the City because I thought I should work. I decided instead to move to New Mexico."

I Love Wild Thunderstorms Myself

In central Nebraska, east and west of Gothenburg, train tracks thread together the tall grain elevators that loom above the flat landscape every ten miles or so. Around each elevator, groups of buildings cluster, sometimes composing a small town with short streets of well-kept houses. In June the unending fields around these villages show off their young blankets of corn and alfalfa but seem less a part of the passing scene than the enormous, overarching sky. Parallel to the tracks, the Platte River cuts the earth, draining the invisible Rockies far to the west. For more than a hundred miles, Andy and I had driven toward those peaks on our way from New York City to New Mexico, along the tracks and the river, past the varied outsized architecture whose corrugated volumes and multiple angled roofs reflected differing ideas of storing and moving grain. Each one stood unique and sculpturally compelling, but the regular repetition in that wide territory felt oppressive.

For the first time, I understood how this land had shaped my father. But that didn't help my central subterranean worry: that something in my genes pushed me to retrace his steps. I feared I'd fail at my life, would have to domesticate my feral dreams. New York and the West would play major, if unclear, roles.

My father had grown up in Gothenburg as the youngest son of a hotelkeeper with Scottish ancestors. His family lived in town, surrounded by a community of Swedish farmers. Struggling to bring in the crops, the Swedes fought endlessly with outsized natural forces, beginning simply with the huge, isolating spaces of the Great Plains. I knew about the elemental struggles of those farmers, not because I'd lived there—I'd grown up in Washington, D.C.—but because my father had been in close communion with a larger-than-life folk character named Febold Feboldson. He had written tall tales featuring Febold as a super-hero for farmers; the tales appeared first as columns in the Gothenburg paper, then as a compilation he'd published two years before I'd been born, when he was forty-three. I, therefore, became his second offspring. There would be no others.

I grew up hearing about the way Febold outsmarted mosquitoes the size of prairie dogs, harnessed tornadoes to his plow, invented popcorn on the stalk during heat waves, busted droughts by sending Yellowstone's geysers through watermelon vines. And so on. But not until I drove mile by endless mile along that ancient river bottom with its matching tracks and lonesome grain elevators did I recognize the deeper source of those yarns.

They were born from desperation. The heat, the cold, the drought, the storms, the plagues—all surpassed human scale. How comforting to concoct a human large enough to at least make an equal fight. I also grasped how my father must have felt to be stuck in the middle of Nebraska, especially as the Depression took hold, as the Dust Bowl churned up clouds of prairie soil and desperate people. The distances were so great, getting away so hard. Getting anywhere was so hard.

These stories, disguised as good-humored, folksy Americana, gave him an escape from a narrow town, from a place and a way of life where he never felt at home. Febold could do with alacrity what my father never could manage, and everyone loved the big Swede for it. In the book's introduction, he explains he collected some of the Febold tales during the time he "made [his] way as a night clerk in a hotel" and talked with the passing circus of voluble guests. He doesn't admit that the hotel belonged to his father. Not until long after he'd died did I hear a revealing story about my grandfather's good heart, though I have no way to confirm it. My father's older brother Hobart—the family's black sheep—had once been married to the elderly woman who told me the tale.

"The longer the Depression lasted, more and more families came through Gothenburg. They were all hungry. First they'd go to one of the churches, but the churches couldn't feed all those people. They said, 'Go over to Beath's Platte Hotel and you can get a meal there.' Well, you know, he fed them all. There wasn't much money around, but no one could stop him. 'They're starving,' he said, and kept giving away food. It finally drove him into bankruptcy." His name, I thought, after all, was John *Goodship* Beath.

At my prodding, she went on, "Paul"—my father—"was always different, always reading. The whole family worked in the hotel, but he didn't have to do as much as the rest of us. He was sort of a dreamer, and Ma and Pa Beath just let him dream."

For two years, I'd flown over Nebraska, from New York City to Tucson and back every two weeks to see Andy, the person with me in Gothenburg's town square, sharing avocados and tortillas, salsa and chips. We remained comfortable companions, but the demise of our love affair had paradoxically prompted my move from East to West.

In a trek across country, what better place to stop than in Dad's old stomping grounds? But I didn't have the searching-for-roots enthusiasm that marks real family-history pilgrims. I felt uneasy in the place. We stood out dramatically in the laid-back, pruned neighborhood where pleasant Victorian houses surrounded the quiet, shady central park, and the U-Haul behind the vintage red Dodge Ram sealed our identification as transients. But that didn't disturb me as much as an internal queasiness. I'd never felt an urge to come back to my father's hometown, to track down his past, to touch the Platte Hotel's front stoop. It just happened to be generally on the way from friends in Cedar Rapids, Iowa, to New Mexico. Gothenburg sits ten miles west of the climate's vertical pivot point, the hundredth meridian—west of that geographic marker rainfall alone can no longer predictably support agriculture. No wonder the Swedes had such trouble before irrigated crop circles. The hundredth meridian marks the start of the West. Craving more than he saw around him, my father looked East. An East Coast urban kid, I looked West. Andy and I planned to head due south out of Gothenburg, cross Kansas, then dogleg over to New Mexico.

🍃

My father had tried to leave Gothenburg early, supported by his parents' goodwill and their meager finances, first going to Illinois to college, then Wisconsin to graduate school. He'd always been attached to books, and in the early 1930s he made his way to New York, where he pegged his hopes on three interrelated paths. First, and most important, he wanted to be a writer, published by a big house, lauded by critics. Second, he thought becoming a college professor would be a useful career that fit well with writing. Third, he wanted to be a player in the ongoing debates about Regionalism. He entered the PhD program at Columbia.

But he couldn't manage. At Columbia he failed his comprehensive exams, and they sent him away. Grad school must have been tougher then. Everyone I know who's been through that system never takes their comps until their profs are certain they *will* pass. He struggled on for a while, trying to make a name in New York literary circles, partly with his Febold proposal. But eventually he had to return to Gothenburg. He'd been banished from New York twelve years before he met my mother on a blind date, and his New York time remained nearly opaque to me until soon after he died. Among his things, my mother found a slim leather portfolio with yellowing typewritten pages of a diary he'd kept sporadically from 1932 to 1971. During their marriage, she'd known nothing about it. I never heard how much she read before she passed it on. I meant to copy it and return it, but she never asked for it back. I don't think she wanted it. Certainly she didn't want it as much as I did.

19 December 1933
Twenty-eight years old today. Full of hope, ambition, energy, education, intellectual curiosity. I have the equipment for a successful literary career. . . .

12 February 1934
Here I am with my exams three weeks off pursuing young and tender female flesh like a priapic satyr instead of reviewing my middle English dialects. And for one who has scarcely looked at a woman before . . .

16 March 1934
This day, after a lousy two hours of orals yesterday, Wright explicitly stated what I have always thought, namely, that I have not the academic mind and classroom technique and should therefore not pursue the doctorate any further. And so that's that.

After his initial flat response, he sinks quickly. In pages that reveal the baldest emotion in the entire diary, he's overly hard on himself in his New York persona. Familiar, if extreme, self-flagellation.

6 April 1934
God! What a fool I am.

Some have written the poison out of their souls. Do I dare set down my weaknesses? Do I dare write that my life is a debacle? The transition from the academic to the publishing world has not come off . . .

My faults: 1) Vanity. I never intended honestly to go on for a degree . . . but I thought I knew enough to get by the department . . . Plainly I have conducted myself with my friends and acquaintances like an ignorant, vain ass; a boor and uncouth yokel. No social sense, no tact; even now after I know better I still make blunders, hurt people for no reason at all except thoughtlessness.

2) Lack of a job or some mechanical duty which would give me a sense of balance, hold me down, chasten my vanity and roving intellect. I can bear my intellectual debacle, but what puts me in a fog of despair is that I've alienated every person I know here . . .

Down, down, down. Is there a bottom where I can start over and correct my errors? I hope so. I must develop social sense, decorum, and cut out the gab . . . Blindness, blindness, ignorance, ignorance. . . .

Shall I blame it on my origins or on myself? Both. Family honest hardworking middleclass. So hardworking neglected social life and intercourse. I turned to books, but of the essential balance, I had none . . . No more paper. Enough. I feel the same as when I started. I crave sympathy, but don't deserve it. Fool, fool, fool, fool, fool.

10 April 1934
As my painful human relations become more and more painful, the knowledge of my faults grows and grows. Explicit statement may help.

I am a liar and a braggart; one implies the other. When asked an embarrassing question, rather than answer directly I fabricate half truths and exaggerate some minor circumstance into something greater.

I am a thief. I have taken money out of the business to come to New York and fritter away my time when my parents are slaving to keep the business going. . . .

I am vain and blind . . . life values have been distorted by a superiority complex. . . .

Defects of my speech (which crop up badly at times) and my eyes have contributed to my faults. I feel held down by both.

I am lazy . . . Perhaps I am lazy also because I lack some driving power, motive, ideal. I have one now: to correct my faults, to write a respectable book or at least an article to rehabilitate my reputation, to find a job, to make money, to marry, to live a normal life.

The entry ended there. When I knew him, he had made a good attempt at a normal life, though a whiff of self-castigation still clung to him. More appealingly, he still had a deep knowledge of literature, a dry wit and a winning fondness for bad puns, and the aura of an outsider with a number of eccentric friends from those years. He'd not alienated *everyone* in New York. Perhaps that moment *had* been the hinge in his life. He'd surely faced despair. The next entry wasn't until three years later and doesn't mention what happened in the interim.

As unsettling as the emotional outpouring was, perhaps most relevant for my translocation from New York to points west were the entries and the artifacts about Regionalism, especially an article he'd published in a 1936 issue of *Saturday Review* several years after he'd left New York. Discussions of the idea that geography influences the personalities, culture, and arts of the people who live in a particular place have a long history and continue today in a mild form. That connection, after all, triggered my own realization about my father as we drove through central Nebraska. But in the 1930s, it was a hotter topic. Grant Wood and Thomas Hart Benton painted the Heartland, and Regionalism had national cachet as a "movement." As a midwestern writer in New York, my father hoped to ride it to some sort of success. The 1936 *Saturday Review* published paired pro and con articles about Regionalism and I was surprised to see that my father criticized the movement he'd been an "active participant in" for six years. Most cogently, he claimed that despite its potential, on the ground Regionalism exalted mediocre writing.

The debate itself didn't interest me much. From this distance, it seems an attempt to weaken New York's publishing hegemony simply by discussing in print the issue of New York versus everywhere else. Does place influence artists? Of course. But I saw that the piece, written in a dry, almost academic style, reflected my father's ambivalence about his own work. He'd been trying to get the Febold tales published as a contribution to a "modern folk tradition." But he'd mostly invented them himself—a fact that later would earn him a place in the category "fakelore" in university folklore programs, but it made the stories more appealing to me. Still, I knew that for him the article represented a partial retrieval of his self-respect.

⬈

Back in Gothenburg for a while, my father did what he could with his place and his ambitions. He also hooked up with the New Deal, became a delegate to the Democratic National Convention, and even once ran for Nebraska secretary of state.

Eventually he left again for good, moving to Washington and law school in the late '30s. His poor eyes, exhausted from much reading, saved him from military service. After the war, he stayed in Washington and worked to fix his life so it looked approximately like the American Dream. No more illusions of writing, no more debating Regionalism. He

hoped to end his financial struggles. He hoped to end his search
for the right woman. He *knew* he'd not live again in wide open spaces.
He became a lawyer, married my mother, published his book, and
had a child. But nothing in the world runs quite as smoothly as any of
us expects.

My father had not liked large parts of his life. He felt like a failure in
much of what he attempted, and by going to law school, he finally jet-
tisoned his dreams and made a more acceptable life. For his only child,
he wanted something better. But, I noted daily, if privately, that I risked
repeating his life in my own way. Not that it caused me to change anything I did. He hadn't really made mistakes; he just wasn't able to do
what he'd imagined would be possible. But he'd drawn a big black line
through it all; he thought he'd wasted so many years chasing chimeras.
Pointless dreaming. As a lawyer, he managed not to compromise his
ideals: he worked for the Library of Congress, for the Kefauver committee when it crusaded for consumer protection and civil rights, and
for the Federal Trade Commission on antitrust cases. His populist roots
never quite atrophied.

I'd abandoned a path to a "good career," though with great relief
and no regrets, and chosen the arts. I'd not sunk into a quicksand of
financial insolvency, but I'd not been wildly successful either. I had
no children, and here I was, moving West, away from the centers of
intellectual and political power. What was it in my genes? Though my
father wasn't alive to see this visit to a place so associated with his
failures, I couldn't muster any interest untainted by my memories of
his unhappiness.

I was closer in temperament to him than my mother. And I shared
his intellectual capacities, his skill at sports, his olive skin that tanned
easily, his height, his green eyes. For many years I also shared his tendency to moodiness and his shyness, though my shyness didn't have the
explanation of the mild stutter he'd developed after landing on his head
in a fall from a second-story window when he was two.

Before I was two, I'd not fallen on my head, but my mother's parents *had* moved in with us to help take care of me, the adored child. Unexpectedly, my grandmother's fierce controlling urges had so disrupted my father's equilibrium that he sank into a deep depression and couldn't work for many months. His American Dream plan had not included a tough Appalachian woman with rigid ideas about how to run a household.

And I still believe that his memory of cool prairie air on summer mornings haunted him, that the stories he'd never written disrupted his sleep.

I kept my emotions closely guarded in those years too, aware of my grandmother's eagerness to control everything about me. My mother had the same impulse, but she'd read Dr. Spock and operated sub rosa. Then one afternoon when I was eleven, I found myself on our screened-in second-floor porch alone with my father in a chaotic thunderstorm, with wind and rain swirling through the branches of the backyard maples. I made no attempt to hide my pleasure in the storm.

He said suddenly, with an intensity of feeling he rarely showed, "I love wild thunderstorms myself." I'm sure I only nodded in response, but I knew he'd seen a wildness in me, a craving for breaking free that I always tried to keep hidden. My sense of danger fought with the pleasure of being seen by someone I loved. Not only seen and not judged, but recognized by someone with the same secret urges. I also felt embarrassed he'd shown so much emotion to me, as sparse as it had been. We hadn't quite opened to each other, but almost, and the clarity of that memory so many years later attests to its rarity in my childhood. And now, I also know what he'd remembered of the violent storms in Nebraska: the enormous building cumulus over the prairie, the dust kicking up, the unsettling rumbles and sheet lightning, the destructive and magical hail. He couldn't have forgotten.

As I grew older, I strained more and more overtly against the domestic scene. Since we'd moved away from my grandparents, this mostly meant fighting with my mother. My father, always a gentle soul, tried to make peace between his two women. After one blowout, he and I stood facing each other in the den, my mother in retreat upstairs. I fumed. He tried his best.

"Now, Mary Lib, can't you and your mother get along?" He put his flat palm to the top of his forehead, onto his balding scalp. He was past sixty by then. "Your mother's under a lot of stress at work. She worries about you. Can't you be a little calmer?"

Clearly not. I was sixteen. I glared.

"I know you feel held down . . . " Then he pulled out a line from one of the hundreds of poems he had memorized long before. How like him to infuse adolescent upheaval with literature.

> *Out of the night that covers me,*
> *Black as the Pit from pole to pole. . . .*

Ah! I have him, I thought. I recognized the poem as "Invictus," and knew the perfect comeback line later in the poem. Without skipping a beat, I quoted,

> *My head is bloody but unbowed.*

I clamped my lips shut.

I meant it as a salvo in battle, but his reaction startled me. His whole body relaxed, and he said, with some amusement and much transparent pride, "You know 'Invictus'!"

Then I relaxed too and smiled in spite of myself. We both knew "Invictus," but we also knew my mother didn't. We were in cahoots.

🪶

When I fell in love with a writer in college, I didn't understand my
father's intense dislike of him for many years. Such animosity didn't
seem at all justified. But he was a writer, and that was enough. My father
saw his earlier writer-self: misguided, struggling financially, on the road
to destruction. Tricks of the universe: we can't control them and can
barely even recognize them.

Andy and I finished our lunch on that sunny June afternoon in Gothenburg, warm but not yet summer baking, and began packing up to leave.
Andy wasn't my sweetheart from college days and certainly wasn't a
writer. He had unmatched skills at manipulating the material world but
had trouble getting a complete sentence down on paper. As I stood next
to the U-Haul, a newish large pickup slowed to a stop next to me. In the
front seat sat three men, all in their seventies. I'd already done one cal-
culation: if my father had been alive, he'd have been eighty-four. Now
I counted quickly: when he'd been writing newspaper columns about
Febold, they'd have been in their early twenties. They certainly would
have heard of him, would have known my grandfather's Platte Hotel.

I nodded and smiled. They looked curiously out the window at me
and Andy for a moment. I was thin and tanned, six feet tall in short
purple shorts and a sleeveless shirt. Andy could have been a pirate. He
had on his favorite ragged cutoffs and a white string T-shirt. The Tucson
sun had browned his skin several shades darker than mine, his muscles
stood out clearly on his lean body, and his hair framed his head in a
greying Afro. The single silver loop in his left ear glinted.

As I wondered what law we might have broken, the man by the window smiled back at me and said with impressive enthusiasm, "Welcome
to Gothenburg!"

"Thanks," I said as I reached out and shook the hands they offered,
meeting their questioning eyes. With almost no effort, I could have asked
if they'd known Paul Beath, explained that I'd come to Gothenburg

because I was his daughter and had not been to this town since I was five. But I stayed quiet, not able to make that leap. I've regretted my silence many times—by now everyone who knew my father there must be dead, and I'd missed my chance—but I couldn't speak. I couldn't make that contact. Now I could marshal my courage and charm, but then, the weight of the past had kept my tongue still.

Before we drove out of town, we made a halfhearted attempt to spot the building that might have been the Platte Hotel. We might have seen it, in fact, but even my memory of that has become fuzzy. Almost immediately, the small road leading south from Gothenburg and across the Platte River left farming fields and entered more compelling badlands.

I've tried to write this story before. My father's quiet diary seemed to be a useful organizing principle. After all, how many people get to have such a window into a parent's life? But that attempt turned out to be my only experience with complete writer's block. I felt so sad for him, I was paralyzed. After three or four days staring at a blank page, doodling now and then, I finally decided I couldn't do it. But perhaps, I thought, I could write a poem, with the language that poetry offers as a tool for exploration. I left grain elevators of prose for rough badlands, and relaxed.

To my surprise, the poem revealed an unexpected truth.

Instead of following my father's ill-fated footsteps, I'd reversed course. I wasn't on a path where I must *give up* my dreams in order to have a chance at a satisfying life. I'd returned from the East to the West, the *real* West, way beyond the hundredth meridian, to *fulfill* the dreams of his younger self, the dreams he'd had long before I was born. This realization struck me like a gust from one of Albuquerque's summer monsoons. I'd been released from a family curse.

By then I'd started to write in earnest. I wrote about the West and my place in its wide spaces. In some disembodied ozone, my father must have been shuddering, perplexed about what he'd done to fail me. I knew he hadn't failed me, only that he'd given me something different than he'd hoped.

I'm much easier in the desert than I ever was in Washington's green swampiness. My efforts at writing have borne fruit, something neither of us would have guessed likely as I grew in the shadow of his abandoned writer's life. The book of poems I've published has drawn attention from three Western *regional* groups. I could never have mapped this out, and I don't know for certain how my father would have reacted to his daughter becoming something resembling what he'd once hoped for himself. But I do know I'm grateful to him. A force with no real explanation seems to have been at work all this time. Carl Jung says somewhere that nothing affects a child's life as much as a parent's unfulfilled dreams. Even unconsciously. Perhaps especially unconsciously.

I can see him now, that unusual child of the harsh prairie, propped against a cottonwood trunk on the banks of the Platte River, gazing at the spring flood, smelling its wet mustiness and dreaming a future.

Hiking Alone

I heard the bagpipe's wail even before I stepped out onto East Tenth Street. Right in front of my building, the piper stood in full kilts and knobby knees next to the front fender of a VW Bug entirely covered with light bulbs. Usually this neighborhood Beetle crept through New York traffic with bright patterns streaming, but that night it sat empty and dark. No matter. The bagpiper, on his own mission, offered the immobile art-Bug a deafening serenade. On my walk to Second Avenue, I passed the oversized Puerto Rican who kept the block safe for the hot weed trade behind the blue door, then I nearly collided with the wobbly transvestite with her pink umbrella, thick makeup, and wild eyes. The sax player visible through his open third-floor window competed with the piper and aimed his aching riffs into the street. At the corner, the small, sour Greek guy who sold flowers had posted a hand-lettered sign on his stall, "For rent, house on Corfu."

One evening, half a block.

But every walk in New York brought the same swamping, unpredictable, exotic, loud excess, whether you wanted it or not. "You can't fight it," a friend said when I'd lived in New York for six months. "The City's like a steamroller. The first year you just have to lie down and let it roll over you." I eventually grew the hard transparent bubble every New Yorker knows: focus on your destination and go. Walk with purpose. If you let in too much, or if you seem too available, you court conversations with crazies, or dustups with flimflam artists. Or too many offers of sex. But maybe the sex offers only hold for women. At the very least, you'll be interrupted. Or the sense barrage will flatten you. But I only discovered the bubble's effectiveness once it disappeared. Whenever I returned to the City after being gone awhile, for three days people would stop me on the street, want the time or directions, or ask innocent human questions. Unused, the shield had dissolved and others could sense my openness. Then the shield would reconstitute itself and no one asked me anything. After a while I thought, Can that be healthy?

At first I left the City only partway, dividing my time between New York and Tucson.

Most mornings I'd wake up surprised by the season outside the window; but contrary to everyone's expectations, I thrived on the upheaval.

Anchored in one climate, Andy eventually had a different take. After two years, in a November phone call he laid out his position, "I can't stand this anymore. As soon as I get used to you being here, you're gone. As soon as I get used to you being gone, you're back." We talked on, unhooking ourselves from each other. I hung up the phone. Past my fire escape, New York's vapor lights reflected off the falling rain—or had it already turned to sleet?—and four separate sirens howled at different distances across lower Manhattan. My head spun. Five minutes passed.

"Damn it, I can live without Andy, but not without the Southwest. I'll just move." I only needed to figure out how. The leg-irons keeping me in the City—the ones I both cherished and resented—had luckily already been sprung open by six weeks alone on western roads. But to really leave, I had to abandon my much-envied studio apartment in the East Village, where I'd lived for ten years. I had to leave behind my favorite Korean vegetable stand, the Second Avenue Deli, and the corner sushi restaurant always more crowded at midnight than at noon. And I had to give up my walks through the dense urban ferment.

By the next Fourth of July, I'd landed in Albuquerque. After three years, I mainly missed the midnight sushi. Instead of focused walking to subway entrances, I hiked the backcountry. Often I hiked alone.

Hiking alone: every guidebook, every ranger warns against it. Women, mostly women, ask, "Aren't you afraid?" Meaning, "Aren't you afraid *of men?*" After years walking New York's streets in communal solitude, I wasn't frightened by much. But I'll admit the first night I'd camped alone on a trip in Andy's pickup, I'd put the tent right next to the tires. The truck and I had been in a rocky clearing just off an out-of-the-way dirt road in southeast Utah, where few other cars or trucks passed, no mosquitoes buzzed, no rain threatened, and the gentle air blew warm and dry. But the tent's thin nylon offered my only imaginable protection. From *whatever*. That early unease had passed with time and many nights alone in my sleeping bag, senses open to the sky, truck in sight or not. Not only did hiking alone no longer make me uneasy, it gave me in concentrated form some of what I craved.

When you step across the threshold at a trailhead, you enter a universe parallel to your other life. When you do it alone, planning to be gone for five days or a week or two weeks, you know you'll need to rely mostly on yourself. You know you'll get a rush from the risk, and the kind of focus you wish for anything you do. Little will be predictable. Sure, the map reveals where to find water, whether the trail goes up or down, how to get out; but faced with complicated real territory, you can't possibly imagine all its details or what you'll find beyond the next sheer drop-off. As you walk through the unexpected landscapes—no matter how *generally* familiar—you can chew on problems so thoroughly you can often resolve them. You can follow ideas or work out projects, your body's rhythms building paths for your mind. Perhaps most gratifying, you can feel your body readjust—under an unreasonable amount of pain and exhaustion—into a hiking trance, into a surprising, if temporary, ease.

Beyond that shift in inner attention, the land itself wraps you in a new skin. But you also feel your own skin turn inside out, then enlarge so you understand viscerally where you are. You swallow the landforms and forests and open meadows whole; and they swallow you. To be among them is addictive the way all joy is addictive.

When I started up into the Weminuche Wilderness, I'd been on more than half a dozen long solo hikes since I'd moved to New Mexico. Enough to have mastered the basics—food, clothes, shelter—but not enough to be entirely sure I knew what I was doing. No matter what new light gear I bought, for example, my pack still felt like a huge moose strapped to my back, dead.

Just beyond the trailhead, I crossed the threshold, more literal than most. A cold, thigh-deep creek split the trail, and I negotiated the rocky bottom with two stripped fir branches as poles, Tevas on my feet, boots banging around my neck. The first day I meant to reach a broad meadow six miles in at eleven thousand feet, two thousand feet above the trailhead. The trail followed the icy creek, always gaining altitude. My early cockiness at settling comfortably under my two-ton pack gave way in late afternoon to the exhaustion that always ambushes me at the start of a long hike, especially at high altitude. An exhaustion I forget. At about mile five, a thunderstorm loosed its rain and hail, the canyon narrowed, the trail steepened, and I needed to stop every few yards and rest my pack on butt-high boulders to calm my racing heart.

Since I'd set out, I'd seen no one, but when I stopped at the top of
a waterfall, human sounds drifted up above the water rush. Two riders
on pale horses negotiated the trail below across the shallow, diminished
stream. Pikas' high-pitched yips had been heralding my own slow progress up through dripping spruce and fir trees, so when I heard their calls
behind me, I knew the riders were near. I stopped, propped myself half-
standing beside the trail, and pulled out an energy bar. The riders wore
identical ochre dusters, broad-brimmed dark Stetsons, perfectly round
wire rims, and brushy moustaches. Twins?

When I saw they also climbed slowly, walking their matched horses
a dozen paces at a time, then resting for one or two minutes, I felt less
like a wimp. Without a word, we smiled and nodded. I rubbed the ears
of their black Lab and vaguely worried they'd claim the closest campsite
at the meadow.

When I finally emerged from the trees, I found myself engulfed
in frenetic, cacophonous blooming along the tiny creek. Reds, violets,
yellows, whites—in the short mountain summer, everything shot out
blossoms at once. Back from the stream, legions of plants stood with
large tropical leaves drooping along tall rust-colored stalks. In my limp-
rag stupor, that operatic display got me through dinner. Mercifully, not
until I'd finally bedded down in my tent did the storm start howling
again in earnest.

After the climb I felt like a tomato plant nipped by a hard frost, and
as unlikely to be revived. I drifted to sleep trying to decide if I could go
on, or if I'd miscalculated my capacities and should head back down.
I felt awful. How could I have done this? Thunder worried my dreams,
and in the morning I woke to the same dilemma. Should I tough it out?
Or be reasonable and save myself? I fretted while I watched the knob
across the meadow appear and disappear in the clouds. I stewed some
more as I squatted by the creek filtering water for breakfast. One of the
riders from the day before carefully picked his way down from their
camp through thigh-high grassy wet, come to retrieve the cream they'd

left in the creek to cool. *Cream?* I mulled unhappily, feeling put upon by myself, in a deep funk amidst cool, luscious splendor. Go up? Go down? I couldn't solve it. An hour passed. The black Lab came by to nuzzle my hands again and sniff my gear. The blond horses browsed the meadow in and out of sight, their dark manes and tails reemerging first when wind swirled the mists. My confusion bore no resemblance to a hiking trance. I sat immobilized, staring.

Then, as if I'd rounded a corner on a high trail, the view opened out. I didn't need to choose between those two alternatives: up? down? I could stay put. I'd planned a layover day later in the trip and had time to spare. At that moment the problem itself blew away like the fog. I knew I could continue up, and head down later. An answer to irreconcilable opposites. Physically, nothing had changed, but I *felt* unaccountably different. What my mind had happened upon had translated immediately into my body. Or maybe I'd missed the order of events. Had my body finally revived and sent a message to my mind: *OK, now I can hike again?*

The mind-body problem is one of the well-worn themes of traditional Western philosophy, and it has been thoroughly chewed on at least since Newton and Descartes claimed an unbridgeable rift between the two. For a time, that duality caused distressing and destructive fallout: cultural opinion held that animals, like the black Lab and the matching horses, had no real feelings because their "minds" couldn't engage exactly in human thought. The same hierarchical conflict between abstract and concrete, mind and body, had once relegated women—that is, me—to an inferior status because we were more "earthy," more subjective, more emotional, more incapable of controlling our sexual impulses than men. This field has been well plowed, but it's not an historical oddity: the basic sense that our physical selves and our mental selves exist quite separately still persists, though thankfully not in such a categorical way.

I'd done my share of ruminating on matter versus mind, and as I packed up my gear, I remembered the book I'd been reading before the hike: *The Dreams of Reason* by physicist Heinz Pagels. He believes the "problem of the dualism of mind and nature will not so much be solved as it will disappear." His answer involves the sciences of complexity, ways of conceiving the world based on new insights and tools made possible by high-speed computers. Complexity acknowledges the importance of biological organizing principles rather than exclusively reductionist approaches. It embraces nonlinear dynamics, deterministic chaos, neural nets, and the paradoxical but satisfying idea that complex behavior of systems emerges from simple, local rules rather than top-down centralized control. All this was much more than I wanted to consider on the edge of the damp meadow, but his personal story in the introduction came back to me clearly.

When Pagels was first in physics grad school at Stanford, he stumbled on the Esalen Institute on the Big Sur coast, a center that had already begun to emphasize nonverbal learning and "positive rather than pathological aspects of mental life." He met gestalt psychologist Fritz Perls and joined some of his workshops. A highly cerebral guy, Pagels describes his reactions: "I learned most from my body, listening carefully to its signals . . . Such experiences would push me to the threshold of confusion and madness, or so it seemed. But those thresholds . . . are the gates of learning, and one always feels confused and unbalanced crossing them, as with any real learning. Reason alone will not get you across. In the end you have to trust the organism." Without that trust, he believes, you risk "falling into the trap of religious, political, or intellectual fundamentalism—a form of certainty that terminates creative growth." Early in his own life he'd melded mind and body into a whole that worked well.

Pagels had entered my thoughts partly because he'd hiked mountains not far to the north of the Weminuche several years back. On one difficult patch of trail, he'd leaped from rock to rock across a small airy emptiness and buckled his ankle when he landed. He fell. And he died. His ankle had been weakened with childhood polio, but, according to

his climbing partner, Seth Lloyd, Heinz had easily managed more dif-
ficult maneuvers in the past. The accident had partly prompted his wife
Elaine, a historian of religion, to write a book called *The Origin of Satan*.
Can there be any explanation for such bad luck?

In *The Origin of Satan*, Elaine Pagels pursues the *in*visible, turning
her historian's reasonable eye on territory where reason stops, but not
to accommodate the body's wisdom. How, she asks, have religions
explained the inexplicable? The Greeks first populated the world with
unseen, potent presences, giving credit for the unaccountable to gods
and goddesses, destiny and fate—forces indifferent to humans. Jews
added morality to the pagans' view, polarizing these forces into good and
evil. But Satan became a full-blown demonic presence with the Essenes,
a second-century-BC Jewish sect whose members believed *their* religion
counted as the most pure. They convinced themselves they took part in
a cosmic battle as "sons of light" pitted against humans who were under
the devil's dark and evil influence. Early Christians adopted this view and
expanded it: affliction became the malevolence of Satan, "other" often
became "evil." *Other* referred at first to Jews, then to all non-Christians,
then even to heretics within the fold. "Heretics," however, often earned
their labels from social conflicts rather than religious dissent. Challenge
the authority of the person in power? Fall in love with his wife? Heretic.
But did that apocalyptic vision of moral struggle stay sequestered in religion? No, says Pagels, it still permeates our secular lives.

In other words, demonize difference. Pagels's religious explanations weren't necessary to recognize what often happened to the "other"
around here. You didn't have to look far to find examples: ranchers vs.
environmentalists, Anglos vs. Hispanics, to name just two pairs from
a long list. But Pagels reminds us that within the Christian tradition
another powerful tension exists between the "profoundly human view
that 'otherness' is evil . . . and that reconciliation is divine."

Reconciliation is divine. Heinz insisted "mind" can be reconciled with "nature." Elaine suggested reconciling one's self with the

"other"—perceived as evil or not—might be an act of grace. Though the content of both books intrigued me, these thinkers' basic urge to dismantle dualities attracted me more. I'd just experienced a similar small epiphany when the conflict up? or down? had resolved itself.

I found it curious that nowhere does Elaine reveal what she believes about her husband's fatally turned ankle. Because she wrote that particular book soon after the accident, she must have felt at least some hidden evil had been at work. Had she been looking for an answer, but in the end abandoned her attempts? Perhaps chance or bad luck has no explanation. Anonymously, I joined in her grief over her husband, whose writing struck such a chord with me.

The storm had cleared out, leaving the high air clear and moist, and I watched the twins on their matched horses cross the stream up-meadow. I propped my pack on a boulder and shrugged it on, tightened the hip belt, adjusted the shoulder straps, fastened the sternum buckle, and finally secured my binoculars under a Velcro loop. Slowly I made my way to the trail that continued upward.

My body's backpacking misery needed no explanation from the invisible; but because I hiked alone, at least no one saw it. Alone, I also never needed to gauge myself against anyone else. I have no idea if I hike fast or slow, those terms with meanings only in relationship. They are not objectively in the world, but rather in experience. But isn't experience itself *in* the world? This was possibly no more than a semantic concern, but it did bring up again the difference between events versus our perceptions and descriptions of those events. Nature and mind, once again. Does experience ever happen without a body? Without a mind? One language solution is "body/mind." And what about the "body" of nature? Without the steep trail up through dark conifers my body/mind would certainly not pump fluids and transform energy at quite the same crazed rate, releasing endorphins, affecting my perceptions and "state of mind." My body/mind responded to the world's body. Then what was nature's *mind*? Certainly not the otherworldly—gods and goddesses—

but perhaps the invisible? Could nature's invisible mind be photosynthesis, animal metabolisms, ecological webs, all relationships that move
and change through time? Nature's mind—like mine, I thought—couldn't
be anything but physical.

We don't "see" such things only because our senses can only per-
ceive a small range of scales in time and space. When Heinz Pagels
suggested that computers might meld nature and mind, I understood
he meant an expansion of our limited perspectives. The intuitive leap
could be narrowed. Those speedy gadgets may eventually be able
to make visible the complex interactive webs that make up all life.
They might reveal this high mountain forest freshly, not discarding its
smells, escarpments, blooming meadows, but bringing deeper workings to light. And we might be able to understand better the nerve webs
enmeshed in our bodies, the sparking neural nets and synapses—the
webs we call our minds.

But I stray too far from hiking, perhaps.

When I finally crept out of the meadow in noon sun, misery—and a
certain grinding away in my convoluted grey matter—began to give
way to delight. On the mountain's steepening flank, the view opened
out through narrow, cone-laden fir crowns to distant, complicated grey
ridges and graceful, green meadows. Patterns and colors and the sense
of largeness called forth calming, deep resonances. A tribe of being had
welcomed me, and I remembered, down to my cells' mitochondria,
what I'd come for. But the moment before I reached tree line, the new
storm I'd heard rumbling up the valley caught me, crackling the air.
While I still enjoyed the protective company of firs, I rigged a tarp shelter and hunkered down, watching the lightning beyond shoulder-high
dwarf spruces twenty feet away.

In these mountains, the earth's crust had humped and fumed, and
glaciers had gouged it in such a way that not far to the west these

volcanic heavings butt suddenly against older granite. Those granitic peaks draw most of the hikers. Four of Colorado's fourteeners spike the horizon, offering themselves to list makers. Bagging peaks can be a kind of geographic scattershot; the Continental Divide Trail gives hikers a linear alternative, if they're after a coherent organizing principle.

The Divide loomed just ahead. When rain faded to drizzle, I inched my way up the final steep approach, feeling my pulse pounding and pounding, breathing hard. Twenty baby steps, then rest. Twenty more. The moment I reached the Divide Trail proper, a pair of hikers topped the rise to my right, beyond a stocky four-foot cairn. I waited, regaining my breath, until they reached me and stopped.

"Some storm!" the guy offered. "I'm Steve, and this is Nancy. We were hanging out just back there til the lightning stopped."

"Mary," I said as I shifted under my pack. "I was down there." They both peered over the edge to the steep trail. "Where'd you two come from?" I asked. The common first hiker question.

Nancy answered, "We started at Wolf Creek Pass. We're doing the whole Divide Trail. To Stony Pass."

"Wow! How far's that?" I asked, letting my voice show my admiration and envy.

"Eighty miles. We're taking two weeks. We've got a couple food caches on the way."

"Gotta get going," said Steve, "happy hiking." And they waved as they trudged on.

I watched them recede up the trail. Twenty-five miles in, Nancy had already begun to hike with one boot and one tennie to save her blistered foot. Still, they moved along much faster than I did.

For a while the trail followed the crest of a bare, hilly, serpentine pucker that glaciers had left gracious and mellow, like New England rolling countryside minus the green. Like gritty hips and thighs. Up close the smooth barrenness supported low clumps of alpine plants that sprouted this year's delicate lemon blooms peeking out from last year's dry stalks. The pinkish-grey stones themselves blossomed with bright green and orange lichens.

With land falling away on either side of the trail, I walked the ridge's back and finally tripped my elation switch. I floated above the world, air and light and space transmuted to limitless possibility. Not one whisper of misery. My pack had nearly vaporized.

For the next two days I ambled along the Divide Trail in rhythms that resembled complex Indian ragas more than the one-two of my steps. Intricate gardens unfurled everywhere, their visible selves accompanied by the song cycles of their names: gentian, bistort, wild bergamont, whiplash saxifrage, cleome, anemone, rosy stonecrop. Along one section, dense, blooming blue columbines covered grey boulder cascades, exuding the well-designed flavor of a Martha Stewart table setting.

Those hours both collapsed and expanded in seamless changing patterns, vast and tiny interwoven. Two hundred elk, a mile away across one wide scooped bowl, suddenly raced in a pointillistic burst like a land-bound flock of chickadees. Half of southern Colorado framed miniscule, purple trunks of blooming elephant's head. I became both small and enormous myself, the paradox part of a deep phylogenetic truth that extended back to the single-cell life that collectively covered the planet, further back to original stardust. Like so much walking, even in New York, the path and the destination not only became the same, but nothing beyond the immediate mattered.

Then I reached the Knife Edge.

Above tree line, the exposed rocky spit extended out from a narrow finger of the Divide. In three and a half directions, the land fell away abruptly into glacier-smoothed bowls, summer's alpine green slipping under dark, narrow, fir triangles. Nothing blocked the oceanic view out. Tiny bright lake puddles reflected rolling cumulus, snow patches still studded the shadows. I spent nearly an hour on the highest outermost boulder and thanked every speck of what I could see for being. I said (I swear), "May I always be here, no matter where I am." Then I hoisted my pack on again and looked at where the trail went next and muttered, "Oh, shit." Maybe the metaphor wasn't a metaphor at all. I'd be, literally, "always here."

From the Knife Edge, where two glaciers had once nearly melded, the boot-width trail crossed near the top of a sharply angled talus slope. On the trail's right, the slope continued steeply unbroken for a mind-numbing thousand feet until it gradually leveled to a grey, jumbled field. Sharp, head-sized rubble and miniscule plants led to the bottom of the basin. Way too visible, if I looked. Nothing to hang on to or break a fall. No trees, no shrubs, no variation in the slide. I hadn't yet begun to hike with poles, and I'd left the two sticks I'd used to cross the first creek by the water for other hikers. As I've become older, something in me has begun to cringe at heights. Though I'm solid where a fall would mean little, at high edges a primal fear races with a debilitating buzz from my ankles to my sacrum to the base of my skull and back. My heavy pack only made my idea of balance worse.

I knew this was why I shouldn't be hiking alone. Heinz Pagels had misstepped and died, and he'd not even been alone, but with a friend. I'd heard stories of other solitary hikers who had been injured and crawled for miles on bloodied knees and elbows, barely surviving. But I couldn't go around this section. If a better way had existed, the trail would not have made this impossible traverse. How far? Two hundred yards? Three hundred? It looked like miles. Others who do more extreme hiking—rock climbers, people who ascend icy peaks—would find my terror laughable. I saw not one carcass at the bottom of the slide. Other hikers with heavy packs had made it across. Nancy and Steve had made it across. But I lived in *my* skin.

Besides turning back, I could think of only one solution: go on. I breathed deeply and evenly, relaxing my shoulders and ribs down into my pelvis, down my legs into the earth. Attach like a magnet. At least a movable magnet. I understood the release technique from dance class: any tension high up works against good balance. Better to be grounded and unruffled. The urge to get across fast struggled with the impulse to take mincing steps to the point of shuffling. But in boots on the rough rocky trail, I couldn't shuffle. Look forward, look at where your feet are stepping, remember to breathe, relax that rib cage, get your heart out of your throat. Luckily the wind stayed quiet. Luckily the sun didn't shine in my eyes. If I'd been one for prayer, I would have prayed. I swore if I got across, I'd always hike with a stabilizing pole from then on. My breath sped up into shallow gulps. I tried to breathe deeper. Halfway across. More. I wished I had blinders on my right eye. The comforting and exhilarating space had become ominous. How could anyone sky dive? Finally, one small bush appeared on the right of the trail, then another, then a clump. The fear passed. No wonder I'd seen few people on this trail. I'd thought the Knife Edge meant the thin rocky spit, but the name had more to do with this nerve-jangling traverse.

I felt more lucky than skillful or brave. Luck helps everything that involves risk, maybe especially solitary hiking. The danger lay behind, and my recovery had been immediate. On the wider trail, I looked down calmly on brilliant blue Trout Lake off to my right and walked easily again through the cool afternoon.

Risk, I thought, has many variations. Physical risk vies with emotional risk as the more dangerous. Facing a fear often involves both. Whenever I watched videos of extreme snowboarding or kayaking, I suspected risk as pure hubris. Or excess testosterone. We've all encountered risks we've not chosen but have still prepared for. Consider driving over icy roads to get home in a storm. We can often take emotional risks only in a safe environment, exposing ourselves with stories we tell someone we know will not judge us. How many people considered my solitary hikes to be taking senseless, pointless risks? But these hikes are risk within a field of relative safety. I do what I can to lessen the risk: I know what gear I need, study maps carefully, try to figure out how far I can really hike. Ten miles a day for two weeks? No way. But we all see the future from a distance, and that field of safety can't ever be total, in mountains or not. Certainty is an illusion that's part of a rigid structure concocted by anxiety. Heinz Pagels's connection of certainty to all stripes of fundamentalisms—religious, political, intellectual—made sense. They "terminate creative growth," he said. Creativity, by definition, must always be associated with some risk. The safety that allows us to take many kinds of risk is not identical with certainty. Safety, far from being part of a rigid structure, implies a flexible, open system. How else do we ever get anywhere?

But the question from other women about threats from men is legitimate. I do choose routes less traveled, not only for safety, but because they're a better deal. For all my inevitable effort, I want an unclouded time. I also disclose the distance-from-the-trailhead rule: friendliness and insulation from human mischief increases in direct proportion to miles into the backcountry. When I talk about hiking alone, I also have to remember my experience with aggressive men may have been limited because I'm six feet tall, though lean and small boned. I've been told I seem self-confident, not vulnerable, regardless of what might be going on inside. Wherever I am, I also have my antennae out, sampling traces of the invisible, trying always to be present, to be aware. Chance dogs us always. But chance, like luck or risk, can never be an objective reality since it relies on each of us for its final form. Its final *mutable* form.

One afternoon I passed near the source of a creek that split the trees in the valley below like a careful, shining part. Across the trail, melted snow flowed from pale pink lozenges resting up the hillside of low brush and jagged stones. This watermelon snow, tinted by the algae growing between ice crystals, would probably not thaw away before the first winter storm covered it. In the tilted meadow, small, rough, ash-colored boulders littered the alpine flower explosion, photosynthesis ovens palpably cranked up in the sun, humming. Directly in front of me I heard a delicate, measured "burr, burr, burr . . . " One of the boulders not only spoke, but moved, along with five smaller rocks nearby. When I adjusted my focus, I could just barely pick out a mother ptarmigan and her brood, their summer camo outfits perfect but for orange crescents above Mom's eyes. That elastic segment of my hiking brain labeled "tasks required to function," and the one labeled "big questions" had both finally shrunken to pea size. I breathed entirely with the ptarmigans' unhurried progress, chicks nabbing bugs, Mom beaming vocal anchor.

Loneliness has no place for me in these hiking trances, any more than I can imagine ptarmigan loneliness. Or cairn loneliness. Though on the high open meadows, the cairns stood like sentinels, within hailing distance but no closer, enjoying great views, but not much conversation.

On the sixth afternoon, I reached my last camp, where I intended to stay two nights, day hiking to a cluster of high lakes. My tent sat barely in the trees next to Squaw Pass, an unimposing 11,000-foot saddle between 12,500-foot peaks, still on the Divide.

After dinner, in shorts and T-shirt, I leaned on a large trunk overlooking Squaw Creek's trickling source, the wind strong from the west behind me, warm in the late sun. Several times I thought I heard voices blending with the spruces in the breeze. I peered hard down the drainage, but saw no one and decided my quiet days must have attuned me to the local spirits. I'd brought a few sheets copied from my trail guide, and I finally looked at them. The instant I read "a sudden wind shift from west to south to east means deteriorating weather conditions," I lifted my face into wind that had obediently shifted from west to south to east. *Deteriorating* perhaps is a technical term, because that night's resounding thunder seemed more like a concert than something inferior to the night before. And I could hardly remember how the thunder had disturbed my first, unsettled sleep. During early morning, the rain on my tent fly stopped, but when I looked out at dawn, the quiet had come not from clearing, but from snow. It was August 10.

Some hours later, after pancakes, I sat in every piece of clothing I'd brought, waiting to see if the weather meant to *deteriorate* any more. I first heard, then saw, on the other side of the pass, a horse party making its way down the path I'd followed the day before. Two riders led two mules, so they couldn't be the twins from the meadow. Except for the through hikers on the Divide, these were the first people I'd seen since the twins nearly a week before. I watched them approach for ten minutes. When they reached the Squaw Pass marker, the lead rider started whistling. So they wouldn't surprise me? So I'd know they came with light hearts? As they closed in, I realized one of the riders was a boy.

I called, "Good morning!"

"Good morning!" the adult returned, "Where the hell're we at?"

"Squaw Pass. I have a map," I said.

Without a word, he dismounted, rummaged in one of his saddlebags and pulled out a fifth of Jack Daniels, green label, and took a swallow. Then with no hesitation, he walked over to me and said, "Want a hit?"

With no hesitation of my own, I put the open bottle to my mouth and tipped in a sip of the sharp liquor. My inner danger-detector had already spit out, "It's OK, he's with his kid," along with my mantra of self-preservation, hiking or not, "Meet anyone as an equal." Or, as I'd once put it to out-of-town friends following me through the crowded midnight subway station in Times Square, "Remember, you're as tough as they are. Look like you'd kill anyone who messes with you." It was your *only* protection in New York, but seemed to work everywhere.

I was one of the guys, with a taste for bourbon before noon, six days of dried food in my gut or not.

"Where'd you come from?" he asked.

"Down that same trail." I turned toward the pass and lifted my chin. "I came over the Knife Edge yesterday."

"Yeah, we were camped by Trout Lake last night and started out the other way on the Divide til I remembered where it went, and I didn't want to do that, so we turned around."

I had credibility.

"I'm Will. This here's my son Jackson." He extended his large hand and I shook it.

He was a fit six-foot-two classic Marlboro Man with forget-me-not blue eyes, drooping moustache. About forty. He wore the same uniform as the twins: dark Stetson, ochre duster, both wet from the rain. Jackson, about twelve, shivered in soaked jeans, cowboy boots, and a too-short poncho.

I thought of how I looked to them: only a bit shorter than Will, wearing yellow rain pants, a crinkly, faded-housepaint green Gore-Tex jacket lumpy over a down vest, powder-blue Patagonia sherpa hat covered by the visored hood from my jacket. Not even REI chic, no matter how functional, but a clear badge of my likely politics. And a woman alone: it must be a sign of something to them.

I hadn't been eager for company and still hoped I could cruise that last high trail if the lightning cleared out. I tried to gauge how soon they might leave. But the drizzly weather dictated both our plans: wait it out. Will seemed pleased to talk to someone besides Jackson. Standing around the cold fire ring, we exchanged our particulars. Outside a town near the trailhead on land originally homesteaded by his great-grand-father, he ranched and outfitted backcountry trips. Once a summer, he did his own pack trip in the mountains. This year he'd brought his son because Jackson had just chosen to live with him rather than his mother and stepfather in Grand Junction.

"She got tired of ranch life. I guess she got tired of me, too. Not many women are up for ranch life anymore." He winked—I swear it—he *winked* at me.

Ignoring his wink, I offered my own gloss: illustrator and designer from Albuquerque who sometimes worked on contract for the Forest Service. I stayed quiet about my relationship status. I certainly wore no wedding ring.

He took the obvious by the horns. "I'm a redneck, and proud of it. Do you mind being called a Yankee?"

"Not at all," I said. What a strange way to put it, especially in Colorado. But maybe I'd missed one of the ways to describe tensions around here.

"I have friends who really take offense at being called Yankees. But I know people who don't like being called rednecks either. I figure that's what I am, why should I mind?" I admired his bravado and knew I couldn't match it with my own self-exposure, too long used to careful camouflage.

Jackson hopped around, trying to stay warm until Will finally asked, "Do you mind if we build a fire? Storm don't look ready to head out any too soon."

I hesitated a moment, couldn't think of a good reason to say no, so mumbled, "Sure, go ahead."

They jumped to action, and though the wet wood didn't seem promising, Will pulled out a signal flare from the closest saddlebag. A no-nonsense fire starter. Overkill, but effective. Camp began to feel cozy, and I knew they had no intention of moving on soon. Jackson brought out his fishing gear and demonstrated his entire repertoire of knots to me, and then, dried out, set off to dig more worms.

From fishing, we moved to our clearest mutual interest: Forest Service grazing policy. With relish Will articulated his pride at being his own version of ranching redneck. Convinced by a traveling IBM sales-man, he'd PC'd up his operations. As a member of a ranchers committee, he negotiated with the local Forest Service about scheduling allotment grazing, sometimes insisting on less grazing than the Forest proposed.

"I think they should raise grazing fees. Now not everyone agrees with me." He tilted back his dark Stetson with his right hand, at the same time ran his palm over his nearly bald head, a few dark hanks of hair plastered to his skull in awkward undulations. "My private grazing costs six times what my public costs. It ain't right."

I nodded. "Glad to hear you say that. But that's the way it's set up."

"Any rancher can't handle higher fees is working too close to the edge, or worse, they're some big absentee corporation that don't give a damn about the land."

He shook his head and looked off toward Jackson, visible past dark wet trunks. "Damn idiots in Washington make rules without knowing a damn thing." He sighed.

"My father and grandfather died in accidents on the ranch. Few years back, my brother pulled over a stuck tractor onto hisself. Crushed him. I reckon the place'll kill me too someday."

As we talked on, I suspected he might be moderating his opinions out of courtesy for my assumed, though barely expressed, environmentalism, but he still confirmed what I believed about many ranchers. They'd been demonized in land fights, but they cared deeply and intelligently about most of the same things as their opponents. Interesting, even more than interesting, but after three hours on grazing, we began to run out of topics. No change in the weather, and lunchtime had long passed. But I also had begun to sense that Will might be on male autopilot. I didn't easily fit any of his categories, except perhaps eligible, attractive, friendly female, with a surprising lively interest in grazing. Jackson, quietly poking around, not talking much, continued to be the safety latch. I'd known since they'd appeared I balanced along a line only necessary because I was a lone female: be cordial, but not overly inviting. Perhaps most women understand the need for that skill; to miss with either one could trigger an unwanted response. Not often on my hikes alone did I get challenged by company in my camp. I liked this better than hanging out in my tent, but the vigilance began to take its toll.

Finally Jackson broke down and asked, "Pop, can we have lunch?"

Will, ever chivalrous, checked with me. "That be OK? We'd like you to join us." He glanced over to Jackson, making sure he caught these good manners. Maybe I imagined it. Maybe Will, a wise rancher, had figured out I really did want to be one of the guys. I wasn't the answer to his women troubles despite my willingness to talk for hours.

"Sure," I said, "but I'll have my own lunch. I need to eat some more, so I don't have to carry it out tomorrow."

"We've got plenty—we'll put some pork chops on for you anyway." And they went into action again. Pork chops from the cooler on one of the mules, a huge can of mixed veggies, a propane stove, a cast-iron skillet, an enamel pot for coffee.

I contributed hoisin sauce for the pork chops, something I used for dipping my jerky.

"This here's great. Can you get it in the supermarket?" asked Jackson in a rare outburst.

"Yup," I said, "ethnic foods section." I ate mostly peanut butter, rice cakes, and chocolate, but the hot pork chops and veggies tasted terrific.

We'd thrown our last bone into the bushes when a lone rider suddenly appeared and spoke just as we saw him, "Have you all seen any horses around here?"

"No." We all shook our heads. Will, Jackson, and I had become a group.

"Where the hell're we at, anyway?" he asked.

"I have a map," I said. What was with these guys who didn't know where they were?

This new rider was camped a ways down Squaw Creek with his family. The voices on the breeze the night before had been theirs. *Living* spirits. All week they hadn't hobbled or belled their pack horses, and they'd stayed near. But last night, in the storm perhaps, the pack horses had taken off.

Even though he didn't know how they'd get their gear out if he couldn't find them, he related his problem calmly. Handsome and dark, clearly with Spanish ancestors, he introduced himself as Sam Aragon. His full black beard without a trace of grey matched his dark eyes. He was younger than Will and lived in the same town. They started locating each other with their mutual friends, with their grazing credentials.

"Yeah," Sam said, "I used to graze sheep around up here before the

Forest Service stopped it." A statement of fact, no tone of resentment I could hear.

"You been fishing?" asked Jackson, always focused.

"Yup. First we were over at Trout Lake a couple days. Not one nibble."

"I hear it froze solid last winter." Will nodded. "This spring there were dead fish four foot deep all around it."

"Then no wonder," Sam smiled.

Another rider approached across the meadow.

"That's my sister's father-in-law, Albert," said Sam. "He's Cherokee."

He was also a vision. His palomino stood a hand taller than Sam's pinto, and his open yellow slicker folded comfortably around his thin legs and finely tooled saddle. A white scarf tied across his forehead held back his long, loose, black hair. He didn't seem very old, but his dark, weathered skin settled across high cheekbones and around his beaked nose like a nineteenth-century photo. But, unlike those Edward Curtis Indians, in the muted light he grinned.

I was riveted. Had I stumbled into a Zane Grey novel?

These three astonishingly attractive men seemed too archetypal to be real, one from each of the famous three cultures. And me. I was not so much an interloper as an avatar from a fourth culture—the culture of hikers wrapped in miracle fabrics, provisioned with gorp and Colin Fletcher and Aldo Leopold—in love with the same high air and rugged land, but lugging different psychic baggage. A culture where gender mattered less, but where abstractions mattered more. I wasn't exactly a Yankee, nor did I care one way or the other. But I *was* an Easterner turned Westerner who practiced yoga and pondered the visible and invisible in solitary hours spent hiking across rolling alpine fields. A concise label for this eluded me, but I knew I was part of a human wave, as much as I regretted it. Like Will, I knew what I was, but in this company, I couldn't embrace it. I had the map, but they knew the territory well enough to finesse their days.

This instantaneous reverie qualified as an abstraction itself, and I recognized it. I tried to get my focus back to the action. We weren't allegorical figures or bloodless characters for a tourist brochure or a government document. We were alive.

Jackson knew a stunning horse when he saw one and went to the side of the Cherokee's mare to ask about her and rub her flanks.

Will offered his help to Sam if the pack horses didn't turn up. Jackson discovered trout practically jumped out of the stream at the Aragon camp and easily convinced Will to let him take his fishing tackle down there and try his worms. Jackson, Sam, and Albert left.

And in a flash I found myself alone with Will. With disconcerting speed he rested his forearms on my shoulders and smiled into my eyes. "I thought they'd never leave," his voice low, intimate.

My immediate inner reaction matched exactly what I'd breathed when I first faced the trail at the Knife Edge: "Oh, shit."

I didn't worry I'd be raped and murdered on the banks of a gurgling trout stream at the hands of a crazed mountain man. I knew then, as now, that Will acted not so much from sexual aggressiveness as from sexual friendliness. I seemed to like him, and what better activities on an overcast day in lovely mountains than kissing and nuzzling? I'm sure he imagined it might even be the magical start of a romance. With a woman who might just like ranch life. And, in truth, in the past I'd happily and with no regrets fallen into the beds of men I'd known a shorter time. But this wasn't one of those moments. He'd misread me, despite my obscure maneuvers, and I only wanted to cut short the uncomfortableness. With no credit to my candor or my kindness, I said, "I think I'll go for a walk." Lame, indeed.

But that's what I did. Out across Squaw Pass, its name a blunt reminder of earlier attitudes and what I was not, past the saddle where the trail down met the Divide, into the drainage that led eventually to the Colorado. The Colorado's much manipulated water perhaps finally found its way into the kitchen taps of San Diego, half a continent away from the mouth of the Rio Grande, the gravity-impelled target of the rain falling at my camp.

The clouds brushing the surrounding peaks had dissolved enough so streaks of sunlight swept the glittering green exuberance. Where an unnamed creek steepened the descent, a small, fugitive rainbow blinked on and off close to the ground. I concentrated on picking my way through the wet brush and grasses until the tension had washed through me and out into the dripping day.

When I returned to camp, the horses stood packed up, and I guessed Will had gone to retrieve Jackson. Soon they both reappeared, Jackson clearly miffed they had to move. With a Girl Scout's urge to smooth ruffled feathers, I had Will write down his address so I could send him a copy of the poster sitting on my drawing table back in my studio. Not a great consolation prize, but acceptably civilized, I hoped. We were both more embarrassed than anything. He'd misread me; I'd not made myself clear. But the standard gender roles had held. He'd made a move, risking rejection. And I'd rejected him, pissed I'd been put in that position. It seemed to me we'd both been ambushed. We hugged good-bye like DAR matrons, and they left, heading down the side trail to look for the missing pack horses.

Happily alone again, I ate dinner and washed my face, barely in time to dive into my tent to escape another downpour. In Albuquerque, as in New York, I lived alone, competently self-reliant but aware the flip side of self-reliance can be isolation. Since I'd decided to leave New York, Andy and I had had a reconciliation of sorts. He'd flown out and helped drive the U-Haul across the country. But though we were still loosely friends, even loosely lovers, the future didn't seem to include closer bonds. As far as Will might be concerned, I *was* available. I didn't have a mate, after all. No paired domestic scene. But in my world, my current situation fit fine. Will had also miscalculated his moves; he might have continued our talk after Jackson left, perhaps ranging into more intimate topics, then invited me to his ranch after my hike. In that situation of greater safety—easy talk—I might have risked more and accepted. I regretted he'd not done that, in fact, since his ranching life attracted me. But that option had disappeared.

The next morning, as I worked on reconstructing my ponderous albatross for the long haul out, I saw Will and Jackson on the pass, leading their two mules with three other horses. They paused, and Jackson rode over to see if he'd left his jacket, and to give me the news. The night before they'd made it almost to the trailhead, eight miles and 2,800 feet down, before they'd found the lost horses. This morning at dawn, they'd started back up. I smiled. Will turned out to be as solid as I'd thought. I wasn't sure I'd have done the same.

By noon I'd reentered dense forest, shed several layers, and thanked the weather gods that *deteriorating conditions* had reversed. While I leaned against a stump for a raisin-and-peanut break, a new couple lurched into view, their horses weighted down under huge blue-tarped loads. The woman said hi; the man asked, "Aren't you scared being out here alone?" By then, tired and mourning my descent, I could only glare at him and growl, "I do it a lot." Period. Get away. Get away with your assumptions and preconceptions and gender bias and unwieldy, monstrous gear.

By midafternoon I trudged down the long switchbacks that eased an especially steep hillside. From above I heard a yell and looked up to see the whole crew from Squaw Pass. In a few minutes they'd caught up with me, and I moved to the side to sit on a rotting trunk as they followed the switchbacks down—four adults, three boys and a girl, and five pack animals. The receiving line ambled past, and I exchanged silent grins with each rider in turn. When they'd reached the next level down, going the opposite way, Sam called up, "I bet it's warmer in Albuquerque!"

"I was just thinking that." I was really thinking I'd love to have them carry my pack out the last three miles. I sure wouldn't ask.

Two hours later I dropped my millstone at the road, just off the asphalt, and walked the mile to my truck, parked in trees at the other trailhead. As I got to it, I heard from a knot of trucks and horses across the field, "Hey, Mary!"

"Hey, Jackson!" I called, raising my arm to his small shape caught in the strong western light.

Later I sat with my dinner cooking on the tailgate as they drove out, horse trailers in tow: Will, Sam, Albert, with their families, all honking and waving as they passed my camp.

No dark intentions had unfolded in this drama, nothing suited for the evening news or even an off-off-Broadway play. I only knew that the hike had not heeded my antiduality musings and had split itself in two: my days alone, at once an internal cleansing and a sensual filling, hard to convey; and the day on Squaw Pass, the story I'd tell when anyone asked, "How was your hike?"

Nothing in the world stays put in the categories we concoct, whether they're pair bondings that tempt us with salt-and-pepper-shaker order, or neatly merged wholes with apparent contradictions reconciled. It doesn't matter how well we observe or how attentively we hammer together our conceptual furniture. Or perhaps I speak only for myself in this. I try to sort through what seems at least partly explainable—visible, invisible, body, mind, luck, danger, risk, other—but they still all cruise the flux. My musings offer some understanding but never tie up all those flapping complications. Maybe that's part of what Heinz Pagels meant when he said, "In the end you have to trust the organism." Unexpected capacity—or wisdom—can emerge from our whole selves exactly *because* our mind/bodies, and the world, are more complex than we can ever conceive.

I'd trusted the organism when I'd decided in five minutes to move to New Mexico. I'd eventually trusted the organism after my first day's miserable climb when I'd realized I didn't need to choose between up or down. I'd been forced to trust the organism when I'd made it slowly across the Knife Edge. And with Will, I'd also trusted the organism.

But that one had me chewing my lip, wondering.

I'd negotiated a much less clear-cut traverse than the Knife Edge, but I ruefully admitted part of that equation had been that I'd been chicken. And I chided myself.

Solitude, whatever else it might be, is a paradoxical cure for loneliness. I couldn't have been happier hiking alone, but in company on Squaw Pass, I'd been rattled. My companion-vacuum had drawn Will in—but I had kept myself aloof. Such an adventure probably would have meant less physical risk than hiking alone, but it promised more human upheaval than I wanted to take on. That may have been wise, but it also seemed like a failure of courage. I had a notion of my solo mountain retreat, and I wasn't willing to have something too far off the agenda elbow its way unbidden into another part of my life. When I'd left precipitously for a walk across Squaw Pass, I'd avoided the whole issue and taken the easiest way out. Still, I felt no ambivalence about the outcome.

Once I'd gotten over my physical misery, I'd relished hiking alone in the late summer mountains, but the day on Squaw Pass had shone a light on my solitude, as if the benevolent spirit of Heinz Pagels had said, "Now that you've learned to trust the organism, remember how, but also don't stop looking further."

In the settling darkness, hidden insects began their night sounds, buzzing and clicking secret messages to each other. A single, shadowed deer grazed the forest's edge. I put away the kitchen gear, closed up the truck, zipped into my sleeping bag, and lay watching the night. Against the backdrop of constellations, unpredictable bright streaks shot across the heavens. I considered: they weren't so different from unexpected brief, sharp encounters in New York's streets. Or in the backcounty. But the shooting stars burned themselves out, while these other meetings left traces. Each one added to the accumulated wonder at the world's variety; each one offered a chance to make a choice; each one opened a window that *might* become a door, its threshold leading outward, beckoning.

The true biologist deals with life, with teeming
boisterous life, and learns something from it,
learns that the first rule of life is living.

—John Steinbeck,
The Log from the Sea of Cortez

The First Rule

Nothing had prepared me for the way the sea's wild flavor pulled me. And nothing on Baja's parched land had hinted at the marine extravaganza just offshore. I couldn't get enough. While the current stroked me, quirky creatures appeared at every fin flip. Foot-long brown sea cucumbers covered with orange nipples crept along sand flats, sometimes by the dozen, their Latin name, *Isostichopus fuscus*, straight out of Doctor Seuss. Pistol shrimp shot off loud clicks with tiny appendages called chelipeds. Thin crenellated arms of brittle stars explored sponge rims with sinuous persistence while bright blue five-inch-long Cortez damselfish nipped at every creature that strayed into their tiny realms, including me. I never tired of the gentle pulse that moved me with the same mesmerizing rhythm as the open anemones and long translucent ribbons undulating in the clear, breathing water. I'd been baptized into the church of perpetual pleasure.

Part of my delight came from the extreme contrast between this territory and New York City, where I still lived. The winter before, I'd illustrated a book about oceans, and as I'd pored over colorful photos of marine creatures, the urge to be eye to eye with the sea's weird and graceful life had grown nearly unbearable. I'd joined a summer class in field marine ecology on the Sea of Cortez to satisfy that hunger. But I also had another more complicated agenda: I wanted to make some peace with science. Fifteen years before, in undergraduate school, I'd been upended by my struggle.

The moment I'd graduated from Duke with a degree in zoology, I'd escaped those labs and cramped, number-engorged notebooks into art. I hadn't found the academic work hard, but the reductionist attitudes and searches for narrow truths had felt like leeches on my body, sucking me dry. In the middle of my sophomore year, I'd felt the lush, messy world begin to open around me, and I'd wanted to feel more a part of it. Scientific method began to seem less like a tool for exploration than a tightly laced corset, and "objective" science had appeared completely incompatible with passion. Given that choice, passion won. I went off to more open-ended, more inclusive, more emotional art school. But my attraction to science's structures and systems of understanding had never entirely vanished. Since those early days I'd grasped that the most complete view came from *multiple* perspectives. Tentatively, I'd circled back to science. I hoped field biology, immersed in the exuberant world I loved, would resemble classes in physiology (*kill those frogs slowly, please*) as much as the Goldberg Variations resembled a session of piano tuning.

I owed these happy wet weeks to Rob MacKenzie, who had for twenty years run his field ecology trips along the east coast of Baja California. He served equally as touchstone for biology's complicated idea-web and as hassle-master for a trip where everyone had to camp in sandy heat and frequent high winds. In his lectures, he flung out information about biogeography, energy flows, keystone species, reef communities, odd behaviors, and fish gestalts. He also came equipped with a genial black Lab named Fred and a way of smoothing tensions without seeming to lift a finger.

He *did* smooth tensions, but perhaps more importantly, he dealt with disasters. After we'd spent a week at Puerto Peñasco learning to distinguish *Chordata* from *Cephalopoda* and *Holothuria* from *Porifera*, we took off for Baja.

We traveled in a long car-and-truck caravan, with MacKenzie's son Dave bringing up the rear in a large, geriatric Winnebago. I drove and camped with Valerie, a student from the University of California, who had grown up in El Paso, Texas. Its dryness had propelled her to the sea. She meant well and surely had a good heart, but after several days, I understood she was twenty-two going on seventeen. I had limited tolerance for her concerns. We shared our camp with Fran and Nora, two women in their forties who had returned to school for master's degrees in invertebrate zoology. They'd brought along their daughters, two twelve-year-old girls. I'd managed to get them to agree to camp with us so they could adopt Valerie as their third charge. It worked well and left me mostly on my own.

We were thirty-four people, both undergrads and graduate students, including MacKenzie's assistants. And a few people like me, without classification. The group had originally included Sandy, the dive master, but she'd been missing since the first week when she'd flipped her old Bronco on a Mexican road. A passing pickup had rushed Sandy and her passenger Jim to the border, not far away. Jim had been helicoptered to Phoenix, his skull probably fractured; Sandy had been driven to Tucson, her wrist broken. We'd stripped what we could from her wrecked Bronco, loaded her gear into the RV, and continued on our way. About midnight we set up our tents in a vacant dirt lot next to a Texaco station. All other campsites had been taken by some of the fourteen thousand Jehovah's Witnesses in town for a convention.

On the rush to the border after Sandy's accident, the RV had blown its dipstick. But Dave had caught it in time and, with no auto parts store in sight, hit on the solution: a perfectly sized green branch from a nearby tree. The RV's top had begun slipping forward on the wheelbase, something Dave would deal with later. For the time being, he drove twenty miles per hour and stopped frequently to check the slippage.

Some days later, the van belonging to Trevor and Ellen, two of MacKenzie's grad students, blew a tire. Trevor had held it steady as it swerved into the ditch, so it didn't roll, but the jolting over rocky ground flattened the remaining three tires and burst the radiator. The second the van stopped, their black dog, Vishnu Schist—an easily terrified creature—bolted out the window into the field, and when we arrived, Trevor and Ellen both stood a ways off, trying to coax him back to the road. Eventually the *federales* and a nearby farmer who had offered Trevor fifty dollars argued over the van booty. Only Tony, a nineteen-year-old traveling in his open Jeep, had enough Spanish to translate. Finally the farmer prevailed, and we finished moving all their gear, including two sea kayaks, the deflated inflatable, and all we could pry off the van, from headlights to rearview mirror to distributor cap, into the rest of our vehicles, now packed to the gills.

Throughout these mishaps, MacKenzie never showed any signs of being flustered. But then, for twenty years he had caravanned through Baja with college students. To my surprise, half his students this summer preferred playing backgammon and Trivial Pursuit on the beach to water adventures. They hated camping and camp food and the heat and no showers. They worried about getting boils from staph in the soil. I didn't understand why they'd come along on the trip. Beach-blanket backgammon? But others, like me, couldn't imagine anything better.

One was Nicky, who traveled from camp to camp on the dive boat *L'Estrella de Mar*, an old diesel workhorse captained by Armando with his son Juan. In our first meeting in a classroom, I'd heard her described, "She's like a ski bum, but a diver." She came with her dog Snow, who was a silky all-white mixed breed and who, like his black-haired mistress, felt as comfortable on a boat as on land. At that point in her life, Nicky lived part time in Tucson, part time in San Carlos. Like all my favorite people, she lived on the edge.

🍃

We'd reached the trip's third week and had settled on a spit of land separating two curving sandy coves. Beyond our tents and tables and piles of books, coolers, and dive gear, the spit widened to a broad, rocky T. Along its crosspiece, the T fell away to a shallow reef packed with marine life. Around the point, the surge swept a liquid plankton market past anchored animals: sponges and latticed sea fans and fringed tube worms. Through clear water, avalanches of sunlight fed the metabolisms of tiny forests of branching soft red algae and pink foliose coralline algae, crusty and compact. The sponge *Codium* reached its dark green fingers up from the bottom next to graceful, upright brown sheets of the algae *Padina*, both moving lazily over fuzzy mats that resembled AstroTurf. Among the life-encrusted boulders, spiny sea stars, urchins, and furtive octopuses crept back and forth on provisioning expeditions. And fish raced around in their own arcane traffic patterns.

Just off the north point, obscure landmarks defined a cleaning station where larger fish tranced out as smaller fish nibbled parasites and algae off their scales. You could be sure to find a lolling parrotfish or grouper there, as relaxed as a man leaning back in a barber chair, his grooming needs delicately tended by a seasoned practitioner. While I'd treaded water two yards away, I'd watched triggerfish hang out while small rainbow wrasses and barberfish worked back and forth along their broad flanks. Whole schools of goatfish tarried, darkening their color while tiny, darting disks striped in yellow and bright blue arcs serviced them. Nothing I encountered reminded me of my formal education.

While I'd been in school in the late sixties, I accepted as gospel *what* I'd been taught in biology. *How* I'd been taught had seemed the only way. Not uncommon reactions from a twenty-year-old. And I'd not had the luck to find a teacher who had a sense of adventure within biology and who could also be easily approached by a shy, confused young woman—a teacher who might have understood both my fear of being trapped and my broad curiosity enough to suggest I try field biology. I don't know if he'd existed at Duke—all my teachers were men—but I didn't find him. Instead, one summer I had a fancy job in a federal research lab connected to a hospital outside Washington. The project I worked on used early methods of genetic sequencing to establish taxonomies of bacteria. Everyone in the lab had been friendly and helpful but seemed so narrow that the idea of spending my life in research caused me to loosen whatever clothing I had on for fear I'd suffocate before I noticed. That summer I also posed in a bikini for the August calendar of the newsletter that served the hospital filled with returning Vietnam vets. I'd been genetic researcher *and* scantily clad calendar girl.

Field biology turned out to be a fabulous amalgam. Every day we dipped into lore from countless other observers and kept our imaginations loose enough to guess what might be going on. We used our ingenuity to cook up projects that would supply insight without trashing the neighborhood. At the same time the human context infused everything. We endured camping in one-hundred-degree heat but were simultaneously blessed by the extraordinary open beauty of desert and sea together. Finally, like all temporary communities, our provisional tribe shook with shifting alliances, both inexplicable tensions and sudden romances.

"I'm very interested in systems where sexual selection is strong," said MacKenzie. He overtly meant unraveling the details of mate choice: Darwin's engine. But sparking love alliances and all manner of human competition were known to fascinate him on these trips as much as the fish and inverts, the whales and sea lions. He had suggested, in the same tone of voice he used for wide-mouthed blennies, that in our journals we analyze our human companions. Nicky told me, "Every summer he has an affair with one of the students. Hard to tell who it'll be this time." True? I had no idea. But I knew I didn't invent the tone of teasing innuendo when he asked on one test, "What qualities should females seek in a male?" Here was one way he'd found to add passion to cold science: human sexual selection.

A female, in theory, will choose the male most likely to give her offspring the best chance of survival; but the particular seductive quality differs from species to species. In fish it's usually size. Matchmaking has been hardwired by eons of natural selection and holds true for any animal with a choice, including humans.

I bristled whenever such determinism was applied to me. But I did note in my answer that I preferred originality in male *Homo sapiens*, though I doubted that would ensure survival of any of my offspring. According to human evolutionary biology, humans, as biological creatures, must strictly adhere to biological laws. To me, one trouble with sociobiology has always been its single-minded, but easily manipulated, *neatness*. In humans, the theory goes, direct links between mate choice and offspring survival have usually atrophied, but the genetic impulses persist, stronger influences than the image on the Shroud of Turin. What I felt as free will in defining my own preferences in men might be beyond my control. Originality might indicate innovative solutions to survival problems, and mean an originality-craving gene had been selected for in countless numbers of my distant ancestors. I just imagined I'd made it up. In this view, genetic determinism didn't swallow the sensations of passion, but cast them in a different light. But perhaps I'd misinterpreted.

Aside from local primate behavior, many other mating oddities surrounded us. Off the next point to the north, light fingered down into narrow sand channels that separated sheer vertical rocky outcrops about ten feet high. One afternoon, four of us threaded along the confined channels that were brightened even more by white colonial tunicates clinging to the walls like thousands of small, pliant light bulbs. Interspersed with the spongelike tunicates, delicate feather dusters spiraled out from their two-inch-tall tubes, and bushy clusters of stinging hydroids kept us aware of our bare arms and legs. White, red, and yellow gorgonians—those branching, skeleton-like *arbolitos del Mar* covered with thousands of tiny tentacled polyps—grew with their broad sides stiffly in the current, getting maximum flow. At the end of one channel, hundreds of fist-sized murexes had piled on top of each other into a huge mound. Undeterred by the spiny projections of each other's brown-and-white banded shells, they extended their soft feet as far as possible, in constant motion. The murexes, not a species with strong sexual selection, were heavy into an indiscriminate mating frenzy.

The ubiquitous sergeant majors, hand-sized compressed fish, usually preferred parading around in small, tight groups and timed their courtship to summer moons. Once a month, the males exchanged their black on yellow banding for an all-over deep metallic blue, finished off with tantalizing white lips. They each descended to the rocky bottom and scraped algae off an upright rock, establishing a closely guarded territory. The females cruised the area, inspecting each male and his spot, gauging whether she should drop off some of her eggs. The more eggs already in a male's domain, the more likely she'd add some of her own for him to guard until they hatched. Each potential papa sergeant major eventually calculated his own genetic cost/benefit balance: if he had enough eggs, he'd protect them until they hatched, fasting the whole time; if his egg patch fell short, he'd simply eat them and not bother. Better luck next month.

But my favorite fish sex adventurers were the *protogynous hermaphrodites*, including many of the wrasses, like the Mexican hogfish. Each hogfish began adult life as a female, eight inches long, with two horizontal dark stripes on a red and yellow streamlined body. Under certain conditions, so far obscure to humans, one female would transform into a *supermale*, two feet long, a large bump above his eyes, with long trailing fins and tail. Supermales changed not only size and shape, but color: to slate grey with a reddish wash toward the head, a single vertical yellow slash in the middle of each side. When I spotted one in midtransformation, I knew I'd been told the truth. But who among the harem gets to be a supermale? And when? And does she have a choice? What if two start to become supermales at once? Do they meet at the cleaning station for a face-off?

I wasn't part of the primate sexual selection maneuverings even if I *had* eyed the field for a few days, alert to any appealing originality. MacKenzie fit the bill best, but even without other considerations I had no desire to become another in his ongoing summertime harem. And that volatile realm was too familiar. What kept me wound up and completely engaged was not the prospect of a human entanglement, but my brief visits to worlds vastly different from my own. Anytime I could find a dive buddy, I spent time in the water.

But today I'd been thwarted. *Aqueous interruptus.* From a hundred miles away, in the night, a storm had churned the water to opacity. The growing surge had confused my dreams with rising decibels, and I woke to elemental upheaval. No diving all day. "That's field biology," said MacKenzie. He hated wind. It veiled the water and sent tarps and plates flying down the beach. It dusted food with sand and badgered people into their worst selves. It constantly invented new harassments. During breakfast I'd barely caught my tent when a gust had lifted the back, dumped out the rocks I'd piled inside, and tried to export it to La Paz.

In mid-July, the minute the sun rose, Baja began to vibrate with heat. Only the water kept us tolerably quenched. I wore a bathing suit and a thin T-shirt at all times and dunked myself whenever I started to sizzle. The water held enough of winter's chill that uncontrollable shivering limited all my snorkels. Baking and freezing regulated my thermostat so well that I only began to steam in my sleeping bag at dawn, when the day's instant heat always woke me in time to watch the sunrise over the Gulf, with silhouetted fishing boats distantly putt-putting into copper brightness under Jesus calendar sunbeams.

Today the north point extended out into a prolonged, wet explosion that must have interrupted all parasite pruning. And all humans stayed ashore. The wind resembled an aerial infestation of fiendish nags, but it still couldn't touch the basic reality. Baja California's baking desert slid away into the Sea of Cortez, and we were camped at the luscious, foaming edge.

I'd been banished from the sea. But not from its shore. No telling what oddities might crop up in the storm's detritus. I picked my way along the sand of the south cove, looking at shells for their forms, the inert remainders of softer lives. As an artist, I transformed real things into representations and recast life into intimations of life, but I understood that I always had to leave out the most crucial element, much like the moon shell at my feet. It coiled in a graceful spiral, but could only suggest its past complicated existence. After my days of snorkeling and diving, land's appeal had dwindled and what once would have satisfied me had become a pale substitute for the real juice. But I couldn't dismiss my own work so easily, nor my love of form and color, of juxtaposition and descriptive categories. Even the strange overwhelming life of the sea had an order. Or many orders. Often I worked to make that order clear, whether I drew the suckers under a starfish's arm or a spiraling serpulid worm case or details that distinguished taxonomic categories. Even if my drawings lay on the page not breathing, I always knew they referred to life. My field notebook had been filling with black-and-white sketches of the fish and inverts I found in my daily dives: a record that was simultaneously art, a chronicle of lived experience, and a way to understand.

In *The Log from the Sea of Cortez*, John Steinbeck gives us a journal of his trip to collect invertebrates with his biologist pal, Ed Ricketts. They traveled by boat along this shore in 1940, when the Gulf of California had been little visited. I'd read its rich detail and philosophical ponderings just before I'd set off from New York this summer, entranced by his descriptions of the land, the sea, the sea creatures, and all his companions. And I'd been taken by what he says at the very start of his tale: they knew that by collecting samples and storing them in alcohol-filled glass jars they could only capture a part of the life of the Gulf. As importantly, he acknowledges they needed to remember the colors and movements and *spirit* of what they encountered. They went with curiosity, knowing they'd change the Sea of Cortez as much as it would change them.

All these, he says, would give a much fuller picture than any single one alone. "And so we went."

Three hours after dawn, an hour after my walk, the sun had begun to singe my earlobes, and I waded into the cove's sandy shallows wondering about alternatives to scientific method. How to remember the spirit of what we—or any scientist—encountered? Did anyone admit to direct understanding? Could mechanism be trumped by intuition? Could explanation be informed by empathy? Could patterns be deciphered more easily when the methodology included love—or should I call it passion? I sloshed back through thigh-deep water to the shade of our tarps for a day stuck on land, tending to my dive gear and thinking about science.

Since 1940, when John Steinbeck and Ed Ricketts collected invertebrates from this coast, much has changed in biology. Today, fewer people catalogued critters—though that still kept a fair number of biologists occupied—and more people pursued different sorts of questions.

With admirable optimism, biologists expected to find explanations, if not causes, for nearly everything. Natural selection isn't a *cause* but has come to be a nearly all-inclusive explanation. Explanations usually followed stories driven by *how* questions, ferreting out local mechanisms. What *exactly* triggers a male sergeant major to change color, leave his schooling pals, and become a loner with powerful territorial aggression? Do weak internal tides in sync with the moon's cycle work a crucial chemical conversion? *How* questions were proximal questions. The "ultimate" questions were *whys*. Why do sergeant majors need to breed that way in the first place? Why don't they release their sperm and eggs in the water column the way many other fish do? The *why* questions were broader, harder, more speculative, and usually avoided. More than simple *whys* were even larger unexplained phenomena. What about the distribution of all fish in the entire Gulf? What about the sudden die-off of the common multi-armed starfish *Heliaster* during the last few years?

What about the way food webs interact? What about the effect Japanese factory ships in the Gulf have on the rocky intertidal?

Most biologists worked to link their observations with mechanisms, the *hows*. Although that seemed a good way to build accurate and predictive models, two ecologists, Valerie Ahl and T. F. H. Allen, in *Hierarchy Theory*, have called mechanism the "dark side of the force." Limiting your focus to narrow *hows* always threatens to limit your understanding. A little, perhaps, like putting critters in jars with alcohol.

Ahl and Allen see that our world consists of complex systems, and our questions and methods must acknowledge that. "A systems approach involves including the observer, and human values, in the process of coming to terms with complex problems."

Several days before, I'd been out to an island just offshore, snorkeling with Nicky. We'd been identifying and counting blennies on one section of shallow reef. Blennies are small territorial fish that usually live in tiny rocky caves along the bottom. Often they're brightly colored. After we'd finished our count, I'd hovered over the reef watching thin barracudas and an occasional cornetfish cruise the water below me. Nicky had retrieved her spear gun from the small inflatable and headed into deeper water, hunting dinner. In twenty minutes she returned with a yellow snapper. We both climbed into the boat, removed our snorkels and masks. Nicky shook herself as if she needed to make some sort of transition.

"When we were counting blennies, I wasn't at all afraid of the sharks around here," she said, "but the second I started hunting, I got really aware I was also prey. It's always that way. I suddenly know I'm part of the food chain." Outside her narrow framework of science—blennie counts—she'd suddenly *felt* herself part of the larger system.

The *how* questions, Ahl and Allen note, are about mechanics. They're reductionist. The science I'd run from earlier in my life had been just such a reductionist, mechanical approach. *Why* questions include meaning and context. I'd not stayed around long enough to discover that some people in the sciences had felt a constriction similar to mine. Perhaps more importantly, they recognized that an exclusively mechanistic approach does not even do a good job of describing the world, and they had set about changing things. I began to see that biology itself was much less static and settled than I'd once believed.

MacKenzie didn't limit himself to mechanisms and often made observations about larger patterns. With great pleasure in the professional competition, he pointed out that the popular ecological theory of island biogeography claimed that an island's number of species *decreased* the farther away it was from the mainland. But that observation only applied to life above the waterline. Underwater, diversity *increased* with an island's distance from shore. Though that didn't pit mechanism against pattern, it still supplied a perfect example of myopia in action. Terrestrial chauvinism.

MacKenzie also observed that some early ecological theories had been developed by East Coast ecologists using simple eastern ecosystems such as salt marshes (i.e., energy flow as the defining phenomenon). Ecosystems in the West tend to be much more complicated—ecosystems such as the rocky intertidal shorelines where we snorkeled and dived. The classic ecological theories don't work on such complex systems. Eastern chauvinism.

I'd bolted from the corral of science the second I'd felt my legs strong enough under me. But with the distance of some years, I understood the narrowness I'd fled was only part of the picture. I'd objected to a slavish adherence to methodologies dependent on numbers and blind to any vision larger than a bread box. I'd objected to tacit agreements to ignore or dismiss loose ends, poetry, social context, political implications, meaning, emotion, and mystery. Anything that suggested passion. Or any biologist's personal life. As I watched thousands of bitsy, segmented isopods dancing on piles of pungent sargassum on the beach,

I knew I still objected to those tacit—or unrecognized—agreements. Still, on this trip I had come to revel in stories that answered those *how* questions. But I also felt hope that others had begun to address the narrowness I'd experienced. Admittedly, my dismay had been a visceral, not very nuanced reaction to something I'd only barely understood at the time.

In 1970, when I was twenty, I believed what I'd been told: women could as easily as men do anything we wanted, limited only by our abilities. I'd been academically more than able; I'd excelled. I'd also been suspicious of the claims of the women's movement about less-than-obvious ways society constrained women. I'd been a tomboy and had never fallen into typical female roles in my activities or relationships. Consciousness-raising groups were for others, not for me.

Recently, though, I'd found Evelyn Fox Keller and her analysis of gender and science. In her early career, she'd been a mathematical biophysicist—she'd stuck it out much longer than I had. She's clear: not only are "male" and "female" largely social constructs, but so is science. In popular mythology, "male" is associated with objectivity, reason, mind; while "female" connects to subjectivity, feeling, nature. Social studies of science, she writes, have failed to take serious notice of two crucial factors:

> First . . . science has been produced by a particular subset of the human race—that is, almost entirely by white, middle-class men—[and] it has evolved under the formative influence of a particular ideal of masculinity. For the founding fathers of modern science, the reliance on the language of gender was explicit: They sought a philosophy that deserved to be called "masculine," that could be distinguished from its ineffective predecessors by its "virile" power, its capacity to bind Nature to man's service and make her his slave (Bacon).
>
> Second, and related, is the fact that in its attempts to identify extrascientific determinants of the growth of scientific knowledge,

the social studies of science have for the most part ignored the influence of those forces (disregarded as idiosyncratic and at the same time transsocial) that are at work in the individual human psyche . . . [But, we can now] explore the interdependencies between subjectivity and objectivity, between feeling and reason (Evelyn Fox Keller, *Reflections on Gender and Science,* 7–9).

I don't know if I would have made any different decisions if I'd been able to read Evelyn Fox Keller in 1970, but my escape to art school had much more to do with what Keller calls "the rending of the human fabric" than I'd suspected. Men as well as women have suffered from the narrowness in science I'd felt at twenty. I'd always been fierce about my equality with men. Perhaps that's why, when I resisted a discipline that seemed to deny half of my humanity, I hadn't associated that choice with my own gender. But I had been unwilling, or even unable, to dismiss a firmly connected part of myself.

Like gigantic brass spheres, the sweltering hours rolled slowly past until late afternoon. By then, wind and waves had both gentled; heat and light shimmered together, scorching everything not in shadow. I couldn't resist any longer. In the next shade island, engrossed in some field guide, sat Gwynn, another of my favorite fellow divers. She studied geology, but took great pleasure in softer materials too. "Gwynn," I called over, "isn't it calm enough inside the north point to go for a snorkel?"

"Looks OK to me." She stood up. "Let's go!" We carried our fins and masks and snorkels and wetsuits the fifty yards to the beach and backed in happily, heels first so we didn't catch our flipper tips. Then we split up, each on our own unknown missions.

Immediately under the surface, the pale burnt desert and glittering sea-sweep flipped into a complicated scene. Frilly hydroids, pink encrusting algae, olive green anemones with red tips, and scattered

bright yellow sponges almost swallowed jumbled rocks. Cortez damselfish and sergeant majors sped around, so familiar I noted them
only in passing. Clusters of long, dark urchin spines jutted out from
crevices and shifted back and forth slightly out of sync with each other,
while tiny brown and green algae filaments pulsed in concert with
the surge. Only two feet above the bottom, I floated nose to nose
with everything.

Almost at once I spotted a small octopus in the open, oddly out
of rock protection. The size of my closed fist, he had tentacles twice as
long as my fingers. The others I'd seen had all retreated into their hide-
outs when I'd been nearby, but as soon as this one saw me, he came
at me. While he rested, his skin remained a deep maroon mottled with
light beige. But when he feinted in my direction, he turned pale blue.
The change happened in a moment, in a wave like a cloud passing from
in front of the sun. He'd stop, resume his darker color as he settled on a
rock, then approach me again in his blue garb. At first I'd been startled
and had backed off a few feet, but then quietly held my ground. After
five minutes his memory of me faded and he began to amble around
the small neighborhood, rock to rock, his tentacles coiling and uncoiling sensuously. He had no obvious agenda—he didn't seem to be
hunting or mating or defending territory, but he changed color all the
time. Whenever he sank over a rock, his tentacles bleached light, and
the double rows of suckers on each arm faded from maroon to pink to
white. Sometimes the tips of his arms turned slate grey. Several times
he strayed into the territory of a five-inch Cortez damselfish—half his
length, but fearlessly territorial. Whenever the damselfish nipped at
him, he responded by turning solid sky-blue and swelling his large
head, so that the many short fleshy protrusions filled out. In about ten
seconds, he'd retreat and darken and continue his fluid wandering. His
eyes, with their dark horizontal irises, usually stayed uppermost, like
two knuckles on a hand with bent fingers. Just behind each eye knob,
a round siphon opened with a glowing yellow-orange lining. After I'd

hovered over him for twenty minutes, he got especially agitated about
something I couldn't see, deepened his mottled maroon, and materialized a bright blue stripe down the exact center of his bulbous head. A
semaphore self. But who could translate?

Finally, he lengthened to a blunt arrow with trailing tentacles, and,
propelled by water jets pumped backward through his siphons, swam off
ten feet. He nestled into a crevice, where he remained visible, quiet, and
monochrome for ten minutes. When he reemerged, he strolled around in
eight-armed grace for two more minutes, then slipped away completely
into a dark, narrow slit under an overhang.

I waited, hoping he'd live a little more of his life in my sight, but
my teeth were chattering, my thumbs already numb. I swam back to
the hot beach.

I'd been excited and almost frightened by all the rapid color switch-
ing, the coiling and uncoiling arms. While I'd floated nearly immobile
in a buffered silence broken only by my loud snorkel breathing, he'd
been maneuvering like mad. I felt as if I'd been doing something out of
bounds—not dangerous, but verging on forbidden. I had a curious and
admittedly sexual sensation of being a voyeur, which I hadn't felt when
I'd spied on the murex mating frenzy or watched fish do anything at all.
Such undulations and baldly exposed emotions were almost temptations
that carried known strictures: "Thou shalt not move as if thou hadst no
bones. Thou shalt not turn blue and maroon in alternating waves." That
I happened not to be physiologically able to commit such sins didn't
mean I wouldn't have if I could have figured out how. Watching put the
notion in my head and made me squirm.

I knew the basic mechanisms. Octopus skin contained two kinds
of muscle-controlled chromatophores: dark, from brown to black;
and lighter, from red to yellow-orange. Activated, the chromatophores
expanded to create fields of color. Octopus skin was also densely salted
with two kinds of tiny mirrors: translucent iridophores that reflected a
broad spectrum of colors; and deeper opaque leucophores that reflected

white light. Different nerves controlled different sections of the surface palette. But despite their keen eyesight and their own dramatic pigments, octopuses were color-blind. Still, they could visually match the *intensity* of their surroundings. Their chromatophores, combined with the reflective capacities of iridophores and leucophores, did an outstanding camouflage job when that's what they intended.

And octopus *intention*? Some species have been watched carefully enough to link color and posture with particular situations. In *Octopus*, M. J. Wells puts it in clinical language: "zebra crouch by young animal in presence of another octopus," or "moving flush when a small object approaches to one side." Mottled patterns might indicate internal uncertainty. Who couldn't identify with that? In each particular octopus, the arrangement of light spots stays the same, as unique as a fingerprint. And their individuality extends to behavior. A captive octopus often develops personal mannerisms, like spraying an attentive keeper with streams of water. A trick I wished I could pull off. Wells observes that primates and octopuses share an evolutionary history that "forced upon us a way of life that depended upon adaptability rather than armor, a capacity to know when to run and how to detect trouble in the making." He also recognizes how easy it is to identify with an octopus as a fellow creature. "They watch you," he says. He might have said instead, "They watch you while you watch them." But, he warns, "the octopus is an alien," even more than any vertebrate. A Cortez damselfish may be Other, but at least it has a backbone.

And yet. I stripped off my wetsuit and my flippers and lay flat on the toasty sand, my body shivering, sucking up the heat. Except for their haunting eyes, octopus sense organs are in their suckers. Octopuses live in a tactile world where they even taste by touch. I wondered what it would be like to taste the sand along my back, behind my calves and knees and thighs. I wiggled deeper in.

Gwynn splashed back to the beach with her own charged sightings: two nudibranchs—a Mexican dancer and a Norris's dorid. Nudibranchs are bare-gilled, brightly colored, shell-less snails that graze on algae patches. But Gwynn had found both separately levitating in the water column as finger-sized, undulating, free-floating jewels. The Mexican dancer's complicated, curly gills fringe its back, tipped with maroon and yellow-orange, above a yellow-green body. Norris's dorid is the translucent blue-white of fine china, covered with purple and orange dots.

Gwynn hopped around, excited, "How could such gorgeous, weird things have ever evolved? And I was right down there with them!"

Warmed up and dried off after our swim, Gwynn and I threaded our way through dark sargassum clumps back to camp.

"By the way, did you see those luminescent waves last night?" she asked, always keeping her eyes open and wanting to share it all.

"Sure did." I breathed in the damp sea smell on the rising breeze and noticed it coiled together with the aroma of garlic heating in oil for someone's dinner.

My own insistent multiple perspectives engulfed me at every waking moment. Octavio Paz's poems tripped along in my nerve net entwined with MacKenzie's lectures about stochastic processes and keystone species. The night-dive image of what looked like a three-foot-long translucent vacuum-cleaner hose appeared in the same frame with my mental note to send the cooler to town for ice. Predawn dreams of my main squeeze, some thousand miles away, mingled with Latin nomenclature and iridescent blue spots on the red foot of a giant tulip shell. I saw charts of data woven with fin whales cavorting alongside the boat and a king angelfish snoozing against a rock sixty feet down. Hermit crabs in hydrocoral helmets crawled through thoughts of far-from-equilibrium systems, accompanied by the sound of water gently slapping rocks.

Science couldn't compete with such image rushes, but it had at least begun to harmonize with everything else that danced in my brain. Every-day science became for me not a rigid system that denied all others, but simply *one* way—or several particular ways—of looking and thinking. In my mind, it had become less constraining dogma than perpetual, expansive inquiry.

I found mechanistic explanations added a density to the intertwining plot lines as rich as any Dostoyevsky novel. I'd also discovered that the last chapters always remained open-ended. Biology turned out to be a vast library full of individual stories, none with final pages.

Like a tidal cycle, my thoughts returned to Evelyn Fox Keller. She wanted to restore to science some of the world, some of human experience that has been mostly relegated to women: the personal, the emotional, the sexual. On this trip we'd tried to distinguish fact from empathy, not wanting to misrepresent the outer world by coloring it with eccentric inner landscapes. Less sharply, we thought we should distinguish information from experiences, separating pages 201–4 in Brusca's invertebrate field guide from an hour snorkeling. But the interpenetration can't be denied. And I returned to the idea of love. Didn't real work—even real science—require a passion that operated in tandem with "objectivity"? Kaleidoscopic memory, expectations, the same quickening of pulse and dropping away of everything extraneous that accompanies sex *must* animate any satisfying work, from trading commodities to tracking barnacles. In a kind of unintended puritan joke, we're mostly taught rigor and discipline, but not that as crucially we need to learn to fly. We make love, we make books, we make children, we make scientific theories. All, at their best, ignited with passions fired by quirky idiosyncrasies.

✺

Evelyn Fox Keller tells the story of the Nobel Prize–winning geneticist Barbara McClintock, who worked with chromosomes of corn. After years of research, she'd proven that organisms can indirectly reprogram their own DNA by a process called transposition. At first heretical to the doctrine that information flows only one way—from DNA to the organism—transposition is now widely accepted. More to the point for me were Keller's observations about how McClintock had worked. Keller believed that McClintock succeeded in demonstrating such a genetic heresy precisely because she'd been able to suspend the boundaries between subject and object without jeopardizing her science. Unlike stereotypic science, hers was *not* premised on a rigid division between observer and world. Rigor became spliced with empathy. Keller quotes McClintock describing her corn's microscopic genetic bundles, "When I was really working with them I wasn't outside . . . I was part of the system. I was right down there with them." For McClintock herself, the word *love* meant a form of attention, a form of thought indistinguishable from empathy. As Keller observes, it allowed for intimacy without the annihilation of difference.

The *content* of science—often based on what questions get asked—also can be skewed, but for now the *quality* of the generative energy had the most effect on my happier relationship with science.

One morning some days later, ten of us lounged on *L'Estrella*, heading back from a snorkel on Isla Coronado, several miles offshore. A school of flying fish kept breaking the surface between us and the sun, clearing the water, staying aloft for twenty feet, or thirty, their skittering takeoffs and landings brightening the water with brilliant spangles. Each time they appeared in the air, several dorados arced after them.

"What's that?" called Nicky, who was trolling with Tony off the back of the boat for lunch. She pointed to a fin above the water. Not a shark. The fin had a strange rounded shape.

Armando circled toward it, then cut the motor, and the boat drifted in the sudden quiet. Over the port gunwales we could see a large dark form close to the surface. It moved toward the bow, then maneuvered itself slowly until its six-foot-wide blunt snout nearly butted up to *L'Estrella*'s squared-off stern.

"What is it? What is it?" we asked each other. MacKenzie must know. His entire demeanor had changed. He fairly sparked.

"It's a whale shark!" someone called. We leaned over the railing, taking in its large flat body, its dark grey skin patterned with an almost regular grid of white lines, a white dot centered in each box.

"This is a small one," said MacKenzie, holding on to the boat's edge, peering into the water. It was about twenty feet long. "It's the largest fish in the world. There's only one species worldwide. I've never seen one in the wild before." He'd seen almost everything in oceans everywhere. "They're rare. It's a filter feeder. Has huge gill rakers. Eats larger plankton than basking sharks."

Nicky had put on her flippers and had her mask and snorkel ready. "Can I go in? Can I?" A filter feeder wouldn't hurt her.

The whale shark seemed as curious as we were and hovered for ten minutes facing the stern.

"Can I go in? Can I?" Nicky jumped up and down.

Finally MacKenzie nodded, and she tilted herself backward over the side. In slow motion, the shark turned from the boat toward Nicky, its small eyes focusing on her from the corners of its broad, flat snout. Nicky treaded water, her snorkel tube bobbing just above the waves, her body tiny in front of the whale shark's huge bulk. Face-to-face, they stared at each other, suspended in mutual, inquisitive uncertainty.

After some minutes, she swam to its back and looped her arm in front of the fin. The shark moved off, at first staying close to the surface, then going deeper. Just then a trio of bottlenose dolphins began to leap in another direction. Armando started *L'Estrella*'s engine and circled in a wide loop to pick up Nicky.

"Whew," she said, back aboard, "I thought you were after those dolphins and were going to leave me out there!"

We laughed. "What did it feel like?"

"Smooth, but rough. Like asbestos gloves, not sandpaper."

A talismanic encounter with mystery.

Barbara McClintock once said, "There's no such thing as a central dogma into which everything will fit."

The whale shark had disappeared, but MacKenzie still seemed to be vibrating. The picture of laid-back calmness most of the time, whenever fish and ecology came up, he took on an intensity rivaling any octopus color-shift. In the end, his interest in human sexual selection seemed mostly a spice, an entertainment for the trip, one way to jazz up his students. His real sustenance came from the rest of creation, preferably wet. Cold science heated with love. I didn't know if he'd ever have admitted it. But perhaps he did know, to use Steinbeck's phrase, the first rule of life is living.

◄

The night before I had to leave the trip early to get back to my job in New York, Nicky stood up at our regular evening meeting.

"I've been on five of these trips, and I have some data I'd like to share with you. An important part of this data is the Bajarmonics Index." We laughed.

"Don't laugh! It's rigorous science!" she glared at us out of her darkly tanned face, barely suppressing a smile. "This index is also known as the MacKenzie Index. It's based on seven factors."

One at a time she wrote them on the large paper pad.

1. Wind

2. Students

3. Interesting and rare animal sightings

4. Availability and condition of marine vessels

5. Disasters

6. Camp food

7. Staff (staph)

"I've done a careful analysis and have crunched the numbers. Here are the results."

And here are her graphs.

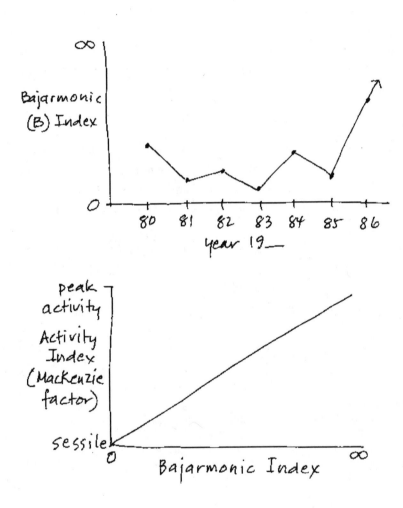

🪶

Early the next morning, Fran drove me with my minimal gear to the small Loreto Airport to start my long trip back. At 8 a.m. I sat by myself, severed from my marine community. The airport vendors sold only cheesecake, beer, T-shirts. In the crowded waiting area, rowdy fishermen smoked cigars. On the plane's loading cart, forty large coolers sat stuffed with their booty: dead fish on ice.

I wrote in my journal, "It's familiar. Leaving again. Taking leave perpetually."

But that didn't cover it at all. Not at all.

Differential Weathering

A Wilderness Lobbyist's Field Notebook

The first time I drove the Burr Trail in southern Utah I stopped at several dozen surveyor's stakes, yanked them out, and tossed them behind the truck's seat. The road was dirt then, in 1987, but Garfield County wanted to pave it from the tiny town of Boulder sixty-six miles through Capitol Reef National Park to Bullfrog Marina. Along the way the most substantial human-made object stood just south of the place where the Burr Trail merged with the Notom-Bullfrog Road. The map labeled it "The Post": a weathered corral for staging horse trips into the backcountry.

Paving dirt roads usually meant more people, more ORVs, and more disruption of the landscape. Paving the Burr Trail—or not—had become a celebrated cause and a symbol for both sides of a heated argument about land use and land control in southern Utah. That argument still rages. The controversy over the Burr Trail introduced me to the Southern Utah Wilderness Alliance (SUWA) at the same time I began to stumble on and over, under and through the Colorado Plateau's dramatic unearthly geology. The group had been formed to protect that magical territory, and I'd found one of their sunflower

yellow fliers somewhere—perhaps at the small, dark store that had
been blasted out of a large hunk of sandstone in Hanksville. I'd wanted
to add my small effort to the resistance.

I'd gently interfered with civil engineering in 1987; the twenty-eight
miles of the Burr Trail east of Boulder finally became a winding, sealed
gravel road in 1991. After I moved to New Mexico in 1989, I continued to write letters about other wild Utah issues following SUWA's
lead. I owed at least that to the heaving rocks, frozen in time, that
had drawn me west. And I owed it to the remaining dirt roads and the
huge expanses with no roads at all. But when someone from the Utah
Wilderness Coalition (UWC)—an umbrella group that included SUWA—
called me in the summer of 1995 to ask me to go to Washington to
lobby Congress about wilderness, I froze with fear. Writing letters didn't
require much besides typing skills and stamps; the idea of talking to
senators terrified me. UWC would pay my way. They'd train me with
fourteen other redrock addicts. They'd match me with a lobby buddy and
provide lots of materials and logistical support. What more could I want?
Even so, at first I refused, claiming a schedule approaching gridlock.
That was true. But I knew the real issue was my fear.

For about an hour I considered this failure of nerve before I decided
fear wouldn't do as a reason to pass up such a chance. Not only could
I speak for a landscape I loved while I got a good look at politics in
action, but I could also return to my childhood city with fresh eyes. And
then, partly to distract myself, I began to think of the trip as if I were a
naturalist traveling to an exotic, distant place, even though Washington
wasn't wilderness.

I had spent seventeen years living in D.C., from birth on. By the time I
left for college in 1967, I'd determined that Washington manifested the
worst parts of city life with none of its benefits and maintained a tone
of disheartening provincialism. We lived at the edges of the District

proper, first in Anacostia, then just inside the line from Chevy Chase, in a neighborhood with cabinet members (I shared my first curiously sucking kiss with the son of the Secretary of Labor), diplomats, and folks mostly better off than we were. My father commuted daily on the bus to his lawyering job at the Federal Trade Commission, an agency empowered to wage antitrust battles and to ferret out false advertising. The agency occupied a building with nothing between it and the west side of the Capitol except vast, meticulously tended lawns, a few minor streets, humid air, and the disparity of power between Congress and career civil servants.

But I had only ventured downtown to museums when my Aunt Helen or Cousin Hazel came to town, to the Fourth of July fireworks at the Washington Monument, and to the inaugural parade every four years. We were allowed to sit in Federal Trade Commission offices that protected us from the January cold and gave us clear views over the bleachers. I only spent real time near those Greek Revival buildings full of federal workers the summer after I graduated from high school. I'd just turned seventeen and my first job was at the Federal Courthouse typing presentence reports for the probation office. The woman who hired me as temporary help—on the recommendation of my mother, who was also my high school's guidance counselor—worried that some of the cases might be too gruesome for a sweet young girl. That would be me. That summer I relished most the murders, their thick files crammed with eight-by-ten-inch glossies.

But politics? Not much. I'd never been to a session of Congress, and only once had my liberal father treated me and several second cousins to lunch in the Senate dining room. On a Saturday, we'd seen no senators.

In the twenty-five years since my folks had migrated to Florida, I had been back to Washington only once. Some years after I'd left, I found my way to the East Village in New York City, where my studio apartment and unvegetated, drug-enlivened block didn't resemble my childhood digs in any way. I hadn't been escaping urbanness as such, but a suffocating gentility where nearly everything seemed counterfeit. In a different way, New Mexico's dry air and open spaces had almost nothing in common with the tidy azalea-filled neighborhoods and the air-conditioned houses where I'd been raised. All my Washington memories rumbled with domestication and constraint. Whenever I speculated on my history, I usually focused on the characters in my family, but Washington's landscape must have had a major supporting role. For this trip my personal agenda vied with the political one. What was Washington like? Had my relationship with the place changed? Would I learn anything about myself?

Once my initial panic about lobbying had subsided, I eased myself into the trip by approaching it like a backpacking expedition. I broke in heels instead of hiking boots, collected appropriate gear (skirts only, please, no shorts, slacks, or neon Gore-Tex), examined my psychic map instead of USGS quads, and studied the UWC's photocopied sheets for crucial information.

✺

One Saturday afternoon in July I arrived into familiar swamp air. I had been booked into a Quaker bed and breakfast on Capitol Hill that was spare, friendly, and cheap—the peace and justice rate. I dropped off my bags and went out to smell my old hometown, though my *real* old neighborhoods were far from that center of government.

I walked to the Capitol past tiny pruned yards surrounded by wrought iron fences that seemed familiar but weren't. Robust specimens of plants I grew in my yard in the desert crowded each other: fringed sage, Mexican hat, prairie coneflower, coreopsis. Even the large stone planters by the Folger Shakespeare Library held purple fountain grass, the same suddenly popular plant of Albuquerque's medians. Almost no traffic disturbed the calm streets, and as I crossed into the east grounds of the Capitol, I recalled I'd never been on Capitol Hill for an evening stroll on a Saturday night. We had accepted as truth the rumor that Capitol Hill after dark crawled with robbers and murderers.

Nothing moved in the openly spaced trees except an albino squirrel that reluctantly ran ten feet up a trunk as I closed in to read an engraved plaque:

U.S. CAPITOL GROUNDS
MEMORIAL TREE
ACER SACCHARUM
(SUGAR MAPLE)
planted by
SPEAKER CHAMP CLARK (MO.)
May 7, 1912

Ah, I thought, an amateur botanist-legislator with a wish to leave his mark on something more durable than shifting coalitions. Then I noticed similar plaques on most of the other trees, and it dawned on me that nature here had been assigned a feudal role. I'd come to argue for wilderness in a place where plants grew only as decoration or examples or monuments, and space existed only to serve the architecture it surrounded.

I hadn't been conscious of this particular urge-to-subdue when I lived here, but it had surely been one of the reasons for my constant desire to flee.

When I followed the walkway around the House chambers to the Capitol's west side, the two-by-four-foot granite blocks under my feet gave way slightly, like a quaking bog, and rebounded with a low grinding sound when I stepped off each one. They hadn't been mortared, and dull clunks followed everyone's passage across them.

On the Capitol's west porch, I found the action. A continual flow of tourists had their pictures snapped by the friendly Capitol police, with the backdrop of the Mall and Washington Monument and the hazed sun sinking just behind the Old Post Office Tower. A breeze carried the sound of cicadas and the music of a single accomplished songbird.

Down the steps past potted palms, more labeled trees, and the weed-free lawn, I made my way to the clump of statues at the head (or tail?) of the Mall. I discovered Grant, stern and heroic astride his horse, flanked at his four corners by four bronze lions facing four directions and comfortably resting. Animals banished to their symbolism.

Aiming back toward the Capitol grounds, I crossed the street to a small ornate fountain at sidewalk level. Two columns topped with acanthus leaves supported a stone pediment that featured a great blue heron foraging in graceful grasses; below that, another panel of braided vines led to an arched stone rectangle carved to suggest the inside of a scallop shell; below that, bas-relief water lilies and cattails formed the backdrop for two copper pipes that emerged over the shallow pool. The pipes twined in an elegant caduceus before they ended in a spout for the simple stream of living water. I wished I remembered more art history. When did civilization start requiring such stylized excess?

✿

The UWC had enticed me to Washington to rally more opposition to an anti-wilderness bill before the House and Senate and to gain support for the more wilderness-friendly Citizens Proposal in the House. Although the bills concerned spectacular land in Utah, they also had far-reaching ramifications for all federal land, especially wilderness in the West. Federal land technically referred to military installations, Indian reservations, federal courthouses, the Jefferson Memorial, the Mall, flower gardens of the White House, and so forth. But the federal land of this controversy was land where differing ideas of the word *waste* butt up against each other.

One world view contrasted *waste* with *use by the most obvious businesses*. Human inactivity meant failure of intelligence or responsibility, or failure to take advantage of opportunity. Conservatives seemed to take this for granted: whatever they intended to conserve, it usually wasn't nature itself. "What a waste!" They claimed protective reserves such as wilderness literally "locked land away." Nature in that case must be stripped of life, at least metaphorically, as if it were a jar of Confederate dollars that could be buried under an apple tree.

Another world view—one that I shared—understood nature as more alive than currency and more intimately linked to human well-being than a money machine. Conservation broadly meant the preservation of the nonhuman and nonhuman qualities. This protection of unhumanness benefited humans, but in more complicated ways than, for example, mining coal. This world view acknowledged that we couldn't completely describe *what* we were preserving. It accepted human limitation and earth-bound mystery. To damage or destroy these nonhuman qualities constituted the other version of *waste*.

Profit and protection weren't as incompatible as so many conservatives claimed. These days, in many places, at least as much money could be made in adventure tours, mountain-bike rentals, freeze-dried food, coffee-table books, and white-water rafting as in coal mining. This alternative usually benefited smaller players. "Undeveloped" land became an economic magnet. Seen more clearly, the conflict turned into a fight between the nineteenth and twenty-first centuries; industrial efforts arm in arm with established political power competed with decentralized, less controllable multiple economies. That often translated into a battle pitting the oversimplified obvious short-term profit against long-term ecological and economic health.

Wilderness, like the word *waste*, had no fixed meaning, but depended on its context. Emotionally, wilderness triggered notions of challenge or threat or ordeal. More mildly, it called up the possibility of solace or personal regeneration. Internal images of wilderness owed much to photographs from nineteenth-century explorers or to TV nature shows. These picturesque "wildernesses" weren't entirely inaccurate, but as experience, they provided only faint and disengaged shadows.

The *wilderness* currently under consideration in Congress was a legal term, codified in the Wilderness Act of 1964. The act acknowledged the need to preserve remaining fragments of roadless territory both for natural systems and for human use, including such nonproductive activities as experiencing solitude. Surprisingly, *legal wilderness* did not mean exclusion of cows and cow pies, existing mining claims, existing water rights, hunting or fishing, horses, scientific studies, or official uniformed managers. But in a country where every square foot must be accounted for, wilderness designation *has* worked effectively to counteract many destructive land practices. The Wilderness Act forbade road building, logging, new mining claims, mechanized transport, and new reservoirs or power lines. Congress, however, could do anything it wanted as long as the votes added up, and the current wilderness bill sought to change the rules so drastically that many protections would be abandoned. A former congresswoman from Utah, Karen Shepard, had noted in an editorial in Salt Lake City's *Catalyst* magazine, that the bill supported by Utah's delegation not only proposed too small an area for wilderness designation, but it contained "two poison pills: First, it permits the building of pipelines, communications apparatus, and dams within the few acres that have been designated. Second, it releases all land not called wilderness in this bill to commercial interests for profit-driven management." That "hard release" provision had never been included in any wilderness bills in the past. In other words, wilderness now or wilderness never.

Before I'd left Albuquerque, I'd looked up *wilderness* in Webster's New World Dictionary and found only this: "an uncultivated, uninhabited region; waste." *Wilderness* equals *waste*? I hadn't expected two such quicksilver words to be bluntly linked as if they were solid ground, but the definition uncomfortably matched the ideas embodied in the bill we had come to fight. The fate of *real* solid ground depended on these fluid meanings, ever open to interpretation. This solid ground was located mostly in southern Utah. The Citizens Proposal identified

5.7 million acres of potential wilderness, an area about the size of Vermont. The anti-wilderness bill offered 2 million acres, but, as Karen Shepard had noted, size was only part of the issue.

My given task in Washington was to speak for the land in a specific context, according to a game plan constructed by others who had been long in the trenches. Conflicting ideas of waste and wilderness can cause wars.

My personal task was to pay careful attention.

At Sunday morning lobby training, I didn't feel panic while I ate bagels with fourteen other volunteers in small third-floor offices on Pennsylvania Avenue, but I was still scared to death. I wasn't alone. On the phone the first words from my lobby partner Dan had been, "I'm terrified." He was a professional photographer from Utah. My roommates at the bed and breakfast confessed equal fear. One taught high school civics in Ohio, the other worked with disabled people on Utah river trips. We had no lobbying experience and bore no resemblance to snake-oil salesmen, but because we all admitted our fears, we bonded quickly and encouraged each other, knowing we were all stretching beyond our familiar roles. And beyond our familiar clothes.

But the strategists had prepared for neophytes. We didn't spend the morning pinning down facts—they assumed we had them in hand—but rather learning *how* to lobby. The lobby trainers' approach included explanations and instructions that bordered on the absurd, but I saw they stemmed directly from a representative government that had become swamped with information and infected with constant reelection worries.

"Being right doesn't have a lot to do with it."

"It's not enough to be right, now we must be clever." (From the post-Soviet Polish government.)

"Members of Congress are not like wise judges. They assume both sides have merit and they want to do what's most popular, because their primary job is to be reelected."

"Your goal is to get your cat fed." (So don't treat the representative, senator, or staffer worse than you would treat your obliging neighbor taking care of kitty.)

"There are two kinds of power: big money and public support. You don't have big money." (QED)

"Keep the con even after you took him." (From *The Sting*.)

"We're going to manipulate them." (Did we imagine anything different?)

"Don't talk on the elevators after your meetings. You have no idea who the other people are." (The opposition could be anywhere.)

"Remember to make the ASK!" (We needed to ask for what we wanted: votes against the anti-wilderness bill and more cosponsors for the Citizens Proposal.)

In the end, it all made more sense than I'd expected. We needed to sell *ourselves* as much as the issue. Good lobbying resembled good conversation. It should be a dialogue: honest, relaxed, full of movement. And like good conversation, each encounter would ripple with the idiosyncratic.

The humanness of the undertaking reassured me, but I still quivered with old winds of doubt. Growing up and for years afterward I had faced the world almost shyly and nearly silently. I had been alert and confident, mostly, but self-contained. After our training I could trace the contours of the strongest source of my fear: in order to speak for the land, I needed to find a new voice that went beyond my familiar but limited range. I needed not only *to focus outward* but *to be out there*. And I must never lose touch with my vocal cords. The personal expanding universe.

Alone in the commons room of the bed and breakfast on Sunday night, I worked on getting fluid with the facts. After half an hour, a person I hadn't seen before walked in. He wore a long loden green cape and a dark Stetson. Odd, I thought, the temperature hadn't cooled much below ninety degrees. He made a brief, easy circuit of the room, then asked, "What is your issue?" A frequent question among the bed-and-breakfast Quakers. After a few sentences, he sat down to quiz me with an alarming intensity. He looked roughly sixty-five, part African American, part Native American; he eventually focused on the Navajo position in the controversy. As far as I knew, none existed, but that may have been my ignorance. As we talked, I realized he was a godsend despite a strangeness that both unsettled and attracted me. As I answered his questions, I began to clarify what I needed to say in my meetings. The twenty-year-old in residence joined us and tried to discover what this unlikely man did. "I am a professor, emeritus now, at several New York universities."

"Which ones?"

"Several. And in Boston."

Ultimately, my good manners overcame my unease, and we exchanged names and addresses. He asked to know how it all came out, then disappeared to find a bed for the night because the bed and breakfast was full. "I have other friends nearby." Quaker Friends? "I drove ambulances with them in the war." Which war, I wondered.

A valuable visit for me. In Washington, a place devoted to surfaces and to trade-offs of tangibles, I could still be visited by Hermes, the Greek god most associated with communication and movement, the one most able to lightly escape all traps. But, after all, who could be a more appropriate archetype for politics?

Zeus, ultimate power, would be a more obvious choice. In fact, a nimbus of hopeful ambition hovered around most of the young staffers I met. But nothing at all could happen if you weren't fleet of foot.

The fall before, I'd been to southern Utah in unusually raw land. One afternoon I faced a baroque pandemonium of buff and russet rock angling abruptly above the opposite side of a black, mile-wide dried river of mud. This dry river flowed only several weeks a year, and in years of little rain, not at all. Nothing fleet about it. Nothing even human about it except the high precarious track where I'd stopped my truck, and the tire marks below, which demonstrated the possibility of driving over the nonflowing clay. I gazed across Muddy Creek at the San Rafael Reef, 1,500 feet high. Behind me stretched miles more of undulating dried dark clay with sparse wisps of bleached vegetation, interrupted now and then with low sandstone outcroppings, and one enormous landform: Factory Butte.

Factory Butte must have been named for its soot-grey color, the narrow ridge of spires that stood like smokestacks along its top, and its looming presence in relatively flat surroundings. In all directions the scene extended vast, silent, light-saturated, otherworldly, intimidating: not a candidate for Hallmark cards. In southern Utah, multitudes of complicated rock personalities interpenetrated each other, all as overwhelming as this one.

In these remote lands of nonhuman scale, naming landforms must have been intended to domesticate wave after wave of nearly incomprehensible visions. Twenty miles to the west, weathering and erosion had carved cream-colored Navajo sandstone into immense, almost symmetrical half spheres. The nearly white outcropping most visible from the road carried the name Capitol Dome.

These landscapes, drenched with distance, had an unaccountable effect on transient humans like me. The sensation diminished successively with translation from physical presence, to photographs and words, then to imaginations asked to conjure up such unlikely country without the aid of memory. These nearly naked rocks revealed the earth-wide forge and the vise of forces that had created them. Through complex routes, these same elemental energies and materials can be traced to our own racing blood. To deny this connection damages the self.

I turned my truck away from inhospitable Muddy Creek, retraced my tracks, and found a campsite broadside to Factory Butte, several miles to the east. Except for the Factory itself and a cluster of boulders like a pile of old VW Bugs, nothing obstructed the 360-degree view. Much of what I saw would not be protected in the wilderness bill before Congress, even though it was clearly wilderness, no matter whose definition you used. Wallace Stegner once wrote, "Factories, power plants, resorts we can make anywhere. Wilderness, once we have given it up, is beyond our reconstruction." After dark the still October air cooled quickly. I crawled into my tent and slept snugly until two o'clock, when sudden wind began to churn the night around me.

The landforms of the Colorado Plateau have been created over millions of years by a succession of geologic processes: sea or wind deposited layers of sediment, deep movements of the earth's crust uplifted the whole area, then wind and water eroded down those layers of raised-up sediment. The bare-bones description of complicated processes. Many of the fantastic forms that give the area its visual power—hoodoos, arches, parfait-like striated canyon walls, isolated buttes that look like temples, massive mesas—result from varying hardnesses of the layered sediments acted on by erosion. A particularly hard layer such as the White Rim, a layer found around Canyonlands, will erode more slowly and in places protect softer underlying rock, but not completely. Geologists call this variability in hardness and consequent erosion *differential weathering*.

Here was a pointed analogy: the contrasts I observed not only between Utah wildlands and Washington, but between the experiences and knowledge of the people in Washington and those who had spent time in Western wilderness also resulted from differential weathering. Weathering not from wind and rain and snowmelt, but from culture—another indeterminate word like waste and wilderness—working through time. We'd been affected differentially by social forces, including the

requirements of the lands where we had grown. We'd weathered differently. Washington itself had weathered in a dramatically different way
than had southern Utah. Culture's creative and erosive forces.

🍃

Underground on Capitol Hill, tunnels threaded together the Capitol and
the six House and Senate office buildings. After you entered one, you
were safe from all atmospheric weather. Dan and I cruised the subterranean routes. From the Senate offices, polished, quiet, pint-sized subways
traveled back and forth to the Capitol, carrying senators and assorted
others. As a teenager, I'd ridden them once with my father for my only
taste of working legislators. This time the accessibility of senators struck
me. No secret passageways: anybody could engage a senator in a three-
minute conversation if luck put you in the same four-person car and you
were up on the latest Congressional mug book. Not all senators were
easy to spot.

At the Capitol, we found our way up as if we climbed out of a canyon through successive layers of sandstone. Different formations and
populations appeared at each level until we emerged finally in the Capitol itself, manic with people and covered on all surfaces with marble,
tiles, mosaics, murals, endless architectural details. It had kept many
craftsmen fed for a long time.

The House tunnels had none of the elegance of the Senate's. A long,
curving, oppressive concrete gallery led to much narrower corridors that
angled past kitchens and storerooms, their exposed ceiling pipes close
over the heads of droves of white-suited food-service workers and over
the constant stream of *us*—people with agendas, in transit.

🍃

Dan and I dropped in to our first office. The overworked staffer had said
we might, but in person he acted even more frantic than on the phone.
We managed only a minimal message and left, feeling like whining

mosquitoes. But we'd confronted the unfamiliar, and our next visit eased us more.

This staffer not only had time for a chat about environmental issues in general, but wanted to talk about moving to Salt Lake. We rambled on with him, periodically trying to rein the talk back to Utah wilderness. He questioned Dan closely about living in Utah and finally asked, "What kind of skis do you have?"

At the office of the representative from the Virgin Islands, we relaxed into a visit more in line with what we'd expected. We made a few points, easily remembered, before the congressman himself walked by and joined us. Sympathetic, he asked, "Is there any potential for mining? What minerals are there?" (Perhaps one of his pet issues?) We remembered to "make the ask," and he agreed to cosponsor the bill. As a delegate from a U.S. Territory, he couldn't vote, but he could be a cosponsor. We laid gorgeous photos on his aide and trekked back to lobby central.

On our first morning, we'd gained two new cosponsors, and the Washington regulars greeted that news with pleasure and surprise. Apparently they weren't sure if we would be at all effective. And we hadn't known one of the basics: it wasn't easy to get new cosponsors.

We tried to sort out what was hard, what was apparently easy. On the way back, we had passed the newly renovated brick building that had recently caused an uproar in town. The funeral-home-turned-dormitory for the teenage Capitol pages had drained five million dollars from federal coffers. Had that been hard or easy?

With every click of my heels on polished floors, I felt surrealism breathing down my neck. This was a bizarre lark. Wilderness? A TV in every senator's reception area broadcast either the Senate in session or Hurricane Erin about to slam into the Outer Banks. It didn't take a Herculean effort of deconstruction to make some leaps about how environment related to assumptions and attitudes. Has there ever been an architect not clued in to the concept? Just look at all the neoclassical buildings peppering Washington. Greek ideals, here we come.

To my surprise, almost immediately my fear had been replaced by a peculiar brew of exhilaration, curiosity, and a deepening pessimism. It seemed inevitable that *here* people would always have trouble understanding wilderness (especially non–Swiss Alp wilderness), or why it should be protected, efforts of memory or imagination notwithstanding. I felt the poignancy of the lasting consequences of decisions made in the midst of this hyperactive, conservatively dressed carnival, where nature meant a framed watercolor or a dolphin tie tack.

🍃

Mountains and Clouds filled the bright atrium of the Hart Senate Office Building. Alexander Calder had designed this stabile/mobile combo, though he completed only the maquette before he died. *Mountains* rested solidly on the floor, five stories tall, fabricated of riveted steel plates; *Clouds* brooded above, in equally huge balanced horizontal slabs. The entire sculpture had been painted flat black as if for a formal state occasion. Unlike most Calder mobiles, *Clouds* appeared not to move one inch. It responded only to the rotation of the earth, with the same creeping speed that many people associated with Congress.

Dan and I stood on the seventh floor, overlooking this macabre playfulness, level with the upper layers of *Clouds*. They needed a good dusting. We were waiting until our appointment with one of my senators, Jeff Bingaman. Usually only constituents can meet with actual senators rather than their staff.

Suddenly a raven's cry echoed through the space. Dan had spotted two of our lobby buddies walking across the floor of the atrium below. But no one looked up to his call.

When a delegation of Alaskan native Gwich'in visited Washington, they refused to walk under *Mountains and Clouds*, spooked by the expectation that *Clouds* would fall because it wasn't real. I imagined that in Washington they'd been spooked by more than these fake black clouds.

🍂

Senator Bingaman's reception area sported graceful New Mexico references: a six-by-eight-foot blow-up of Ansel Adams's *Moonrise, Hernandez*, and a series of Georgia O'Keefe Santa Fe Chamber Music Festival posters. Part of my value in Washington was to have this specific meeting with one of the few Democratic senators from the West. The strategists wanted to know if he'd carry the fight against the bill in the Senate. None of them could just ask him, apparently. They needed a New Mexican first to get past his gatekeepers, then to make the case personally that New Mexicans cared about wilderness in Utah and that this issue ultimately affected *all* public lands in the West, even if it focused on Utah's roadless territory.

In a state split between liberals and conservatives, Bingaman always had tough reelection fights. As the ranking Democrat on the Senate Resources Committee, he watched out as well as he could for New Mexico's land, and I was grateful to him. But I knew he walked a fine line with many of his rural ranching constituents, and I wasn't surprised that he didn't jump at the chance to be a hero for Utah. He was cordial and attentive, and sympathetic in principle, but he made it clear that ultimately he had to think first about his—and my—own state. We passed on to him our info along with the high-end photos of the proposed Redrock Wilderness.

"Thanks for coming by," he said as we shook hands. "I'll study this and see what I can do to help."

As we left the office after our meeting, we stopped at a small water sculpture by the door. Gurgling up through layers of stone and copper, water spurted out a small aperture in the top so that a truffle-sized sphere of clear quartz spun and spun, moving, but not moving in any direction.

Back at lobby central later that day our information came as a disappointment to the legislative experts who had hoped for more risk taking. Might Bingaman introduce the Senate version of the House Citizens Proposal? Might he filibuster the bill? Not a chance.

When Dan and I visited the offices of other senators—Richard Bryan and Harry Reid of Nevada, Daniel Patrick Moynihan, Ted Kennedy—we spoke with staffers assigned to environmental issues. Without exception, they met us with attention, earnestness, and good general knowledge, but not with much information about Utah wilderness. They questioned us closely. Their senators were all Democrats, and though they couldn't speak for their bosses, they assured us they'd be sympathetic.

Senator Reid's staffer told us he had "cut his legislative teeth" on the Nevada National Forest Wilderness Bill. As the process was set up, separate bills designated wilderness state by state, agency by agency. He expected his senator would be concerned about a chunk of endangered desert tortoise habitat that bordered Utah, near Las Vegas. Currently a landowner wanted to engineer a land swap, hoping to exchange exceptional tortoise habitat for several acres of prime casino habitat in downtown Las Vegas.

Washington's isolation from the land it attempted to administer shone so conspicuously that it was no surprise "locals know best" has become a familiar rallying cry. But a dismaying history of locally sanctioned plunder challenged this logic. I considered: in areas that have so far escaped the tentacles of industrial civilization and have remained virtually roadless, humans usually struggle to make a living. In marginal circumstances, wouldn't hungry locals be tempted by promises of increased incomes? Their good intentions soured by narrow perspectives and perhaps by greed, wouldn't they give only scant attention to ultimate costs?

Westerners also have a tendency to chafe against nonlocal government while embracing nonlocal large companies that care little about long-term damage to the land or to the community. But when specific issues of land management come up, no clear-cut jurisdictional formula exists. Too many shades of grey.

⬧

At each end-of-day debriefing, we passed around Band-Aids for feet blistered by new shoes and told our lobby stories to the staff directing our efforts. They were the ones strategizing and collecting the pieces of information we brought back. The best story, selected by democratic vote, won a pint of Ben and Jerry's ice cream.

⬧

I headed back to the Capitol alone to watch an evening House session. Opposite the Speaker's platform, the visitors' gallery perched high over the floor. The place seethed in disarray, packed with small conversations in changing combinations, in the aisles, in the curving pews, at the doors. For a full half hour, these noisy clumps entirely ignored the Speaker's percussive gavel.

When I tried to sort out sides, I settled on the hair test. On the left, one representative looked surprisingly like Allen Ginsberg: loose, below-shoulder-length greying hair, a shining bald head, and a full beard. On the right, I spotted numerous bald heads whose owners had opted for the comb-over. No question where the Republicans sat. How clear the sources of stereotypes.

One single head of blond, curly, surfer's hair bobbed rapidly from person to person, touching base. I guessed correctly: Joe Kennedy.

Hours later the big event rolled around: a revote on an environmental-protection amendment (one establishing a lower level of asbestos in drinking water) that had passed the previous week, against Speaker Newt Gingrich's wishes. He'd scheduled the vote again, twisting arms in the meantime. It must be legal, but seemed awfully squirrelly. The two sponsors (one Democrat, one Republican) gave short, passionate speeches before the revote. The keeping-up-with-the-times House voted electronically, with plastic cards. Instantly these votes lit up on the score-card that shone through the brocaded wall above the Speaker's platform.

Time clicked down on an LED display glowing from dark-stained wood molding. As the close vote neared its end, the Democrats started chanting, "Newt, Newt, Newt, Newt," as if they cheered at a football game. Was it an obscure tradition to chant the Speaker's first name on a close vote he might lose? Or an attempt to mimic the British House of Commons? Newt wasn't even here; he was at someone else's fund-raiser. Finally, the last Republicans voted. It was a tie; the amendment failed, even without Newt. The next day, a faxed analysis explained: only one changed vote, but many conveniently absent swing Republicans.

Adjournment, 10 p.m. I accidentally found my way to the wide marble stairs leading down to the main hall, where I crossed paths with House members and many Domino's Pizza guys carrying two-foot-tall stacks of pizzas.

Several days later, 10 a.m. Press conference at the edge of the Capitol parking lot, at the "House Triangle," a favorite grassy spot for press encounters. Towering marble architecture lends solemnity to anything.

Our Utah wilderness bill had been scheduled for markup in commit-tee later in the morning. This meant it would be amended and probably voted out to the floor. We opposed this current bill, but an alternative Citizens Proposal had been sponsored in the House for the past four ses-sions, since 1989.

The unlikely current sponsor of the Citizens Proposal was Represen-tative Maurice Hinchey, from central New York State. The previous Utah wilderness champion, from Utah, had been defeated when he left his House seat to run for Senate. Mr. Hinchey, an articulate soul who clearly loved his job, would speak to the press first, then three lobbyists from the West: a professorial guy from California; Dan, from Utah; and me, from New Mexico. All three of us half hoped no press would show up.

The evening before, I'd gotten much advice about how to quell stage fright. No one had addressed the ghosts of my childhood violin recitals. This morning, however, I'd begun to have an odd sensation. Given my history, I expected to be filled with dread, but I sensed only a mild buzz. For one thing, I hadn't censored myself at all in my statement. I'd said what I really believed. Was that some sort of inoculation?

Next to a wooden podium, an easel had been set up with two large photos of vast stretches of luscious mesas and badlands, very dry. Sweat already soaked Dan's cotton shirt.

Our fifteen-minute knot of Utah-focus eventually included five reporters, dutifully staring at the speakers. Around us the life of the Capitol continued, orchestrated in almost-clichéd counterpoint.

"Listen for a moment . . . to the sounds of the city, and think . . . ," said Dan in his statement, then paused.

Above the general growl of traffic, horns honked, a helicopter flew over.

". . . the buzz-bomb whine of chain saws . . . ," said our friend from California.

A chain saw obediently started up nearby, began to prune over-enthusiastic trees.

" . . . 'we must unhumanize our views a little' . . . ," said I, quoting Robinson Jeffers.

Immediately behind the podium a groundskeeper micromanaged the dead blossoms in a stand of coral canna lilies.

House Resources Committee hearing. *Resources* are animal, vegetable, mineral, and, I was reminded, *Indian*. On the long side wall of the committee room hung six muted paintings in wide gilt frames. Two others hung over the respective Democratic and Republican doors up front, but

I couldn't quite make them out, since I'd left my binoculars in New Mexico. The paintings within my range of vision all depicted Indian scenes:

- an Indian maiden tending a stretched hide on a drying-frame
- a snow scene with tepees
- tepees with orderly confabs, the Indians in appropriate clothing (two paintings for this governmental activity)
- an Indian family group traveling on the edge of the plains, with horses pulling pole travois
- a "brave" standing victoriously over his victim, hand held high, clutching a scalp

I'm sure none of the regulars even registered these paintings anymore. But I wondered if other cultures so thoroughly romanticized what they had largely destroyed. I didn't know the answer.

Before Utah wilderness came up on the agenda, the committee treated us to a lengthy discussion of "management of free-roaming wild horses" in Ozark National Scenic Riverways. "Management" turned out to include worry about liability for whatever damage the "free-roaming wild horses" might do if they happened to roam freely out of the Scenic Riverways and behave wildly. At least one representative noticed the irony: "We used to want a home where the buffalo roam, and now we're worried about free-roaming wild horse damage."

Not once did anyone refer to these horses as "horses," but always as "free-roaming wild horses," a phrase that clashed so dramatically with the suited beings who uttered it, that back in the peanut gallery we exchanged quizzical looks.

The outcome of the committee vote to send the Utah wilderness bill to the floor had never been in question; Republicans outnumbered Democrats, and the doting father of the bill—Utah's Jim Hansen—chaired the committee. The official chair, Don Young from Alaska, had scheduled open heart surgery instead. A legendary fire-breather, Representative Young had once pounded and shaken an *oosik*, a walrus penis bone, at Mollie Beattie, Director of the U.S. Fish and Wildlife Service, while she testified about the Marine Mammal Protection Act. Now I heard whispered from my right, "Young taught Hansen everything he knows."

We'd been warned, "It won't be pretty." No chance of victory, that is, to kill the bill outright, but a distant chance to amend a few provisions. And a chance to kick up a fuss, air objections, maybe find out who was troubled about what and why. And to score any hits imaginable. On the list of nearly thirty possible amendments, the first one was to change the name of the bill from "Utah Public Lands *Management* Act" to "Utah Public Lands *Development* Act," a more apt description.

Suddenly the discussion veered off in a way I hadn't expected. The issue at hand concerned the need (or not) to build roads and "permanent structures" *in wilderness areas* (!?!) to "protect archaeological sites." What could they be thinking? Did they have any idea what wilderness was? What archaeological sites were? Not an unforeseen topic, but as the discussion went on, it became clear that most of these folks didn't have a clue what they were talking about. They were operating by analogies, and the analogies didn't fit.

Representative Hinchey tried repeatedly to bridge the gap between the *idea* of the experience and the experience itself, but it didn't sink in. For days I'd seen evidence of this dissonance—a steel cloud was *not* a cloud—but here it had popped up in the flesh, or rather, in the *word*, and I was taken aback. Despite all signs, I had still supposed the controversies would be based on disagreements or obscure mutual backscratching, but not on misunderstanding and befuddlement.

Beepers around the room went off abruptly, bells rang, the clocks flashed all their lights, and the committee recessed so its members could scamper off to vote.

After it reconvened, the hearing quickly drew to a close—lunchtime had long passed. The vote reported the bill out, with a number of Democrats voting yes with Republicans. I was confused. In the milling around afterward, a friendly Democratic member who'd voted with us stopped in front of one of our strategists and asked, as if he'd read my thoughts, "Why did I vote no?"

Why did he need to ask that? Why had so many Democrats voted with Republicans? Why had some of the discussion been so wiggy? The answer, given nondefensively by one of the Washington Utah people: "We didn't do our job."

"Our job" meant this: inside the constant whirling information storm, to provide sufficient dots so they could be connected into a gestalt strong enough that it would be acted on. "Information" was not just facts, but a rich soup of friendships, personalities, experiences, staffers, contributors, messages from home, ambitions, loves. All in constant flux. And "our job" had to be accomplished in the face of the given: wilderness is not Washington.

After days of barreling from office to office to committee room to debriefings, I grasped that we were part of the muscle and bone, the living conduits of this information flow. The "cleverness" from our lobby training had more to do with attentiveness than with guile. The best way to serve the land in southern Utah was to be neither rigidly idealistic nor cynical—each a form of blindness—but to accept the complexity, try to see it clearly, and to act within it. This did not mean compromise of goals, but flexibility in means.

In an irony contrary to the darkly hilarious examples of what our culture did with nature, I sensed an ecological parallel between Capitol Hill and natural systems. Ecologists often describe ecosystems as flows of energy (a kind of information) with every element located in a web of interrelationships, explainable and graspable. Early research with this perspective used the simple ecosystems of the East Coast, such as salt marshes. The same theoretical framework doesn't work as well in the West, where ecosystems tend to be much more complicated.

Information (energy) flow still provides one approach, but the intricate connections prove much harder to pin down. The more complex the system, the further away in time and space a *cause* can be from its *effect*.

Despite the long history of western civilization's impulse to control and romanticize nature (once it seems to be controlled, it's safe to romanticize it—I remembered the Indian paintings), the dynamics of *this* little corner of western civ in Washington operated on the same principles as nature itself. Living (human!) actions and interactions were indispensable and drove the system in ways that could only partially be predicted. Luck played an enormous part. Everything connected to everything else.

In the popular mind and most of the press, politics has been simplified to the point of destroying any understanding. But even this oversimplification acts as an ingredient in the complexity. One not only considered current sound bites but also, for example, kept in mind the fact that Senator Bill Bradley had just finished writing his book and could once again concentrate more on legislation. We couldn't predict what our impact would be, but every push had the potential to cause a reconfiguration in the system.

The realization that ominous phantoms of central control might be figments of our imaginations was comforting to me; I hoped I wasn't being hoodwinked by my own optimism.

Like natural systems, Capitol Hill also didn't exist in a vacuum. Our lobby training had included a car analogy: lobbyists are the wheels, but the car won't go anywhere without an engine, and that engine is public uproar—messages from home.

On the last lobby day I headed out alone on a delivery run to take additional info to the congressman mystified by his own committee vote. I stepped into the first subway car in the sub-basement of the Hart Senate Office Building and settled myself on one of the two-person benches.

Two men in discussion followed me. When I looked up, I saw sitting across from me Pete Domenici, my other senator, much less sympathetic to environmental causes than Bingaman was. I hadn't even tried to make an appointment with him, since I knew he'd support his Republican colleagues. But I had three minutes on the run to the Capitol. I introduced myself, and Domenici launched into his cordial constituent-interaction mode. I deflected it and explained briefly why I was in Washington, then made my pitch:

"I urge you to oppose Senate Bill 884."

He grinned his Cheshire-cat grin. "I hear what you're saying. I urge you not to believe everything that's being said about my grazing reform bill." This bill only tangentially related to Senate Bill 884.

I grinned back. "I hear what you're saying."

Before we reached the Capitol, I had just enough time to hand his aide a packet of Utah material. As the senator hurried off, his aide paused long enough to give me his card and urge me to contact their office with any issues I had. Any issues at all. Good constituent relations.

Domenici's politics were so different from mine that I'd never have chosen to try to convince him of anything. But I'd seen the opportunity and grabbed it, even relished the minor sparring with an ease that surprised me. It was a tiny moment, but Utah wilderness had reached his computer screen in the form of one of *his* constituents, in Washington.

At the last debriefing, this subway hit won a pint of Chubby Hubby ice cream for the best lobbying story of the day.

Lobbying wrapped up. I stayed a day longer to sightsee along the Mall, to contemplate grassroots action, and to consider the difference thirty years had made in one corner of my psyche.

In the Museum of Natural History, I collapsed on the carpet and rubbed my sore feet through three showings of a video collage about the ocean. The huge, uncontrollable, North Atlantic storm waves impressed me most. Wet wilderness, beyond Congress's control, unaffected by neoclassical Greek architecture.

The overwhelming size of some issues can paralyze us; having any impact often looks impossible. The deep ecologist Joanna Macy has addressed this feeling of insignificance and futility among activists. The danger of despair. She suggests, in the Institute for Deep Ecology Education's newsletter, one way to save yourself: "Act your age. You weren't born yesterday. Remember that every atom in every cell of your body goes back through time in an unbroken succession of life, of survivors and adaptors right back to that initial fireball which created space and time . . . When you're in that Congressman's office . . . you are [acting] out of the full authority of your five billion years. Feel the dignity that graces you with and you simply can't go crazy."

Rebecca Solnit, in her book *Hope in the Dark*, reminds us that ordinary people have made a difference over and over. She writes, "To hope is to give yourself to the future and that commitment to the future makes the present habitable. Anything can happen, and whether we act or not has everything to do with it."

Southern Utah Wilderness Alliance organizers were then considered the most innovative grassroots group in the country, giving themselves to the future in as many ways as they could cook up with their expansive imaginations. One way was to recruit neophytes like me: people who had to stretch to even imagine meeting with a senator, but who were still willing to move forward with their fear. "Anything," after all, "can happen." For one thing, the sincerity of innocence carries a certain weight. The Utah Wilderness Coalition's Washington people had given us excellent training, great materials, accurate direction—a careful structure—then trusted us to discover our own abilities. I'd found I not only could do what they'd asked, but, to my surprise, I felt like I'd been born to it. And, I could improvise! On the carpeted floor while I watched the video of tough lobstermen in wet slickers, I could only shake my head in mild consternation. Had I banished my fear of speaking up forever? My effort had been a tiny piece of the ongoing Utah wilderness story. But here in Washington, the mesas and canyons of Utah had given me a different sort of gift than when I hiked their dry, rocky trails. They had given me the chance to grow in a distinctly social way.

As for my personal agenda, this hadn't been the Washington of my childhood, despite my memory of its architecture and imperial boulevards. The thread to my past had been my reaction to the place. As a kid, I'd found the city contrived and narrow. This time it felt the same, but in a more ironic and hilarious way because I could leave when I pleased. Returning confirmed that the constriction and banality I'd felt growing up had not been merely extensions of normal rebellion magnified by the sixties counterculture. They had been fact.

But Washington depended on its mix of unreality, power, and complexity. Anyone who aimed to affect decisions had to accept its form and work within it. Despite all that, after my experience in congressional offices, I clung to my hope that human acts, human personalities, human relationships, one by one, two by two, could have a substantial impact. Washington might be filled with fakery; nevertheless, it was populated not with automatons, but with *people*, in all their complication and capacity.

Eventually the bill we'd opposed died on the Senate floor as Senator Bill Bradley droned on in a filibuster. Not enough votes for cloture. He came from New Jersey, not the West, but he believed we had it right and didn't mind antagonizing a few colleagues to stop the bill. One principled human had acted alone, though UWC had long worked with him, and he understood the size and energy of the grassroots opposition.

🦅

After I'd had my fill of the heaving North Atlantic on the video screen, I wandered into the Hall of Mammals and paused in front of the moose diorama. As I gazed at the static scene, I felt the stopped energy. My muscles involuntarily gripped. I could think only of my solitary campsite at the end of a five-day backpack along the Beckler River in Yellowstone. That early-season trip had been the only time I'd felt the animal richness that once existed in parts of North America's wilderness. Next to my campsite in a grove of conifers, the river raced down stair-step rocks, sending up sprays of icy water. In four days, I had seen no human in that out-of-the-way corner of the park, and I had been drained by the day's hike. As I concentrated on making dinner, four feet away at the edge of the clearing, a large bull moose browsed the fresh growth. He ignored me, acting as if I were just another creature intent on enjoying the spring's bounty after a long winter.

In the Hall of Mammals I also thought of my first drive along the unpaved Burr Trail. I'd stopped at Upper Muley Twist Canyon near the top of the narrow, hair-raising switchbacks that climbed the east side of a massive wrinkle in the earth's crust, the Waterpocket Fold. For several hours, I'd walked along the winding wash bottom, the sand damp from a recent rain, many fresh yellow cottonwood leaves plastered flat on the dark ground. In one section, the moist earth showed clearly the tracks of a mule deer. They crossed and recrossed the wash until I noticed another set of tracks had entered from the left. Fresh cougar prints, the first I'd seen in the wild, followed the deer's path. This canyon happened to be in Capitol Reef National Park, not officially wilderness, but I remembered the signs of this hidden drama as a reminder of our limited points of view. I made sense of the tracks in the ways I could, with the information I had. The people who made laws in Washington operated with their own limited information, with many preconceptions, and with their multiple agendas. Still, anything that clarified the real issues and increased their understanding, or even triggered a personal connection, made it more likely that they would act with wisdom. I could always hope.

✺

In the years since 1995, a few changes have come to southern Utah and to Washington, D.C. In 1999 President Clinton established the Grand

Staircase–Escalante National Monument. Controversies about unpaved roads in Utah continue unabated. A concertedly anticonservation administration has been in office since 2000. Responses to the attacks of 9/11 have likely made much of the easy access I experienced in Washington impossible. The Bureau of Land Management has limited ATV and dirt-bike use on land surrounding Factory Butte. No bill designating wilderness on Utah BLM land has yet passed Congress.

It is well to be informed about the winds,
About the variations in the sky,
The native traits and habits of the place,
What each locale permits, and what denies.

—Virgil, *Georgics*, circa 30 BC

Zuni Maize

Faint southwest wind, clear October light, toasting sun. Locale: Zuni, New Mexico.

In a field filled with whispering corn stalks bleached pale, I found myself happily surrounded by complication. A race of Zuni blue corn stood in tousled ranks next to a variety of modern hybrid corn; my companions were an equally unlikely mix. I had come to the Zuni Reservation with a corn physiologist from Iowa State University, and we'd been joined in the field by five Zuni men. The corn physiologist was Deb Muenchrath; this experimental field and the nearby canyon were part of a National Science Foundation-funded collaboration between the Zuni Tribe and a group of scientists trained in the same schools that churned out agribusiness researchers. The five Zunis working with us that morning lived with beliefs and practices stretching back millennia, but they had also become experts in speaking with satellites via the latest GPS technology. Expected categories became fluid and intermingled.

While the ancient Anasazi inhabitants of this landscape abandoned many settlements, they didn't evaporate into the dry desert air, despite the theatrical appeal of such a mysterious disappearance. Modern Pueblo peoples, especially Zunis and Hopis, have no doubts those Ancient Ones simply moved on and became their immediate ancestors.[1]

Although Zuni traditional farming can't be mapped directly onto prehistoric Anasazi agriculture, enough evidence exists to make a confident leap: Zuni strategies for growing crops in their semiarid environment had their genesis in a past more distant than the heyday of Chaco Canyon's great houses.[2] That dynamic continuity over such a time span suggests those strategies succeeded without exhausting the land and could well offer unexpected lessons.

Deb's test field sat at the mouth of a small canyon, in a gently tilting expanse of dried grasses, asters, blooming tangerine globe mallow, and indeterminate brush full of pesky prickers. Up into the canyon, the slope increased slightly as the fractured sandstone walls slowly closed in, their burnt orange sides streaked with umber, visible behind scattered piñons and junipers. The central runoff channel, which meandered up and back about a mile, had not cut downward, and its braided sand patterns smoothly merged into the surrounding ground, unlike the deep erosion I'd seen in most drainages in the Southwest. In the last several years, this particular spot had not been farmed, but scattered potsherds, stone tools, and ruins nearby told archaeologists it had probably been sporadically cultivated for at least eight hundred years.

A dirt track curved away from the field through low sage and spent sunflowers toward the paved road that bisects the reservation. The seven of us had been working about an hour when we all stopped abruptly and turned our faces into the wind. A wavering, high tone seemed to blow past us and up into the canyon. In the bright air, the stalks swished around us like the rush of a fast rocky stream. Above us, chalky contrails crisscrossed the deep blue distance.

"What *is* that?" asked Deb.

"Someone on the highway, maybe?" said Dixon, tentatively.

The high note glissandoed higher, jumped a major fifth, then stopped abruptly when the wind died.

We all shrugged, shook our heads, and turned back to the harvest. Deb, in a broad-brimmed hat, white T-shirt, jeans, and her multipocket field apron, set a plastic bin filled with blue corn ears on the electronic scale perched on boards suspended between two stepladders. We'd established our harvesting/data-collecting rhythm. Low earthen berms gridded the field into twenty-five plots, and within each plot corn had been planted in nine hills, either Zuni blue or modern hybrid. Deb had treated each plot with one of five water/fertilizer regimes, including the organically rich runoff water from the watershed above the field. Our task was to find each plot's median hill by harvest weight, so it could return with Deb to her lab in Iowa: the median hill would provide a statistically significant figure without needing to ship all the corn. In Iowa, Deb would remove all the ears' water to determine each hill's dry weight. One hill at a time, Lowell and Dixon slashed down the stalks with machetes and brought their unwieldy armloads to the green tarp next to the scale. Deb, Niles, Monroe, and I shucked the ears. Then each hill's harvest took its turn on the scale. Curtis, whose year-old broken toe had been bothering him, monitored the scale and called out the weights for me to record.

In the quiet fall morning we joked easily as we cut and shucked and weighed the harvest. I felt welcomed and honored to work alongside these five men who repeated an activity they knew down to their marrow, but this time repeated it with a twist.

Zuni, a favorite western New Mexico hangout of ethnographers from Frank Cushing in the 1880s to Dennis Tedlock in the 1980s, has lately shifted tribal gears. ("Here come the anthros, better hide the past away," goes a popular song.) In the 1980s, Zuni Pueblo sued the U.S. government for stealing its land and trashing its resources—both intentionally and through high-handed ignorance. During the legal proceedings, the ecological disaster and associated cultural disruption became well documented. In a painful irony, Zuni corn varieties, grown on Zuni land, with Zuni knowledge and technology, had been producing sustainably for well over two thousand years. At least Zuni agriculture had been sustainable *before* the westward-ho U.S. government had done its damnedest to make Zuni a distant suburb of Kansas City. Even a much condensed list of havoc-wrecking government policies offers some sense of the magnitude of environmental sabotage visited on the Zuni people:[3]

Before 1846, the Zunis' aboriginal land covered more than 15.2 million acres. It extended from Mount Taylor in the east to the San Francisco Peaks in the west, providing territory for grazing, foraging, and farming. Zunis farmed mainly west of the Continental Divide, along the tributary streams feeding the Little Colorado, from near Pie Town in the southeast and Crownpoint in the northeast, to Winslow, Arizona, in the west.

Without compensation, the government took Zuni land for military uses, national forests, railroads, and non-Indian homesteading. Today, Zuni trust lands include just under 420,000 acres, less than 3 percent of their original territory; in the mid-nineteenth century, Zunis cultivated 10,000–12,000 acres, compared with less than 10 percent of that acreage in 1991.

The remaining Zuni land has suffered severe erosion, beginning in earnest around the turn of the twentieth century. Off-reservation clear-cutting in the Zuni Mountains, combined with a severe, region-wide drought, partly caused the extreme land degradation. Overgrazing also played a part, triggered by Zuni flocks squeezed into a smaller and smaller range. In addition, large, government-built dams caused extensive down-cutting of rivers and streams.

During the lawsuit, in response to the Zunis' claims that official policies caused erosion, the government at first denied any responsibility. Spokespeople insisted that erosion is a natural process in the West and simply "an act of God," despite ample evidence from many locations that human activities influence how, where, and how rapidly erosion occurs.

Socially, official policy aimed at assimilating Zunis into main-stream American culture. Although such cultural sledgeham-mering is all too familiar throughout Indian Country, at Zuni the policy had a specific effect on farming. Traditionally, Zuni land was held communally, with extended family parcels inherited through women of the family. This communal and female-oriented system of land tenure must have mightily irked the individualistic males who ran the show at the Bureau of Indian Affairs (BIA), and they forcibly changed land control to individual plots (of a mere ten acres) *owned by men.* Those plots then could also be bought and sold, not only precipitating social disruption but also pro-viding another push into a cash economy. Currently, bitter land disputes can be traced directly back to that intrusion into a well-functioning Zuni system, effectively preventing farming on a great deal of otherwise productive land.

The most dramatic and ecologically ignorant government encroachment at Zuni has been its attempt at large-scale dam and irrigation projects. Traditionally, Zuni farmers cultivated relatively modest fields, providing necessary water with small-scale, dynamic water management. Their methods were effec-tive and appropriate to the land, though they often required continual, labor-intensive maintenance. Five farming districts, at some distance from the main Zuni Pueblo, provided most land for cultivation: upper and lower Nutria, upper and lower Pescado, Tekapo, Ojo Caliente, and Halono:wa. But small-scale, ecologi-cally effective water management conflicted with the narrow empire-building water attitudes at the Bureau of Reclamation and the BIA. Perhaps the policy makers harbored benevolent visions of providing the Zuni people with lush and fertile fields watered by their new dams. More likely, those bureaucrats were caught up in the twentieth-century rush to dam every flowing watercourse in the West, their technical capacities for impounding water far outstripping their understanding of geology, ecology, soils, sedimentation, or local cultures.

One example of such misguided irrigation projects will suffice.

Black Rock Dam, just upstream from Zuni Pueblo on the Zuni River, was built between 1906 and 1909 with no consultation with the Zuni people. At the time, it was one of the largest public-works projects in the country. Its waters were meant to irrigate cornfields downstream, although Zunis knew the intended cornfields were composed of tight clay, badly suited for cultivation. Once filled, the reservoir drowned and destroyed a sacred spring that had been used for traditional ditch irrigation at the settlement of Black Rock.

Though the dam had been built on surface basalt, pure sand lay under the hard rock. As soon as the dam was put into service, it collapsed, causing major erosion downstream. This added to the erosion caused in 1906 when an upstream dam had failed before Black Rock had even been completed. Once repaired, the dam provided enough hope to Zuni farmers to draw them to the new fields, away from the farming districts. Deprived of labor, the carefully maintained water-management systems no longer functioned well. The reservoir behind Black Rock Dam silted up quickly and within twenty years held only 27 percent of its original capacity. In 1931 the BIA drained the reservoir to add a sluice gate in an attempt to flush the sediment. Once refilled, the reservoir still could irrigate only 10 percent of the land originally planned for the project. In 1932 the dam failed again.

Dismayingly, blind governmental behavior apparently isn't limited to the early part of the twentieth century. Though twenty feet of fine silt entirely filled the reservoir, in the 1980s Black Rock Dam was declared the second most dangerous dam in

Indian territory. The $13 million that Congress had appropriated to repair it needed to be spent. When I stopped by with Deb in the fall of 1998 to take a look at the construction, the heavy equipment and hard-hatted men had rebuilt an impressive structure. However, not one of the contractors was from Zuni. When I asked the construction foreman about the sediment stretching upstream in a flat, scrub-covered plain *level with the top of the dam*, he shrugged and said, "The Zunis are in charge of that."

While Zuni had been struggling through the labyrinthine legal system to claim some small justice, on the margins of Big Agriculture a handful of scientists had been rediscovering the value of "land races," heirloom crop populations whose genetic variability gives them resilience in the face of pests, disease, and erratic environmental conditions. Since the domestication of plants, especially in the biotically diverse Third World, growers have practiced intense artificial selection, season by season, and mingled geographically distant populations. As a result, crops have evolved into many varieties adapted to local conditions. Within any one crop species, thousands of genetically diverse land races exist: rich, heterogeneous variations on a theme, much like the members of an extended family. The Zuni blue corn growing in Deb's test field was a land race, not a "pure" single genetic strain like modern hybrid corn, but adapted through centuries to the particular conditions at Zuni. Usually land races flourish in the fields of small farmers who depend more on their grandparents' knowledge than on official science. Land races also rely on cultivation methods that contrast sharply with the highly mechanized, synthetically fertilized, and pesticide-treated fields of Big Agriculture.

Some early data from this project suggested the nitrogen content *inside* some traditional Zuni fields surpassed the nitrogen in the surrounding ground. Most fields showed more soil microbes.[5] Both results were exactly opposite from U.S. Corn Belt fields where persistent

nutrient loss required annual additions of nitrogen and other supple-
ments. And Zuni fields used no synthetic fertilizer, had no pesticide resi-
dues, depleted no groundwater, lost no topsoil.

This collaboration at Zuni challenged a commodified mainstream
that had little real understanding of any vision outside a narrow band
of acceptability. That challenge to mainstream intolerance most deeply
explained why I'd joined Deb at Zuni. Although I relished the particu-
larities of Zuni corn-growing and the details of the puzzles Deb and her
colleagues worked to decipher, I found solace in their refusal—on the
part of both the Zunis and the researchers—to buckle under pressure
from the juggernaut of twentieth-century American culture. That juggernaut usually barrelled along blindly, dehumanizing, standardizing, sim-
plifying, and destroying any insubordination in its path. Like many other
small, quiet ventures, this project questioned business as usual, not with
romanticized notions, but with careful, open-minded explorations of a
working system.

What the Zunis could teach wasn't an easy lesson for a culture like
ours, convinced of linear reasoning, of singular answers, of quick fixes
and absolutes. Loosen that limited set of logical apparatus, I imagined I
heard the Zunis saying, throw out those badly fitting templates and open
your eyes to what will, given time, work: flexibility in the face of inevitable uncertainty, innovation as a response to living on the edge.

Paradoxically, this long-standing, fluid accommodation contrasted
with the immutability given to traditional practices absorbed into religion. Where to unbend? Where to hold firm? Corn is sacred. The Zunis
will not sell their corn.

The eerie whistle renewed its silvery song. We all stopped again, looking
for some explanation.

"I know what it is," said Niles finally. "It's the wind in these lines."
He tossed his head toward the glittering gossamer threads stretched

east to west, every three feet, across the seven-foot-tall enclosure. Deb needed the fence to keep out the hungry elk, the fishing line to spook the marauding crows and ravens. In the center of the field, hanging from one taut line, a large, inflated plastic pumpkin grinned at us. The monofilament succeeded in keeping the birds out, but in its delicacy and unexpected regularity, it looked unmistakably like high-tech art. And in the wind it sounded like a playful gremlin making mischief from some other realm. No wonder the ravens left it alone.

Deb Muenchrath and her colleagues from Iowa, New Mexico, Montana, and Wyoming approached this canyon and the experimental cornfield as an integrated *system*: "crops, biophysical elements, and human management." Oddly, such systems approaches that encompass multiple factors crossing disciplines are almost anomalies in science today. They're hard to get funded and equally hard to publish in a journal market that seeks short, highly focused articles. Soil journals concentrate on soils, not plant physiology, for example, despite the relationship between the two. And not until recently would such a project have embraced indigenous knowledge as the skilled orchestrator of the whole shebang. The pressurized atmosphere of scientific publishing, partly geared toward getting authors jobs or tenure, seemed to add unnecessary roadblocks to legitimate attempts to truly understand the interrelated complications of the real world.

This project had three goals. First, the researchers intended simply to describe Zuni runoff farming analytically (the basic hookup to science) and in the process glean a better understanding of semiarid ecosystems. Second, they meant to add to research on sustainable land use. Third, they would offer what they learned to the Zuni Tribe for its agricultural revitalization. A kind of loop-de-loop: from Zuni through the digitized university house of mirrors and back to Zuni.[6]

For nearly three years, they'd been measuring rainfall and water flow, analyzing soils, surveying plants, and mapping the topography of the diminutive drainage. Runoff from the rare rains normally would wash nutrient-rich sediments into the field near its mouth, an ancient farming method that used neither conventional irrigation nor artificial fertilizer. But now a temporary, boxcar-sized reservoir caught the runoff so Deb could treat the twenty-five plots in this test field with different water/nutrient regimes.

Despite ZSAP's welcome, some Zunis remained skeptical: after all, before their world had been disrupted, they'd successfully farmed corn, beans, squash, and peppers for a hundred generations. After the Spanish had arrived, they'd added wheat, melons, and peaches to their fields. In waffle gardens closer to houses, women grew coriander, garlic, onions, some cotton, and encouraged wild plants such as amaranth and edible greens. In the mid-nineteenth century, ten thousand acres were planted in corn. Although today Zunis farm only about one thousand acres, planting cycles and ceremonial cycles still depend on each other's elaborate rhythms. But ZSAP had spotted issues that needed science's stamp: whether tractors bought with Ford Foundation money worked the soil more effectively than hand tilling; verification for the New Mexico Organic Commodities Commission that their runoff farming produced crops organically without depleting the land; maps of eastern Zuni indicating suitable future farming spots so the inevitable Pueblo housing expansion might be wisely located. Practical Zuni goals interleaved with the project's more general ones.

Deb's attention to Zuni's traditional farming attracted me, but I'd also caught her contagious fascination with corn.

The plot whose ears we shucked at the moment had been planted with Zuni blue corn and treated with runoff water, but no sediment, from the drainage—one of Deb's five treatment regimes. The ears had grown long and thin, with mature, filled-out kernels. While we laughed at Niles intoning again "tamale, tamale, tamale, tamale, tamale"—those Southwestern steamed delights of spicy meat and cornmeal wrapped in corn husks—I peeled away one ear's pale, translucent, paper-thin sheaths. Exposed, the dark corn glowed in the October sun, the overall deep blue-violet kernels interrupted in places with red ones the color and richness of burgundy. Five or six yellow ones from cross-pollination with the non-Zuni hybrid in other plots had also shown up. Next to the dark kernels, the hybrid ones looked sallow and opaque. This ear had a rare variation: on certain kernels a delicate starburst of dotted white lines radiated from the center top, down around the kernel's curved sides and bottom. An ear full of jewels.

"That's from a mutation in one gene," said Deb when we all stopped shucking to admire the ear. Since we needed to harvest and weigh twenty-five plots, nine hills per plot, we tried to work fast, but not so fast we couldn't slow down to exclaim at an oddity—a tassel ear or an extra-large corn worm—or a beauty.

Corn. *Zea mays*. Maize. Without maize, what would the Incas, the Aztecs, the Maya, the Anasazi have been? What would the Rio Grande Pueblos, the Hopis, the Zunis be? How many times have we heard that story? Yet maize still grips us like the sight of a much-loved person, ever renewing its magnetic pull, grounded in need but ultimately mysterious. What, after all, would *we* be without maize?[7]

Corn is so uniquely mysterious that no other crop provides so much to the industrial world. In 1987 the National Corn Growers Association crowed, "Anything made from a barrel of petroleum can be made from a bushel of corn," from biodegradable plastic to ethanol to lightweight building materials. It's been claimed that in a supermarket everything but fresh fish has had contact with some product or by-product of corn. And then there's its use in rubber tires, dynamite, and embalming fluid.

"Corn is our mother," say all the Southwest cultures whose roots extend deep into the land's past.[8] "King Corn is Supreme," proclaimed midwestern cities in the booster years after 1880 when corn palaces with domes, flying buttresses, and allegorical mosaics seemed to sprout everywhere. In 1891 Sioux City's corn palace included a balcony scene from *Romeo and Juliet* that was constructed entirely from white corn. An annually refurbished corn palace still graces Mitchell, South Dakota.

In the Southwest, tracking corn cultivation has provided work for legions of archaeobotanists, who currently place its arrival from the south around 1800 BC. Dating the appearance of corn's companion crops—squash and especially beans—has been even more difficult. But one thing can't be argued: they supplied what corn lacked as a protein source, the amino acids tryptophan and lysine. We can explain molecularly why that made sense, but those ancient chefs had their own ways of knowing. They also discovered that corn must be cooked with an alkali, like wood ash. The lime improves the flavor, but it also promotes the release of the important B-vitamin niacin. Early Europeans who first imported corn neglected to import the alkali processing, and an epidemic of the niacin deficiency pellagra followed, with its skin sores, aching joints, and dizziness. But in a study of fifty-one Native American societies depending on corn, fifty-one used alkali processing.[9]

During the nineteenth and twentieth centuries, plant breeders have chased after "corn improvement" with high passion, rarely recognizing that the plant they aimed to improve was already highly bred. No one knows what became of the missing link between corn's presumed wild ancestor—teosinte—and its cultivated descendants, but countless myths explain that maize was a gift whose usefulness arrived full-blown. The corn geneticist Walton Galinet says, "The American Indians were not simply the first corn breeders. They created corn in the first place."[10]

Unlike other cultivated grains, maize *needs* humans. A human must plant corn kernels before a new crop will grow. Wheat or barley or rye will sprout into producing plants if wind broadcasts their seeds, but corn will not. The corn stalks we cut and weighed at Zuni took their place as the most recent installment of an *unbroken* chain of corn-human-corn-human-corn-human that extends back perhaps seven millennia to somewhere in central Mexico.

That staggering continuity hovered in my mind while I wondered about the unspoken, closely guarded, and, for me, all but unknowable ceremonial and sacred lives of the five Zunis joking with me and Deb as we all weighed and shucked her scientific harvest. I say *"her* harvest," but after she'd dried and analyzed a portion of the corn, Deb would return it all to Zuni.

"And which one wins a free trip back to Iowa?" Niles asked in his game-show voice as I tallied the weights and determined the median hill.

"Number nine, number nine, number nine," I chanted, Beatles-style, though my reference to that sixties album might have been lost on everyone. While Deb and Monroe, in his Nike hat, stuffed the ears and stalks of pile nine into the string cabbage bags the Iowa State University Agronomy Department bought for just such purposes, Curtis, Dixon, Lowell, and I added the other stalks from this plot to one big heap out-side the field. The shucked ears we laid in their new, ears-only group. Five plots down, twenty to go.

I was, of course, an outsider admitting a curiosity shared by gen-erations of curious outsiders, through the long line of ethnographers to the thousands of visitors who until 1995 had been welcomed to watch the intricately costumed and masked kachinas of Sha'lak'o.[11] The best-known Zuni celebration, Sha'lak'o takes place near the winter solstice, the return of light. The dancers dance to ensure harmony and to bless newly built houses, the earth, and all humankind.

But the word "curiosity" is too lightweight and simplistic to describe what I felt. I also admired the tenacity and inventiveness it took to live where summer heat rivaled winter cold, and where meager soils, scarce water, violent spring winds, and dramatically unpredictable weather made farming a chancy venture. That same tenacity had helped maintain the Zuni culture in the face of the devouring, disease-laden European onslaught beginning in 1540, and the even more destructive U.S. gov-ernment policies after 1846. I envied their attachment to this land of sandstone and light, still largely free from the most unsightly marks of the twentieth century, despite the eroded arroyos, depleted game and forests, and stolen water. I was both attracted and discomfited by the contrast between the inappropriate HUD housing and the Zunis' richly complicated beliefs, which whirled everywhere like the invisible wind through sage and junipers.

The ancient heritage these corn plants embodied mirrored the threads of the past in the Zunis themselves. Culture/agriculture: not exactly the same, but here as closely mated as the husks hugging the ears.

Deb, on the other hand, had grown up in the culture of the Corn Belt, the still-beating heart of the Green Revolution, where hybrid varieties have been bred for optimum conditions, where air-conditioned John Deere tractors work enormous feed-corn fields nourished with synthetic fertilizer and drenched in pesticides, fungicides, and herbicides. A familiar scene: soil as black as night, corn as high as a crop plane's eye and fields as far as the eye can see. A picture of abundance, with a not so subtle whiff of crushing mass production. The Industrial Revolution turned to chlorophyll.

Sometime in Deb's graduate career, after she'd had a part in developing a new patentable genetic strain, she decided she didn't relish trafficking in the guts of life. She turned then to corn's physiology. Her dissertation research had been on land races of corn from the Tohono O'odham, who live in the Sonoran Desert near Tucson.[12] During that work, it had dawned on her that Native culture and local growing techniques were inseparable from corn's biology. They had evolved together.

A short foray into the staggering behemoth of Industrial Agriculture is in order here, to put in proper context local growing techniques, corn's land races, and Native cultures.

Some have suggested that Big Science didn't start with the Manhattan Project, but with the successful hybridization of corn in the mid-1930s.[13] Modern hybrid corn—the carefully controlled crossing of inbred parent lines—had two immediate physical effects: to dramatically reduce genetic variability and to decouple "grain" from "seed." Farmers could no longer save seed from their own corn crops, but needed to buy it anew every year or suffer declining yields. That has meant enormous profits for seed companies who have always promoted use of hybrids rather than other approaches, such as population improvement, which would have left them without such a sellable and proprietary product. In fiscal 1997, for example, Pioneer Hi-Bred, the planet's largest seed company, sold seed corn worth $1,374,000,000 worldwide.[14] In 1982 biologist Richard Lewontin flatly stated, "If the same time and effort had been put into [improving open pollinated varieties], they would be as good or better than hybrids by now."[15]

But hybrid corn has also been linked with two other legs of the so-called "high-profit trio": plant more thickly, fertilize more heavily.[16] In the United States, between 1950 and 1994, the number of acres in corn *decreased by 4 percent*, and the harvest *tripled*, while the tonnage of nitrogen fertilizer applied to corn *increased by 1,700 percent*.[17] More luxuriant corn growth in larger fields encouraged insects, disease, and weeds, which meant more insecticides, fungicides, and herbicides. Over the years, pests have adapted to those chemical controls, and applications have increased. More row planting and less fallow time encouraged topsoil loss. In 1992 corn accounted for 58 percent of U.S. agricultural herbicide use (223 million pounds!) and 37 percent of insecticides. Yet, since 1940, the price of a bushel of corn in constant dollars has steadily *fallen*.[18] The term *high-profit* implied farmers would be better off. In reality, seed companies and the agrochemical industry made out like bandits. Green, orderly abundance came with a dark underbelly of pollution, erosion, loss of topsoil, and capital concentration. In October 1998, in a year with a near record crop, a depressed Asian market, and a shrunken federal safety net, an Iowa State University survey predicted perhaps as many as 30 percent of Iowa farms would go under.[19]

While technology has continued to refine its tools—first, hybridization, and now, gene splicing—commercial seed companies have succeeded in gaining patent protection for plant varieties and genetic strings. With utter solemnity they have engaged in acrobatic doublespeak: their germplasm sources (varieties from the gene-rich Third World or from

Native America) are the "common heritage of mankind" and therefore
should be free to all comers, while their saleable seeds should be protected by property-rights laws. Once again, the already powerful are
attempting to increase their power and profits by manipulating the law.

When I asked Deb how she connected her research in the outback
of the arid Southwest to more mainstream agriculture, she said, "There's
a lot to learn from traditional systems," and paused. "But it's not easy to
convince people in Iowa of that."

≈

In the Southwest, nothing is more important to agriculture than water.
Traditionally, Zunis would have used storm runoff from the small watershed above Deb's test field to provide it with sufficient moisture. Runoff
fields concentrated the rain from an area significantly larger than the
field: in some examples of similar "akchin" fields at Hopi, the planted
area at the mouth of a canyon measured less than 2 percent of the
watershed's total area.[20]

At Zuni, from late winter until the end of March and again during
the monsoons beginning in July, short and intense rainstorms quickly
saturated the thin soil over rock. Then the rainwater washed across fallen
pine needles, juniper berries, gritty sand, cryptobiotic soil clinging to
bare earth; past sage, saltbush, and mullein; finally tumbling down the
watershed to the field at its mouth. These floods, rare but usually frequent enough, not only brought necessary water to the corn but also
supplied what Zunis call "tree sand"—the decaying organic matter that
slowly made its way down the drainage. A moving compost pile delivered without pitchforks.

These storm-runoff fields struck me as ingenious and quirky. The
land, often with a few added low rock barriers, focused the flash floods
where they could be used, the way a lens can focus light. Ingenious,
maybe, but Deb told me such runoff irrigation wasn't limited to a few
out-of-the-way spots in the American Southwest. In Israel's Negev

Desert, a group of biologists and archaeologists had renovated ancient runoff irrigation systems into several large, thriving farms with vegetables, wine grapes, and orchards of peach, fig, olive, apricot, and almond trees. Pastures of alfalfa, barley, oats, and wheat stretched out next to barren ground. Hardly what anyone would expect in a desert without pumping groundwater or rechanneling a river.[21]

Deb and her colleagues weren't oriented to truck farming, but to deciphering *this* system, and that depended on understanding the biology of maize, a plant so adaptable it seemed to be a botanical chameleon. Corn's wild promiscuity, extreme even for a flowering plant, partly explains its dramatic adaptability. It's the most widely distributed crop in the world, from twelve thousand feet in the Andes to sea level, from the humid tropics to Southwest deserts, and in all climates between.[22]

Fourteen million pollen grains, give or take a few, blow from each of the male tassels that fountain up from the tops of corn's leafy stalks. Carried mostly by the wind, the pollen finds its way to the silks of proto-ears on the stalk below or on nearby plants: one pale, delicate silk per kernel. On each plant, the tassels usually shed their pollen several days before its ears are ready, which makes cross-pollination between plants more likely. In a land race field, theoretically, each kernel on an ear could have a different set of genes. But corn has an additional trick that keeps its variability high: specialized DNA sequences that shift around a little like jackrabbits. They're called "jumping genes." Not surprisingly, though it is a single species, corn claims more varieties—thousands worldwide—than any other crop.

Corn's genetic blueprint, by itself, dictates only *some* corn attributes: the colors of the kernels and whether the "meat" of the kernel will be sugary, flinty, floury, or "dent"—a type mostly used to feed livestock and named for the dimple in each dried kernel's crown.

But everything else, including cob and kernel size, yield of grain, growth and development, height, number of leaves and ears, side stalks, and so on, depends on the genes' interaction with the corn's local environment. No matter what a kernel's germplasm encodes, its growing conditions can mean the difference between large full ears and small, poorly filled ears. Sometimes temperatures a few degrees colder than normal during germination can doom a future plant, or not quite enough water when an ear silks out in July can mean fertilization never happens. No fertilization, no kernels, no harvest.

I imagined corn's messy heterogeneity first prompted the *idea* of orderly hybrids, with their matching sets of DNA, long before technology could make it happen. Why not track down the "best" traits and construct ideal, predictable plants, instead of settling for the hodgepodge from promiscuous, open pollination? And that's exactly what has happened: the handful of Corn Belt hybrid varieties will grow uniform plants with one ear per exceptionally stiff stalk, perfectly suited for mechanical harvest, and will produce large yields when all conditions are *optimum*. And that insistence on optimum conditions has led down the path of industrial agriculture. Keep the plants standard, like dolls off the assembly line, and go after the *maximum* yields. But keeping conditions optimum requires enormous inputs, especially in difficult, variable conditions, and drastically diminishes any flexibility.

Deb had planted hybrid dent corn that New Mexico State University had recommended for Zuni's conditions, to compare with the local Zuni blue.

"I once planted some corn from the extension service," Niles told us. "Tall, beautiful. Giant stalks, though—two inches across." He circled his thumb and forefinger. "But I didn't get *one* ear." He shook his head half in amazement, half in disgust.

Among most traditional farmers, certainly in the less-than-optimal arid Southwest, the goal has been to minimize risk. When survival literally depends on your harvest, as it did for several thousand years, the less risk the better.

Instead of attempts to *control* the environment, the Zunis, like other traditional farmers, have worked to *buffer* its lack of cooperation. At the same time, they have selected seeds that tolerate their harsh and uncertain world. Maize and Zuni have evolved together.

This distinction bears repeating. Industrial Agriculture aims for high yields in the short term, under the best of conditions, no matter what the eventual collateral damage to the environment might be. Traditional farmers have always sought consistency of production through genetic variability and multiple, flexible growing strategies. Minimize risk.

At Zuni, harshness and uncertainty meant scarce and sporadic water, cold temperatures at germination and toward the end of the season, high midseason heat, low soil nitrogen, spring wind so violent it could rip seedlings right out of the ground, and pests. This year the worst pests had been field-inhaling grasshoppers, elk forced down from the mountains by new houses, and "two-legged deer" in pickup trucks. But Zuni's varied topography—its mesas and canyons, elevations that range from 6,030 feet to 7,000 feet, springs and seasonal streams—partly counterbalanced those difficulties by offering many microclimates.

The Zuni potpourri of planting techniques reminded me of a well-stocked larder, full not of food, but of effective strategies.

Sometimes the Zunis nestled their fields by a mesa for wind protection or next to heat-holding canyon walls that trumped frost; they might locate one field a little higher, one a little lower, hedging their bets.

They planted up to twelve inches deep—where the growing plant would be more likely to reach water and to be protected longer from those late frosts—deep roots providing solid anchor. Zuni varieties had evolved to grow much longer sprouts than varieties planted closer to the surface.

They planted four to ten plants together in widely spaced hills. The stalks supported each other against the violent spring winds and debris-laden swift runoff. The hills' distance apart increased effective moisture and required less labor to plant and tend.

Traditionally—though not since ready tractors—they planted kernels using a digging stick. Undisturbed by plowing, the soil evaporated less of its precious moisture and didn't compact under heavy equipment. They tended to their soils by rotating crops and allowing fields to lie fallow. Not only do beans, with their microbial collaborators, fix nitrogen from the air, but so do wild plants like larkspur and cliff rose. Lightning also transforms atmospheric nitrogen into a usable form. Cryptobiotic soil, which covertly takes over on ground untrampled for some years, supplies a surprisingly large proportion of the nitrogen available to plants all over the Southwest.

At Zuni, an unexpected regular genetic shake-up takes place, beyond cross-pollination, beyond jumping genes. Night dances include a large communal seed bowl: everyone contributes, everyone leaves with a handful of *different* seeds that have been blessed. Extra care goes into planting and tending those sacred seeds.[23]

My head spun with the details. But I thought of these Zuni farmers beside me who I knew often laughed good-naturedly at this project's effort to translate their "system" into the framework of science. What to me seemed novel and complicated had been codified in their culture, each detail easily related to the others—details of land and weather, of ceremony and the sacred, of corn stalks growing green and kernels ripe with the future.

Yet Zunis are no more monolithic than any other group. Some ZSAP fields closer to the roads, including one of Deb's test fields, had been vandalized this year (1998)—squash smashed, ears of corn half shucked and thrown on the ground. Reverence abandoned. No one knew who. No one really knew why.

But this year's assistant director of ZSAP could work only until December, when his yearlong religious duties kicked in again. Reverence maintained.

And jurisdictional ironies abounded.

The renovated Black Rock Dam in front of its silted-up reservoir seemed unlikely ever to function, though the Zunis themselves welcomed it, retaining some hope for new irrigation water.

The crop-damaging elk roamed the reservation with impunity, illegal game unless a hunter had a permit. They had been pushed down from the Zuni Mountains in the past five or six years by extensive new house building off the reservation. Even though the New Mexico Department of Game and Fish provided free hunting permits to farmers in the Eight Northern Pueblos in north-central New Mexico, I'd been told, they hadn't extended the same privilege to the Zunis.

I could easily portray this Zuni system as jazz improv counterbalancing the Sousa marches of mainstream agriculture, but that didn't honor the complications and the internal paradoxes. To me, the most positive impulse at Zuni seemed the attempts not to *resolve* their paradoxes, but to *corral* them into an encompassed synergy. The success of the Zuni corn system came from its flexibility, responsiveness, redundancy, human resourcefulness and idiosyncrasy, and its specificity to local, often wildly unpredictable conditions. Powerful outside forces had interrupted it, but its heart remained intact.

As far as the Zuni effort can be generalized, it seemed meant to buffer their culture against internal nuttiness (such as field vandalism) and external nuttiness (such as capricious policies of the BIA, Game and Fish, HUD; TV and mainstream culture) just as their corn has been buffered for millennia against the potentially destructive forces of a difficult climate. Much as they cultivated *with* the topography, the soils, the wind, the rain, the heat and cold, they were trying to work *with* the twentieth and twenty-first centuries and *with* science. And not be swallowed. But the going was tough, partly because science can never claim the ultimate certainty of religion, despite its apparent handle on "truth."

🌿

A few days before the corn harvest, I'd joined Deb and several others following Niles and his ZSAP boss down a rocky dirt track on a mesa southwest of Zuni Pueblo. The bumper piñon crop hung heavy on the branches, ready to be shaken loose. The nuts' smooth, oblong meats were as rich in protein by weight as beefsteak, with a full complement of amino acids. Chamisa bloomed egg-yolk yellow. Prickly pear, dried grasses, and snakeweed mingled with flame-shaped junipers, covered with their own yields: dull purple berries traditionally used as food or flavoring or to make a tea for stomachaches.

The track angled downhill to an outcrop of pale sandstone boulders. To our left the edge of the mesa fell away abruptly to a series of gently sloping benches of maroon, purple, and cream gravels dotted with dark piñons and junipers. Directly ahead and several hundred feet below, a broad, flat expanse of golden desert separated us from two short red mesas, then more distantly, a taller light mesa, its top frosted dark green. The trail rounded the boulders to a steep, winding slot through the rocks. Stepping carefully across stones and dust, we picked our way down to a small basin that faced the warm sun to the southwest. About one hundred yards long, thirty yards wide, the nearly flat shelf nestled below the mesa's faceted persimmon face, but still above the desert floor: a natural porch. Clumps of big sage and more delicate sand sage shared the ground with the pale delicate grasses. And, remarkably, within the porch's sandstone boundaries grew a reviving peach orchard.

When the Spanish had muscled their way into this territory, they'd brought not only a mission to convert the "heathens," but also plants from home. They'd carried with them from Spain several peach varieties that would grow from pits, already adapted to an arid climate, with small fruits perfectly suited for drying. The Zunis had established orchards on many terraces just below mesa tops where runoff would water deep sandy soils. They dried their new harvests on their roofs alongside corn and chile and gourds and beans. But in the 1950s a catastrophic freeze had wiped out most of the thousands of trees.

For years the bare trees in this lovely, protected cove had stood neglected, left for dead, with cactuses growing at their feet. The two stone field houses had nearly disintegrated. ZSAP had mined their community's knowledge, consulting with an older Zuni farmer who kept his own flourishing orchard, and went to work. They cleared out the cactuses and dug around among the roots. If the roots weren't brittle, they still lived. The crew cut away the dead fibers, split the stumps aboveground, and pruned some of the old branches. Around the grey, cleft bases, they piled up sand. Just downslope from each tree, they built a curved earthen berm to catch again the winter snows and summer runoff from the mesa top.

And in a year, or two, or three, these small, moribund fruit trees had sprouted back to life, into ragged, five-foot-tall, healthy, leafy peach bushes: truth as convincing as any I could imagine.

I couldn't miss the obvious analogy. In 1879 the Smithsonian's Bureau of Ethnology had been created to document Native Americans just before they "disappeared completely." And yet—

The wind whipped up over the raised sandstone lip of the shallow basin, stirring flaxen grasses, lifting the curved, dark green peach leaves, and brushing the higher mesa's steep walls, where rows of ancient petroglyphs scored the soft stone. We all grabbed for our hats.

~

For a certain sizable segment of the agricultural world, the results of the collaboration between these scientists and the Zuni Tribe would matter little. Most seed companies demeaned traditional systems and land races as insignificant, marginal oddities. Deb had paraphrased their attitude, "If land races had any merit, they'd already have been used." I doubted seed companies could grasp any reason for the Zunis not to sell their corn, either.

But for a small and perhaps growing minority, all the data crunching and correlating, the computer modeling and simulating would perhaps add evidence that, in part, for practical science as well as for poetic vision, *the way forward is the way back.*[24]

"Look at this," said Niles as we shucked yet another pile of corn from Deb's test field. He rubbed off the last silks from a dark ear the color of oxidized silver. The kernels grew entirely to the tip, a perfectly filled potential. All the other ears had either not grown to the end or had been nibbled away by corn worms. "Save this one out," he said as he handed it to me. I took it and turned it and watched the sun reflect off each of its burnished kernels. I bent my head and inhaled its delicate, buttery smell, then laid it carefully in the small cardboard box on top of several dozen new wooden row stakes.

"Hmmm. All done," said Dixon later, with clear pleasure, as he gently turned the perfect ear in his own callused hands.

🪶

> Asking for his life-giving breath
> His breath of old age,
> His breath of waters,
> His breath of seeds,
> His breath of fecundity,
> His breath of good fortune,
> Asking for his breath.
> And into my warm body
> Drawing his breath,
> I shall add to your breath . . .
> May . . . you be blessed with light . . .
> May your roads all be fulfilled.

> —from a Zuni prayer
> translated by Ruth Bunzel, 1932[25]

Notes

1. David E. Stuart, *Anasazi America* (Albuquerque: University of New Mexico Press, 2000).

2. Carol B. Brandt, "Traditional Agriculture on the Zuni Indian Reservation in the Recent Historic Period," in *Soil, Water, Biology, and Belief in Prehistoric and Traditional Southwestern Agriculture*, ed. H. Wolcott Toll, New Mexico Archaeological Council Special Publication 2 (Albuquerque: New Mexico Archaeological Council, 1995), 291–301. Although Brandt notes that "ethnographic examples must be used with caution when modeling prehistoric agriculture," she continues, "it is likely that [the Zunis'] technological and biological innovations have their origin in antiquity." Strategies that are common both at Zuni and in the archaeological record include waffle gardens, field locations, features within fields for controlling soil and water erosion, irrigation systems, and crop repertoires.

3. David A. Cleveland, et al., "Zuni Farming and United States Government Policy: The Politics of Biological and Cultural Diversity in Agriculture," *Agriculture and Human Values* 12 (3) (1995): 2–18; T. J. Ferguson, "The Impact of Federal Policy on Zuni Land Use," in *Seasons of the Kachina*, ed. J. L. Bean (Hayward: Ballena Press/California State University, 1989), 85–131; Richard I. Ford, "Ethnoecology Serving the Community, A Case Study from Zuni Pueblo, New Mexico," in *Ethnoecology: Situated Knowledge/Located Lives*, ed. Virginia D. Nazarea (Tucson: University of Arizona Press, 1999), 71–87; E. Richard Hart, *Zuni and the Courts: A Struggle for Sovereign Land Rights* (Lawrence: University Press of Kansas, 1995).

4. James Enote, et. al, *The Zuni Resource Development Plan: A Program of Action for Sustainable Resource Development*, 1st ed. (Zuni, NM: Zuni Conservation Project, Pueblo of Zuni, 1993); Hart, *Zuni and the Courts*; Cleveland, et al., "Zuni Farming and United States Government Policy."

5. Jay B. Norton, et al., "Observation and Experience Linking Science and Indigenous Knowledge at Zuni, New Mexico," *Journal of Arid Environments* 39 (1998): 331–40.

6. Since this essay was written in 1998, some of the project's results are reaching publication: Muenchrath et al. 2002; Norton, Pawluck, and Sandor 1998, 2000; Stahl et al. 1998. The National Science Foundation grant was in Ecosystem Studies, Award Number 9528458.

7. Betty Fussell, *The Story of Corn: The Myth and History, the Culture and Agriculture, the Art and Science of America's Quintessential Crop* (New York: Alfred A. Knopf, 1992). Exhaustive elaborations of the information in the following five paragraphs can be found in this lively and extensively illustrated book.

8. Richard I. Ford, "Corn Is Our Mother," *Corn and Culture in the Prehistoric New World*, eds. S. Johannessen and C. A. Hastorf (Boulder, CO: Westview Press, 1994), 513–25.

9. Fussell, *The Story of Corn*, 176.

10. Quoted in Fussell, *The Story of Corn*, 67.

11. Sha'lak'o was reopened to non-Natives in 2000.

12. Deborah Ann Muenchrath, "Productivity, Morphology, Phenology, and Physiology of a Desert-Adapted Native American Maize (*Zea mays* L.) Cultivar" (dissertation, Iowa State University, Ames, 1995).

13. Jack Ralph Kloppenburg Jr., *First the Seed: The Political Economy of Plant Biotechnology, 1492–2000* (Cambridge: Cambridge University Press, 1988).

14. "Pioneer Reports Decrease in Corn Market Share: Net Earnings for the Year Are Up at $243 Million Despite 2% Drop in Market Share," *Feedstuffs* 69 (45) (1995: 971103:6).

15. Fussell, *The Story of Corn*, 93.

16. Kloppenburg, *First the Seed*.

17. U.S. Department of Agriculture 1950, 1997; Kloppenburg, *First the Seed*.

18. U.S. Department of Agriculture 1995; Biing-Hwan Lin, U.S. Department of Agriculture, Economic Research Service. *Pesticide and Fertilizer Use and Trends in U.S. Agriculture*. (Washington, D.C.: U.S. Department of Agriculture, Economic Research Service, 1995).

19. Gary Strauss, "Turn into Lean Acres; Strong Global Financial Climate Slashes Crop Prices; Many Farms Could Be in Final Season," Green Acres, *USA Today*, October 13, 1998.

20. John R. Hack, *The Changing Physical Environment of the Hopi Indians of Arizona*, Papers of the Peabody Museum of American Archaeology and Ethnology, vol. 35(1) (Cambridge, MA: Harvard University, 1942).

21. Michael Evenari, et al., *The Negev: The Challenge of a Desert*, 2nd ed. (Cambridge, MA: Harvard University Press, 1982).

22. Deborah Ann Muenchrath, et al., "Maize Productivity and Agroecology: Effects of Environment and Agricultural Practices on the Biology of Maize," in *Soil, Water, Biology, and Belief in Prehistoric and Traditional Southwestern Agriculture*, ed. H. Wolcott Toll, New Mexico Archaeological Council Special Publication 2 (Albuquerque: New Mexico Archaeological Council, 1995), 303–33.

23. Carol Brandt, personal communication.

24. Lao-Tzu, *Tao Te Ching*.

25. In *Zuni Ceremonialism* 1992 [1932].

Bibliography

Bowannie, Fred, Jr., and Andrew Laahty
1993 The Nutria Irrigation Unit, the Zuni Sustainable Agriculture Project, and the Nutria Pilot Project. *Zuni Farming for Today and Tomorrow: An Occasional Newsletter of the Zuni Sustainable Agriculture Project* 2:1, 3–5.

Brandt, Carol B.
1995 Traditional Agriculture on the Zuni Indian Reservation in the Recent Historic Period. In *Soil, Water, Biology, and Belief in Prehistoric and Traditional Southwestern Agriculture*, ed. H. Wolcott Toll, 291–301. New Mexico Archaeological Council Special Publication 2. Albuquerque: New Mexico Archaeological Council.

Bunzel, Ruth L.
1992 [1932] *Zuni Ceremonialism*. Albuquerque: University of New Mexico Press.

Cleveland, David A., Fred Bowannie Jr., Donald F. Eriacho, Andrew Laahty, and Eric Perramond
1995 Zuni Farming and United States Government Policy: The Politics of Biological and Cultural Diversity in Agriculture. *Agriculture and Human Values* 12 (3): 2–18.

———, Donald Eriacho, Daniela Soleri, Lygatie Laate, and Roy Keys
1994 Zuni Peach Orchards, Part III. *Zuni Farming for Today and Tomorrow: An Occasional Newsletter of the Zuni Sustainable Agriculture Project* 3:25–28.

Cushing, Frank Hamilton
1920 *Zuni Breadstuff*. Reprinted 1974. Indian Notes and Monographs 8. New York: Museum of the American Indian, Heye Foundation.

Eggan, Fred, and T. N. Pandey
1979 Zuni History, 1850–1970. In *Southwest*. Vol. 9 of *Handbook of North American Indians*, ed. Alfonso Ortiz, 474–78. Washington, D.C.: Smithsonian Institution.

Enote, James, Steven Albert, and Kevin Webb, eds.
1993 *The Zuni Resource Development Plan: A Program of Action for Sustainable Resource Development*. 1st ed. Zuni, NM: Zuni Conservation Project, Pueblo of Zuni.

Evenari, Michael, Leslie Shanan, and Naphtali Tadmor
1982 *The Negev: The Challenge of a Desert*. 2nd ed. Cambridge, MA: Harvard University Press.

Feedstuffs
1997 Pioneer Reports Decrease in Corn Market Share: Net Earnings for the Year Are Up at $243 Million Despite 2% Drop in Market Share. 69 (45) 971103:6.

Ferguson, T. J.
1989 The Impact of Federal Policy on Zuni Land Use. In *Seasons of the Kachina*, ed. J. L. Bean, 85–131. Hayward: Ballena Press/California State University.

Ford, Richard I.
1994 Corn Is Our Mother. In *Corn and Culture in the Prehistoric New World*, ed. S. Johannessen and C. A. Hastorf, 513–25. Boulder, CO: Westview Press.

1999 Ethnoecology Serving the Community, A Case Study from Zuni Pueblo, New Mexico. In *Ethnoecology: Situated Knowledge/Located Lives*, ed. Virginia D. Nazarea, 71–87. Tucson: University of Arizona Press.

Fussell, Betty
1992 *The Story of Corn: The Myth and History, the Culture and Agriculture, the Art and Science of America's Quintessential Crop*. New York: Alfred A. Knopf.

Hack, John R.
1942 *The Changing Physical Environment of the Hopi Indians of Arizona*. Papers of the Peabody Museum of American Archaeology and Ethnology, vol. 35(1). Cambridge, MA: Harvard University.

Hart, E. Richard
1995 *Zuni and the Courts: A Struggle for Sovereign Land Rights*. Lawrence: University Press of Kansas.

Johannessen, Sissel, and Christine A. Hastorf, eds.
1994 *Corn and Culture in the Prehistoric New World*. Boulder, CO: Westview Press.

Kloppenburg, Jack Ralph, Jr.
1988 *First the Seed: The Political Economy of Plant Biotechnology, 1492–2000*. Cambridge: Cambridge University Press.

———, ed.

1988 *Seeds and Sovereignty: The Use and Control of Plant Genetic Resources.* Durham, NC: Duke University Press.

Lin, Biing-Hwan

1995 U.S. Department of Agriculture, Economic Research Service. *Pesticide and Fertilizer Use and Trends in U.S. Agriculture.* Washington, D.C.: U.S. Department of Agriculture, Economic Research Service.

Matson, R. G.

1991 *The Origins of Southwestern Agriculture.* Tucson: University of Arizona Press.

Maxwell, Timothy D.

1995 A Comparative Study of Prehistoric Farming Strategies. In *Soil, Water, Biology, and Belief in Prehistoric and Traditional Southwestern Agriculture,* ed. H. Wolcott Toll, 3–12. New Mexico Archaeological Council Special Publication 2. Albuquerque: New Mexico Archaeological Council.

Muenchrath, Deborah Ann

1995 Productivity, Morphology, Phenology, and Physiology of a Desert-Adapted Native American Maize (*Zea mays* L.) Cultivar. PhD diss., Iowa State University, Ames.

———, M. Kuratomi, J. A. Sandor, and J. A. Homburg

2002 Observational Study of Maize Production Systems of Zuni Farmers in Semiarid New Mexico. *Journal of Ethnobiology* 22 (1): 1–33.

———, and Ricardo J. Salvador

1995 Maize Productivity and Agroecology: Effects of Environment and Agricultural Practices on the Biology of Maize. In *Soil, Water, Biology, and Belief in Prehistoric and Traditional Southwestern Agriculture,* ed. H. Wolcott Toll, 303–33. New Mexico Archaeological Council Special Publication 2. Albuquerque: New Mexico Archaeological Council.

Nabhan, Gary Paul

1979 The Ecology of Floodwater Farming in Arid Southwestern North America. *Agro-Ecosystems* 5:245–55.

1989 *Enduring Seeds: Native American Agriculture and Wild Plant Conservation.* New York: North Point Press.

Netting, Robert McC.

1993 *Smallholders, Householders: Farm Families and the Ecology of Intensive, Sustainable Agriculture.* Stanford, CA: Stanford University Press.

Norton, Jay B., Roman R. Pawluck, and Jonathan A. Sandor
1998 Observation and Experience Linking Science and Indigenous Knowledge at Zuni, New Mexico. *Journal of Arid Environments* 39:331–40.

2000 Farmer-Scientist Collaboration for Research and Agricultural Development. In *Soil Science Society of America Special Publication*, ed. W. A. Payne and D. Keener. Madison, WI: Soil Science Society of America.

Sandor, Jonathan A.
1995 Searching Soil for Clues about Southwest Prehistoric Agriculture. In *Soil, Water, Biology, and Belief in Prehistoric and Traditional Southwestern Agriculture*, ed. H. Wolcott Toll, 119–37. New Mexico Archaeological Council Special Publication 2. Albuquerque: New Mexico Archaeological Council.

Stahl, P. D., C. I. Havener, S. E. Williams, J. B. Norton, J. A. Sandor, and D. A. Muenchrath
1998 Influence of Zuni Agricultural Practices on Some Soil Biotic Properties. Unpublished manuscript.

Strauss, Gary
1998 Green Acres Turn into Lean Acres; Strong Global Financial Climate Slashes Crop Prices; Many Farms Could Be in Final Season. *USA Today*, October 13.

Stuart, David E.
2000 *Anasazi America*. Albuquerque: University of New Mexico Press.

U.S. Department of Agriculture
1950 *Agricultural Statistics, Yearbook 1950*. U.S. Department of Agriculture, Washington, D.C.

1995 *Agricultural Resources and Environmental Indicators*. Washington, D.C.: U.S. Department of Agriculture, Economic Research Service.

1997 *Agricultural Statistics, Yearbook 1997*. U.S. Department of Agriculture, Washington, D.C.

Web Pages

Corn Production, Agronomy Extension, Iowa State University
http://www.agronext.iastate.edu/corn

Food and Agriculture Organization of the United Nations
http://www.fao.org

Indigenous Agricultural and Environmental Knowledge Systems
http://www.ciesin.columbia.edu/TG/AG/iksys.html

International Development Research Centre
http://www.idrc.ca/index–en.html

Native Americans and the Environment
http://www.cnie.org/nae/

Native Seeds/SEARCH
http://www.nativeseeds.org

Rua
Eda Amargura

Bodysurfing at the Equator

Alcântara hovers in my memory as a place out of time, a place of primal presence. Yet this is not about that isolated town on the Brazilian coast, nor even about Brazil, though both serve this tale. This is about Sara, a woman I knew in New Mexico, where she taught Afro-Brazilian dance some years after I'd been in Alcântara. It's about bodies dancing and about spirits that animate our lives the way energies cross the equatorial Atlantic to animate waves breaking along Alcântara's beaches. It's about Sara's inexplicable fragmentation and about spirit possession.

⁂

One afternoon just south of the equator, Andy and I lay salty with sweat and sea on the bed in the world's most beautiful room. It sat at the end of the second floor of the only hotel in Alcântara, the small village we'd reached after three hours on a ferry powered with straining red sails. The room formed a perfect cube eighteen feet on a side, eighteen feet high, with whitewashed walls and nothing on its worn, wide-planked wood floor but one chair and the bed. Four dark, irregularly shaped wood cutouts made up the headboard. On one side, sepia and cream doors shuttered tall windows and a tiny balcony, shading us from the afternoon heat. Opposite the windows, a wide, built-in niche served as a table, and on every wall, carefully placed hooks offered attachments for hammocks. In the exact center of the room hung a single bare bulb. The lone switch by the restaurant controlled it with all the other lights in the building: electricity on at 6:30 p.m., off at midnight. To give the rooms maximum airflow, the inner walls stopped six feet shy of the ceiling and the constant soft swish of palm fronds in the trade winds blew over us. Our room looked out on the town's bare main plaza, the ruins of a church at one end. On three sides stood buildings with decaying facades entirely covered in brightly decorated Portuguese tiles first brought on fierce Portuguese ships. Across from us, the plaza's fourth side dropped two hundred feet to the sea.

I'd come to Brazil to visit Andy on his two-week break from an archaeological dig along the Amazon. When we'd registered at the hotel, we checked to see when the last American had been there: eight months before, a petroleum engineer. The owners, who spoke no English, cheerfully called us the "gringos."

That morning we'd haphazardly made our way toward the ocean along hilly cobbled streets where tropical growth worked on reconquering the abandoned built world of the Portuguese. Fragments of immense, umber stone walls still stood, partly vine covered, slowly disintegrating. One hulking fin had kept its street sign tile: blue on white, in delicate script, wreathed by brush curlicues, Rua da Amargura. Street of Sorrow.

We finally found the path down to the broad strand and made our way across tidal flats that were separated by pockets of scrub and low trees. Where the sea drew near the land, pulsing energies that had traveled thousands of miles across deep water rose up to perfect waves, at body temperature. We felt them lift us, catch us, carry us along as part of their blind, ceaseless, graceful flow. The beach flashed with mica; the sea glittered with sun. Due east lay Congo, the source of these perfect waves.

We bodysurfed for hours.

Nothing separated the earth's breathing and our own. The formless water had been shaped by invisible energies into something that held us and carried us, and we tuned our movements to those larger movements. Lifted along such a wide circumference, I believed I might someday understand my place among creatures and stones, my place in this complicated world.

Our simple, whitewashed room triggered a similar sense of rhythm, of proportion, and of the way our physical selves can recognize a barebones perfection: our bodies fit harmoniously into a larger scale that had grown from unfamiliar and mostly unknowable circumstances. Nothing extraneous distracted from the room's deep *rightness*.

In the afternoon heat, in that spacious shadowy room, the wind's white noise covered the sounds of the sea. We could feel the long past of the place, the people who had struggled to piece together their fragmented worlds. This isolated town showed the sadness created by the Portuguese who had understood little of this tropical territory. Their dreams to colonize the land with their African slaves had possessed them, but their difficulties had finally destroyed their ill-conceived plans. Rua da Amargura. The damage they'd done in the meantime remains, palpable. But their West African Yoruba slaves had brought with them their food, their religions, and their dances, and those have not only survived, but have flourished.

The term *spirit possession* calls up certain images: a true, if temporary, transformation of personality; speaking in tongues; moving in bizarre and unlikely ways. But the exotic or the seductively foreign can't claim a monopoly on animating spirits. Most of us have brushed up against their capacity to move beyond an ambient availability and possess us. I've felt it when a second wind kicks in, or inspiration arrives from some invisible muse. Sudden feats of strength or astonishing grace in athletes and dancers leave us breathless. Actors become the roles they play. Novelists speak of their characters hijacking plots. Solutions to problems appear in dreams. A long-standing fear defuses itself. Glee erupts. Love. And possession's darker aspects always lurk, ready to seize control unexpectedly: the drive to pursue a dream into a hopeless thicket, the grip of raging anger or despair, the damning words that spew forth of their own accord.

Something from the outside has entered you, something from far off. You feel only a whisper of its distant power, but that is enough. Those attached to the Bible might call it God or the devil. Physiologists might attribute the sensations to internal biochemical cocktails; psychologists, to a complicated amalgam of personal history and collective commotion.

But no explanation satisfies completely.

As a teacher and as a dancer, Sara's generous strengths coexisted with a surprising fragility. Her successes never calmed her gnawing hunger for something more. Sara seemed possessed.

We wore white to honor Yemaya's feast day. Sara gazed at us and pointed to her right eye: we must watch her. Then we danced. Across the floor, forty of us followed her steps and movements, listening to the drums, aware of other dancers, once, twice, three times across the space til the mind's counting began to be taken over by the body. We heard the rhythm shifts, felt the repetition not as rote learning, but as deepening patterns that grew from melding bone marrow with vibrating air. The vault of the old gym echoed with the drums, and we forgot how odd this might be: ancient dances first made in African villages, transformed in Brazil, then repeated in a university in the American Southwest. We danced on.

Yemaya is a Brazilian orisha, the animating spirit of the sea. Her energies gush around us as flow, foam, wave, sex, flirtation. More deeply, she embodies the mystic cooling antidote to violent conflict and the sword of radical female sexuality. This radical sexuality, the great leveler, fights the separations of class and social hierarchy; it undermines and loosens male domination.

But Sara didn't tell us much in words. We danced. We danced to Yemaya's rhythms, the sea in drums. It was like bodysurfing at the equator.

One day, over plates of mussels with pasta, Sara told me about her time in Brazil, in Bahia, the home of *condomblé*, the religion that had its source in the slaves the Portuguese brought from Africa. Although Sara was officially a grad student in New York, she had arranged to live in Bahia with some in-laws of her dance teacher. Early on, she'd discovered the University in Bahia taught only bad ballet and modern, so she hit the streets and found her teachers there.

And she told me this story.

"Two weeks after I got to Bahia, I was invited to a condomblé ceremony. It was at someone's house where they always had meetings. I don't think it was the house of the woman who was being initiated, but I never found out for sure. We sat in a circle around a small room, quietly, waiting. I was the only white person. I didn't know what to expect. I didn't understand Portuguese then, and no one had told me anything, just invited me to come along. We sat like that for ten or fifteen minutes, then suddenly the hostess started to shake and slumped over in her chair. And I felt a really strong fear. My heart was racing, and I felt a sensation that started in my first chakra, rising up. My fear kept pushing it down, but it would rise up again, the fear would push it down. Then the priest came over to me and put one hand on my forehead, one hand on my heart, which was racing like crazy, and said, 'You are from far away, but I am standing very near you.'"

"In English?" I asked.

"No, the woman I'd come with translated, but it didn't help. Then someone across the room shouted, and I felt whatever was rising up pop out of my chest. Just straight out." She touched her chest with her hand and flicked her fingers outward. "When a certain orisha arrives, the person being possessed shouts. But whatever it was came back almost immediately, and that time I let it go, and it gushed out the top of my head, like water, and I fell over on the floor. Everyone seemed to know what was going on. They splashed me with lavender water, then the hostess held her hand *above* the top of my head and lifted me off the floor. I sort of got myself together."

"Were you still afraid?"

"No, I wasn't, just sort of freaked out. The ceremony went on, and later another woman slumped over in her chair with her hands at shoulder level, turned in toward her heart. Everyone got up and went past her and grasped her hands. She squeezed back. It seemed like she was imparting something—or the orisha was. When I got to her, she *really* grabbed my hands hard in both of hers, and held them to her cheek and rocked back and forth. It was such an embracing act, so loving. I cried, it was so loving. Then later, when I was leaving, the house mother—the priestess, kind of—said, '*You* can come back *any*time.'"

"Did you go back?"

"No. It seemed like I got too busy with dancing and drumming. I've felt that same rising sensation a few times since then, but I've always left the room. It's been in this country, but I just couldn't deal with it."

"Did anyone ever explain it to you?"

"No, not in so many words. Brazilians are very noncommittal about all that. But they did tell me I was a daughter of Oshun."

Oshun: like Yemaya, an orisha of water. But Oshun is the spirit not of the sea, but of the powerful, roiling river. In Yoruba legend, her great beauty and passion led her into marriage with the fiery thunder god, Shango. She bore twins, a magical occurrence in many mythologies. In Yoruba culture, everyone showers twins with gifts. Those gifts had the effect of adding great wealth to Oshun's already great beauty. When Oshun died, she took her beauty and wealth with her to the bottom of the river, provoking much jealous witchcraft. The only way she could counteract such evil was by constant giving, by constant, complicated generosities. Oshun's spirit seems darker and weightier than Yemaya's, for Oshun is also known for her masculine abilities in war, mixing deadly potions, and brandishing knives as she flies through the night.

As a teacher and daughter of Oshun, Sara gave almost beyond measure, wringing herself dry in every class, physically, emotionally. Periodically she'd lecture us when her frustrations at our occasional group-drifting bubbled over. "Be present! Leave your other lives outside the door. Focus on what's going on *here*. Otherwise we can't do it. If your mind's wandering off somewhere else, it pokes a hole in the dance container, and the energies fly off up there." Fly off into the room's high cavern, instead of feeding the group electricity. "The drummers and I can't do it alone." They couldn't supply all the zapping power, the invisible, unifying drive. And the days we meshed, it did feel as if together we'd become a wide, roaring river.

She'd learned Portuguese in two months in Bahia by letting it wash over her. "I first had to let go of my western mind, stop being 'in school.' I listened to the radio, watched soap operas, and read the paper out loud before I understood a thing, before I could even pronounce the words right. I took care of my linear mind by studying one verb a day at breakfast." But she absorbed it mostly without "thinking" about it. She learned samba—the secular version of orisha dances—the same way. "I watched and watched the street dancers; I kept trying, kept trying, kept watching. And one day it just clicked." And when they danced on and on, nonstop for hours, she tried to keep up until she learned, in her flesh, that the only way she could do it was to let go, let the effort be non-effort—effortless effort. Let attention sink to a deeper level, below the conscious mind, but still utterly present, present *only* to the moment. Otherwise it was not possible. Not difficult, just not possible.

At the end of one semester, nearly in tears from watching the short dances we'd made in small groups for our final projects, she spoke from her heart, gratified we'd learned some of what she'd been trying to teach us, and said, "I do this for one reason: peace. I'm trying to make some peace in the world. A tiny bit more peace."

Later, over our plates of mussels, I asked her why she taught, what she aimed at, and got an answer from her trained mind, but no less true: "Balance, grounding, rhythm . . . " The basic tools of dance, a good thing for me to quote sometime, but it did not come from her heart. But then she said, with an open, compassionate wisdom from the orishas, "I finally figured out I can't make it happen, but I can provide the *opportunity* for it to happen."

🪶

I didn't know why the university had invited her into its precincts in the first place, beyond the official line: widening horizons, cultural expansion. But that reminded me of my sixties Sunday-school classes in a fundamentalist protestant church. For months we chose a religion a week and reported: Christian Science, Catholicism, Judaism, Lutheranism, maybe Islam, but I don't remember Buddhism, and absolutely not a word about African religions. We weren't expected to explore viable alternatives, but to defuse rivals, to create little religion puppets that after the play could be put in the box while we proceeded with the *real stuff*. In the dance department, the *real stuff* meant ballet and modern, maybe flamenco; and in the larger university, dance itself was, well, not rigorous.

Ignoring her marginal status, Sara taught her classes the way she danced: intensity woven with liberating pleasure, concentration festooned with lit sparklers. This wasn't like any other classes, though she seemed largely oblivious to what she could generate. She thought she was doing her job and didn't quite grasp how much more she gave her students. But her classes at the university had three times the enrollment of other dance classes, and in town her classes overflowed. Beyond dance forms, songs, traditions, and attitudes, she offered a way to inhabit one's own body. With the experience of her classes, anyone could find personal strength and open outward as surely as a river will tumble over a sudden rocky drop-off. She could make it possible to fulfill yearnings just barely perceived.

❧

Not long after I started taking Sara's class, I dreamed this: not far below the sea's surface, I swam effortlessly, green light filtering around me in broken, rhythmic patterns. Swells lifted me and released me, invisibly. Schools of fish flashed silver against the darkness below. I passed through a narrow breakwater, boulders piled on either side, and entered a quiet harbor, shadowy hulls and anchor lines all angled the same way by the tide.

Abruptly I found myself on a steep, barren cliff overlooking the ocean—no sign of the harbor, no way down to the sea. Wide open, alone. Small white birds with red-orange patches behind their bills came and went, fluttering into nests around me. Wind raised the down on their breasts. To one side a recently dead albatross lay, feathers splayed awkwardly, specks of sand dusting one wing edge. Then the dead bird revived, turned over, and unfolded, releasing tiny dark birds in a whirring cloud. Still dreaming, I fell asleep in the warm sun, imagining myself in a soft cocoon, wrapped, enclosed, comfortable. This sense of protection contained none of my familiar struggle against suffocation whenever I'm stopped from moving. Instead: unexpected happiness and anticipation.

In my dreams, at least, Sara's classes had shaken loose some tenacious knots.

❧

On the surface, Sara seemed perfectly suited for what she did, a teacher you always hope to find. She had vast knowledge of Congolese and Afro-Brazilian rhythms and dances and songs; but she also warmed us up carefully, kept the class moving, revved our energies. She attracted explosive drummers who'd haul their table-high drums to class even when they weren't being paid, just for the pleasure of playing. In our mix of bright wraps, we reached and stretched and stepped and loosened the muscles and tendons around our hips and ribs and shoulders—the ones that even in modern dance you usually hold in check. Certainly normal life contains a taboo against gyrating pelvises, with exceptions, perhaps, for Elvis impersonators, Mick Jagger, and NFL cheerleaders. Much too much implied sex. But here, the looser, the better. Sara encouraged us by demonstrating and dancing across the floor with us, watching everyone while she moved through our lines. Usually a few young children cavorted to one side, their parents dancing: here, dance meant community. Once, when Sara couldn't shake off a lingering flu, a group of drummers and dancers held a healing ceremony for her, dancing and drumming through the night. She got better; the malaise pulsed and sweated out.

Sara seemed always tanned, her dark skin striking under black straight hair she held in check with intricately patterned fabric scraps. Her dancer's strength had molded her body, not twig thin, but like wild Rocky Mountain bighorn sheep—solidly grounded, but also spry and a little skittish.

I'd first crossed paths with her several years before I found myself in her university class. In a tiny alternative space, with no drummers, she ran classes for three or four students, just barely getting by. And that quality of struggle always clung to her, despite her apparent confidence and growing local renown. She gave me an inkling of explanation once when she quoted the experimental filmmaker Maya Deren. In *Divine Horsemen*, written about her time spent absorbed in Afro-Haitian spiritual life, Deren describes a deep impulse: "Conceive beyond reality, desire beyond adequacy, create beyond need." Reach. Always reach. Even if where you are has not been fulfilled: a rousing but ambiguous directive. Although Deren's words weren't mystic formula, Sara embraced them almost ferociously, as if they were instructions on a lifeboat.

During the two years I danced with her, her struggles began to come into focus. Most obviously, she was a white woman teaching African dance. In this land of Hispanics and Native Americans, African Americans are a minority among minorities. At first, half a dozen took Sara's class; they were always the most adept and graceful, the most able to capture crucial nuances, especially if their bodies were generous and undancerly. Although members of the small Black community had once voted Sara an "honorary nonwhite," eventually they all left the class, feeling finally, according to Sara, that a white person shouldn't teach an African class. I once asked her about race, and she said she'd never run into a problem with Africans or Afro-Brazilians— only African Americans. She knew, she said, she'd never be teaching on either coast, where plenty of great Black dancers taught African classes. But here, she was the best.

The coasts. We shared separate pasts in New York City, and we both knew how its enticements mingled with its hellacious pressure, how living there seemed like cohabiting a gorgeous walled garden with a voracious tiger. I'd lived for ten years in East Village nuttiness and left with little regret when I figured out hiking in the desert would be easier if I didn't have to go through LaGuardia Airport. She'd bailed out at the last minute, barely in time to salvage her sobriety, a refugee from the City's inexorable steamroller. She'd only accidentally come to a temporary halt in this dry outpost, intending to land instead at the edge of the Pacific, on the other coast. Here, in this in-between hideout, she'd regrouped, slowly revived by wide spaces and her own extraordinary teaching. But when she worked with a visiting Mexico City dance company and felt again the catalytic heat of urban ferment, even at a distance, her dissatisfaction grew. She itched to assault New York again: she craved a place where she could learn from peers and swim in a thick, turbulent human brine. She didn't want to live anymore at the end of the world.

🪶

A visiting Haitian dance teacher once made a point about connection, not thigh to hip, shoulder to ribs, but across time. I understood she meant a connection that might allow deeper harmonies, perhaps realer peace. The dance forms—the literal, specific movements of these dances—arrived with slaves from Africa, from the Yoruba, in the case of Brazil. The dances retain their original integrity, and by dancing them we each participate in a realm of continuity, as if the movements live an autonomous life, and our individual bodies give them temporary haven. These dances exist separate from us, but in another way *only* exist through us.

As a dancer, I link up with those Yoruba dancers from centuries ago, when they fought the Dahomey, even before the Portuguese. And all dancers since. It has a New Agey ring, and a whiff of channeling Galileo or Gurdjieff, but because it is physical, it depends less on obscure mystic doctrines. What could be more real than rolling hips and torso above bare feet stepping across a wooden floor?

In Haiti, the Brazilian/Yoruba female sexuality orishas have been consolidated into one female *loa*, as they call their animating spirits: Erzulie. Erzulie is beauty and sex, but more than that, she is love. Maya Deren says of Erzulie's love: "that human luxury of the heart which is not essential to the purely physical generation of the body. She is lavish with that love as she is with her gifts." But Erzulie doesn't embody the antidote to conflict or the power that the orishas Yemaya and Oshun offer, but an all too human condition. Deren describes it: "She who is the most complimented, most beloved . . . protests she is not loved enough." Lavish giving of love will not assure an equivalent easeful receiving of love. Even in the spirit world, what seems like a flow blessed by cosmic order can be blocked by some obscure barrier.

Sara attracted swarms of students. They loved her as a dancer and teacher and performer. They also admired her as a woman able to bring nonacademic and even edgy activities like drumming and African dance into a mainstream institution. On stage with her classes, she emitted an impressive charisma. At the same time, her openness and vulnerability seemed to make her available—to dissolve the curtain that often surrounds forceful figures.

Then one day when I'd stopped by her office before class on some routine matter, she said to me, out of the blue: "This is exhausting. Some of them want me to be their friend, some want me to be their mother, some want to jump my bones, some want a mentor, some just want to hang out all the time. It's not just the students; it's the faculty, too. It's *everyone*. I just can't deal with it."

Including me, I guessed. I kept my distance, but I paid close attention, since for me too she glowed with a strange, magnetic light. Her powerful public self blazed with sophistication and capacity, but something else drew me. Without her teacher/performer mask, she melted into an uneasy, regular kid, almost a child. The dissonance nearly overwhelmed me: a dramatic version of something we all know, a divided self. I lacked her public self-confidence, my childhood shyness lingering long into adulthood. And I craved more access to the "irrational," the loosening that seemed connected to dance trances or to putting yourself on the line in performance, perhaps one variety of possession. But I did have my life running relatively smoothly, practical matters in hand—so much so that in the past an old boyfriend had always teasingly called me "reality-bound."

Sara seemed caught between two worlds. She'd not been born straddling cultures, but she was temperamentally at odds with herself. In her first world, she knew a great deal through her body and elaborated with her mind what her body knew. She could impart her arcane knowledge to others so effectively that it seemed like magic. Her magic needed effort, sweat, hard breathing, sore muscles, but still it was magic. That world—the movement and traditions of Congolese dance, of Afro-Brazilian dance—wasn't a world she'd been born into, nor did she live there. She lived in a second, different world where cars required repair, tires needed replacing, her salary had to be negotiated, dance demonstrations needed scheduling with dancers she could guarantee would show up. And she was obliged to connect with people without her performance mask, without a teaching structure, without a dance container. She had to interact with people who weren't straddling the same two worlds, who didn't have as a reference point six hours of nonstop samba in the streets of Bahia, who didn't have a library of rhythms and songs readily accessible in the file of their brains. The second world, in short, was the one where most of us must live, one way or another. Sara managed, but readily admitted that she just barely held it together most of the time.

Sara's second world perversely intermingled the demanding, ordinary present with the possible future. In this second world, New York loomed, and both internal and external approval depended on a context beyond the traditional, a context of Art.

But I imagined that a deeper fallout from her inner split plagued her more. In the realm of her first world, where her essential understandings made her seem possessed by powerful beings, she had few peers. Yet when a situation required a more down-to-earth individual dialogue, she tiptoed uncertainly, meandered tentatively, backed off. One of my dance buddies said, "She doesn't listen." But how could that be, when she listened so well in her own realm? Her openness in her first world perhaps made her so vulnerable, so much in demand that she needed to put up barriers so she wouldn't drown. But perhaps she'd never found the fluidity of exchange with people one at a time that she had with groups. Perhaps she'd never learned the attentiveness within an individual focus that brings release and nourishes a groundedness of the emotions. I didn't really know. But her distance, her dependence on groups and community and performance, could lead straight to Erzulie's plight: "She, the most beloved . . . protests she is not loved enough."

Sara didn't protest—at least not to me—but she did finally leave town. She left propelled by the fire of her ambitions to make Art, driven by desire the way birds sail before a storm.

She returned to New York in December, cruising over snowy highways with her two cats, on tires she'd been given as a going-away present by her students. She meant to re-create herself in her second world, hoping she might learn to fly through the night with knives, like Oshun leaping cultures. She began again: taking modern dance classes, catering for a living, commuting into Manhattan on the subway from Queens. She was possessed by an orisha without a name, without a clear personality: an orisha who valued Art above all else, and who always struggled to reassemble scattered pieces into a workable whole. Sara didn't have to describe this orisha to me, because when I'd lived in New York's East Village, I'd pursued my own version of Art-in-the-City, seeking a way to piece together my life into a form that made sense.

In my old New York neighborhood, a street artist had repaired the crumbling curbs and broken sidewalks with collaged mosaics: smashed orange and red fiesta ware, delicate roses on porcelain chips, and his favorite, willow ware. The placid river flowed under the bridge while the willow hung elegantly frozen on the bank. Pieces of the blue and white story lay embedded in concrete next to shards of mirror that flashed underfoot in the sun and in the unblinking yellow streetlights. When I stepped over these oases of color and high-end recycling on the grimy streets, they always pleased me, and I never stopped admiring the anonymous artist's inventiveness. But as metaphor, their message struck hard. Here the shards had been put back together into rigid decorative surfaces, much as Portuguese tiles covered the crumbling walls in Alcântara. A fragile illusion. I sought instead the perfect equatorial waves at body temperature, Afro-Brazilian rhythms on the drums, Yemaya's energies. I'd finally unbound myself from New York-possession and left. Back in the City, Sara might be able to find a way to rely on an animating spirit who could lead to greater wholeness. But I thought of the mosaic sidewalks and the effort the City required, and I doubted she'd be able to give herself the empowering ease she'd given so many of her students.

Still, it's too easy to claim that Sara's answer would be close to mine. I'd left New York and found immediate release in New Mexico's open spaces and broader rhythms, and then a way to expand. But the impulse to a calmer, more integrated life usually fights with the impulse to complication. Maya Deren's directives reflect these inherent urges: "Conceive beyond reality. Desire beyond adequacy." Sara's answer might *not* be "wholeness." The power of possession by orishas—or any pantheon of animating spirits—is that they are multiple and coexisting. What I'd felt bodysurfing at the equator implied an all-encompassing order and an intimation of my part in it, but our lives rarely offer such experiences. Nor are they always reliable as a way to deal with the multiplicity of the world. Those waves at Alcântara broke evenly and predictably that day, but other days they must have been so strong and chaotic we could not have bodysurfed at all. Sara's classes, with her evocations of the sexuality orishas, tapped into physical energies that relate to sex, but are not identical with the charged exchanges between two humans. The varied languages of Art would give her an additional way to use her knowledge and expertise to make something new—something of her own—and perhaps even teach her more about herself. The City offered one of the more savvy places to follow that path.

Sara fascinated me precisely because she continued to trust her vision of what *might* be, of what she *could* do, despite her struggles with practical matters and personal relationships.

How often had I chosen the practical course, chosen *against* unpredictable, inexplicable animating spirits?

Maya Deren's third directive offered a touchstone for us both: "Create beyond need." *Always reach.*

A Cloud of Impetuous Rivers

"I can tell you the whole story. I can't really tell anyone else everything," Kit began, then tensed his forehead, lowered his chin to
his chest, and let out a single deep belch. "Excuse me, again. I think I
probably have a hiatal hernia—fasting really made me feel it. And only
noisy burps seem to help." Kit should know, I thought, he's a doc. For
twenty years, he'd run the health clinic in a small community in western
Massachusetts. In the bright afternoon shade of my patio, he sat across
from me in an intricately patterned shirt, framed by a tall stand of cane
rattling in the breeze. Scabs from healing blackfly bites covered his
well-muscled tanned arms and legs, and he seemed disoriented in a way
I couldn't identify. In the garden's sun, a black-chinned hummingbird
thrummed from hollyhock to prairie coneflower, then sped off.

He went on. "You're interested in the process, but you don't have any agendas for me." I smiled and dipped my head in agreement.

I'd known Kit for twenty years but had seen him only twice in the past decade. I'd met him when he married one of my friends from art school in the late seventies, and although we'd always been comfortable with each other, we didn't have a close friendship. His two visits and his openness about his life surprised me. Three years before, he'd sat across from me in the same chair, in New Mexico then, as now, to do a vision quest. From the little I'd known of vision quests at that first visit, it seemed an odd activity for a fiftyish doctor with two kids, a house, and a minivan. But he'd always been able to dive into things with a sincere and almost innocent enthusiasm.

For both quests, he asked me to be his first audience, a chance to practice the "story" of his adventure before he dropped back into a life he readily admitted resembled sticky emotional flypaper. And he clearly believed a quest could make a difference.

When I'd learned he planned to return to New Mexico for a second quest with the same guide, I thought it sounded like a promising topic for an essay. Lots of quirky details. With that in mind, before Kit arrived this time, I researched quests, fasting, and the neurophysiology of altered states. And I'd already signed up for a vision quest of my own in the fall, with the same guide. But unlike Kit, who sincerely sought help to untangle his life, I meant to go as a spy.

I listened to Kit with great attention.

"This time was different from last time. Entirely different."

Since I'd last seen him, he'd grown a beard for his role as a villain in a community operetta. Two black streaks radiated down from the sides of his mouth, interrupting the trimmed grey hairs. But the beard did little to change his open, friendly face. "I felt bad the whole four days we fasted, and for the last twenty-four hours I just lay on the ground in a fetal position. Every once in a while I tried to throw up. I only moved to follow the shade around my little clearing. But I didn't have energy for anything else. You remember the last time I fasted, I went on a long hike and did a bunch of rituals. This time I couldn't even wade back across the river by myself."

"How did you get across?" I asked, concerned, even though he'd clearly gotten back OK.

"Sparrow was there on the other side, waiting," Kit said. Sparrow had led both Kit's fasting adventures. He lived in Vermont, where he also guided quests and ran men's workshops. "It had rained a lot while we'd fasted, and the water had gotten so deep it was up to my chest. First Sparrow came over and carried my pack across, then he came back and put his arm around my waist. He really held me tight. Very strong. Very reassuring." He paused for a long time, his blue eyes focused a little to the side, and seemed to remember how it felt to be helped when he needed it, the current pushing against his shaky body. "We waded across together and went extremely slowly. He said in thirteen years leading quests he'd never seen anyone as wiped out as I was." I thought I detected a touch of pride for pain endurance. I remembered that two years before, he'd run a marathon.

"What happened, do you think?"

"I'm not sure. It's got something to do with whatever's wrong with me—the hiatal hernia, probably. I could feel the acid sloshing around in my stomach every time I turned over. And the pain seemed to be coming from my heart. It wasn't, of course, but this part of your stomach,"—he placed his hand on his left ribcage—"right below your diaphragm, is snuggled up to your heart."

"Ugh. Grim. Did drinking water not help?"

"Nope. It seemed like my whole digestive system had just shut down." He chuckled. "But I'd come out here to feel, to be open to whatever happened. I live way too much in my head. Too rational. After everything that's gone on, it's no surprise that finally I felt it in my body. Essentially, my heart ached. My vision wasn't visual or auditory, it was *visceral*."

Given the troubling details of "everything that had gone on," his relaxed tone unsettled me. But I understood he trusted me to keep those details to myself.

Two months after Kit told me his quest story punctuated by pain-relieving belches, he sent me a copy of the e-mail he'd posted to his quest companions and the guide Sparrow. This medical detail struck me with force:

> . . . I decided to heed my dreams and do an electrocardiogram on myself. To my amazement the tracing that rolled off the machine was that of someone having a heart attack! I faxed it to a cardiologist who recommended I get myself to a hospital pronto even though I was having no acute symptoms at the time. I spent the night hooked up to IVs, monitors, oxygen, and the next day was transported to a big hospital where they injected dye into my heart and discovered that I had a perfectly normal heart. So, with the info that my physical heart was OK, I am left with the opportunity to explore the more metaphorical dimensions of the meaning of a heart breaking—open . . .

He didn't linger over the strangeness of his heart fooling the EKG, but went on to metaphorical matters.

But I didn't understand how an electrocardiogram could pick up "heart attack" from a heart struggling through metaphorical mire. A machine trusted to reveal the body's inner workings to the outer world had been tricked into printing out traceries of a crisis deeper than the physical.

Western medicine has long struck me as limited in its approaches to healing, but I've kept my faith in the gauges that measure the body's quiverings and flows. Also, those measurements provided the raw material for the neurobiological explanations I'd been sifting through. Though

I still trusted the data that medicine's tools collect, Kit's aching heart and his duped EKG gave me hard evidence for something more.

Kit's almost matter-of-fact telling of his story couldn't disguise the depth of his distress. Or that of some of his companions. He described them, first looking up over my head to the darkening sky. "An Episcopal priest who's forty-nine. His wife is in alcohol rehab, and he has three anorexic daughters."

Now there's an irony for someone on a fast, I thought. Kit continued, grinning, "He was really worried about snakes. Guess who was the only one who saw a snake?"

"Ah, Lucifer. And a priest." I laughed. "Classic."

He went on. "A forty-two-year-old male nurse, a real hulk of a guy, but sweet. He does ICU care. His girlfriend died in a climbing accident three years ago, and he came out to try to release that and move on. He reminded me a little of Peter." Peter had been my first love, the one who'd opened my life. "Kind of morose, but with a sense of humor." I laughed at his breezy but accurate description.

I saw that people who went on these vision quests weren't flailing around on the margins, but, like Kit himself, were respected community members whose lives had somehow become painfully snarled. And apparently the standard sources of help in our culture—psychotherapy and religion—hadn't been able to loosen their inner knots.

"Then there was a fifty-four-year-old librarian who wanted to lead writing excursions in nature. She was partly there to figure out how Sparrow worked."

He paused. "And Sparrow's daughter."

"Really?" I raised my eyebrows, surprised.

"Yeah, she's twenty-one, and she just graduated from Stanford. She'd never been on a quest with her father."

"How was that? Don't a lot of issues with parents come up?"

"Yes, but Sparrow was very gentle. It was touching to see them interact with each other. A good relationship. Now they're backpacking together in Colorado for a couple weeks. Sparrow's grown and matured a lot in the past three years. He was good last time, but this time he was right on the mark with everybody. Impressive."

"Who is he?"

"Sparrow? Interesting character. He's been jerked around a lot in his life, but he's come out just fine. He was a local townie with an abusive father, but he won a scholarship to one of those fancy prep schools—Andover or Exeter. You know, they get off on feeling like they're being generous once in a while. Give one of the riffraff a chance." He made a sour face. "Then he went to Stanford on scholarship. Phi Beta Kappa in poli-sci." I clicked my tongue. "But he's always invented his own life. And he walks his talk. A couple years ago, he ran a hundred and nine miles from Vermont to Boston for a fund-raiser. For cancer research, I think."

I winced. "That's *four* marathons. Jeez."

"I did a men's workshop with him a while ago. He knows what he's doing."

By the time Kit had arrived for his second vision quest, I'd lived for ten years among New Mexico's abundance of spiritual paths, so I was surprised I could still harbor a substantial skepticism about such an activity. My explorations had been broad, if not especially deep, and I'd long believed that our bodies and minds and even spirits inform each other. No Cartesian divisions in my world. But at first, the idea of a vision quest rested firmly on the far side of my flakiness line. It's so easy to make fun of the unknown, and I questioned an activity—so obviously borrowed from Native American traditions—that used such stylized and stilted language. Judgment by lexicon. But despite my skepticism, I understood I must remind myself over and over that what we know of the world is much like the visible spectrum. Compared to the range of energy waves traveling through space, what we can see is narrow. Much more exists if we can just tap into it.

Still, since I didn't have Kit's capacity to jump in trustingly with both feet, I'd done my research.

Before Kit arrived at my house, I had picked up one of Sparrow's brochures at REI, where they shared wall space with leaflets for river rafting, trail repair, llama treks, and hawk watching: all outdoor activities that were neither overtly psychological nor metaphysical, except as nature could inherently be both. But Sparrow laid out his position clearly, linking what he did in the wild to ancient and persistent healing traditions nearly eradicated by Western culture.

Sparrow's brochure sent me off on research about the source of vision quests. Two of his teachers had been Steven Foster and Meredith Little, who ran a school for vision quest guides in Lone Pine, California. According to anthropologist Ruth Benedict, the traditional vision quest is (or once was) the single most widespread religious practice of Native Americans. Non-Natives likely know it best from John Neihardt's classic *Black Elk Speaks*. In the early 1970s, Foster and Little developed their contemporary version of the vision quest, combining traditional solo fasting in the wild with Jungian archetypal imagery and a pan-cultural rite-of-passage framework first described by French anthropologist Arnold van Gennep. Van Gennep's book *The Rites of Passage* first reached an English-speaking audience in 1960, fifty years after its original publication. He laid out the three stages of any rite of passage. First, you leave your day-to-day world and die to your past: *severance*. Second, you endure your ordeal in a liminal state, alone except for your assorted personal monsters and spirits: *threshold*. Third, you return to the world transformed and reborn, bringing with you what you learned: *incorporation*. It matched Joseph Campbell's mythological hero's journey.

Although Foster and Little included *heroines* in their language, a quest sounded uncomfortably like a familiar male adolescent fantasy, one in which ego triumphed in the end, banishing paradox, ambivalence, and confusion. Along with defeating monsters, the hero excises the richness and complexity of life in favor of a happy, heroic ending. I'd grown up not with dolls but with Superman and Batman comics, their covers frayed by my constant attention. Once in a while, buxom and leotard-clad Wonder Woman made an appearance. Superheroes vanquishing evil had taught me to read; but I'd learned more about the world's complications since then.

According to scholar and historian Jill Ker Conway, in *When Memory Speaks*, the quest is the original male narrative in the West, a form from ancient Greece that has persisted, with variations. The *Odyssey*, St. Augustine's *Confessions*, and *The Autobiography of Malcolm X* all conform to its basic pattern. She points out another crucial aspect of this male story, besides the essential quest structure: the hero's power to act on his own behalf.

But women began telling their stories differently, in a way that reflected their experiences as women in Western culture. Conway locates the source of the overarching female narrative in the medieval monastic tradition. In those enclaves of self-direction, women found the only possible places to pursue fulfilling lives as something other than men's chattel. Those cloistered women recorded direct experience of divine illumination, mostly achieved through meditation. We have rich examples from such mystics as Hildegard von Bingen and Teresa de Avila.

Women's spiritual stories and poems often use the language of the earth-bound erotic. *Women in Praise of the Sacred: 43 Centuries of Spiritual Poetry by Women*, a collection edited by poet Jane Hirshfield, amply illustrates this connection between the experiences of sacred joyous unrestraint and sexual exuberance, even if the sexual experience may be largely imagined.

The quest-for-God story eventually evolved into an overtly erotic quest. In nineteenth-century secularized romances, the quest became a search for the ideal mate and often for wealth and power through family. In this *ur*-female narrative, the important element is the heroine's lack of power to act on her own behalf—either in her quest for God or for a human lover. Unlike the hero's quest, the romantic heroine's *agency* doesn't drive the tale. The *quality* of the heroine's *emotional response* fuels the narrative engine.

Yet, agency denied doesn't disappear. It goes underground and becomes more passive and more coercive and can often become destructive. While romances can be considered mainly female narratives, many men have the same experience of losing the ability to act directly in their own lives.

Through time, these two overarching story forms in the West have evolved into many variations: adventures of both women and men in exotic lands or on the frontier; stories of rebellion; women asserting themselves against the injustices of patriarchal domination; the postmodern abandonment of a single narrative perspective; gay and lesbian literature in which erotic experience often gives meaning to life; and plots in which the heroine *does* live her own odyssey.

These essential male and female narratives are recognizable gender stereotypes that still grip us today, as much in internalized life scripts as in expectations of others. Conway believes that the negotiation between the public image, which often matches a more conventional form, and the private reality gives real-life stories their punch and wide appeal.

I'd cringed involuntarily at the term *vision quest* not only because it suggested cultural theft and vibrated with a male perspective, but because it triggered my hokey-detector. Could any self-conscious, mostly humorless, combination of traditional forms lifted from other cultures, even when informed by Jungian and post-Jungian theory, be anything but contrived comic-book theater? But after I'd nosed around in the literature, I could see *appropriation* might describe the transfer from a traditional to a modern context better than *theft*. I could also, with some effort, suspend my hokey-detector: what might seem corny and cloying in the telling needn't be that way in experience. I only had to remember how most descriptions of falling in love fell flat.

I could also see that a quest could be an antidote to a sense of personal powerlessness. Inhabiting a quest story, if only for a short while and in a contrived setting, might provide an invaluable experience of the power to act on your own behalf, to take responsibility for your own life, whatever your gender.

Vision quests were much more common than I'd suspected. The collection of essays *Crossroads: The Quest for Contemporary Rites of Passage* focused mainly on adolescent passages into adulthood and listed nineteen groups around the country that offered guides or programs. Contributors to *Crossroads* claimed our culture suffers from a lack of meaningful rituals and functional rites of passage at all life stages. In the transition from childhood to adulthood, the standard fare—proms, graduation, confirmation, and so on—barely scratch the surface of anyone's psyche, but initiatory practices crop up anyway, notably in gangs, in doing drugs or alcohol, in getting pregnant at a young age. Modern vision quests can fill the ritual void and not only provide personal grounding but get at some of our social ills, too. One aspect of adolescent rites of passage did make me squirm: in traditional cultures, the initiatory ritual served to reinforce and maintain cultural and social norms. Luckily I found little normalizing agenda in language about adult vision quests, which aggressively claimed a dogma-free perspective.

One certain cranny for vision quests, then, existed along the margins of counseling and therapy.

That these quests happened in the wild hooked them into eco-psychology, where psychology overlapped environmentalism. By enlarging our selves beyond our skins to include the natural world we could link restoring the land to healing our minds, in a reciprocal way. Like the modern reinvigoration of therapeutic rites of passage, I could get behind ecopsychology, but I had to admit neither sparked any internal fireworks.

But this detail gave me an unexpected jolt: any real rite of passage required a non-ordinary state of consciousness. Writer after writer, in addition to Kit, claimed these experiences *worked*. In the midst of measured language about inner lives and community lives, about social turmoil, personal confusion, and threats to the environment, I found references to the vision quest's kernel of effectiveness: physically altering consciousness. Quests achieved these altered states not with drugs, but with drumming, ecstatic dance, extreme hiking in the wild, breath work, meditation, or fasting. Sparrow himself referred to vision quests as offering "non-ordinary ways of dealing with the ordinary."

Why did mention of altered states have such an effect on me? Even in the sixties, drugs had made only a cameo appearance in my life. But *altered state* implied more than a quick hallucinogenic buzz. I tapped the mysterious muse—a state unlike my normal state of consciousness— for creative work, though not easily and never reliably. In my shorthand, *the irrational* stood for everything outside a limited, lead-footed, exclusively reason-driven understanding, and it was surely related to non-ordinary consciousness. I had also recognized a new way for my body to dance with my mind. And I had long felt an impulse to expand beyond my physical boundaries—an urge that could be called "spiritual," though I didn't refer to it that way.

To work, in this context, meant two things: first, to shake off binding, invisible ropes in order to inhabit a needed change or an inevitable change (of age, of health, of circumstance); second, to unfold, to open to self, to others, to the world, and perhaps to something beyond. A century ago, William James recognized that neither mind nor brain was "a thing," but rather that both were processes. And I thought I'd found the heart of the matter: the process of mind/brain/body merged with the process of the vision quest, and something happened.

Even before Kit's aching heart had fooled the EKG, I'd begun to believe vision quests could be more than an empty excuse to go out into the wild. But two specific things connected viscerally to my own history: not eating and rituals.

In my skin-and-bones childhood, I hated food. I ate only fried potatoes and grilled cheese sandwiches in picky moderation, balanced with the occasional Jolly Green Giant frozen pea. I didn't like the idea of putting things into my body, whose insides I believed resembled the Visible Man's: distinct, nontouching organs, nothing gooey or messy. I meant to protect my insides. Complicated items such as strawberries and tomatoes, with their tiny seeds, and onions, with their sharp taste, stayed out.

"You don't know what's good," said my grandfather as I refused again a juicy tomato slice. "When you grow up, you'll like them." Sitting at the grey Formica table, listening to his transistor radio propped up beside him with the baseball game in the fifth inning, he positioned the top slice of white bread on his tomato-and-onion sandwich and took a bite. I fled the kitchen in disgust. "You wait," he called after me.

With the same skewed logic that convinced me a carefully moni-tored periphery assured the most safety, I kept as much of myself to myself as I could. In those years I allowed little food in, I allowed not many words out. I would barely eat, and I kept my silence. Inside and outside did exemplary duty as nontouching polestars.

The flip side of my body-as-plastic-educational-toy was my body as the one thing I could claim and use as a weapon in the disguised control wars in my family. I certainly wouldn't use my voice. I grew up an only child of an only child and lived with both my parents and grandparents.

Unaware of my own motives, I'd first tried temper tantrums, sink-ing to the floor, screaming, kicking, and flailing my arms. I must have been four or five, and I let loose at home, in the grocery store—place didn't matter.

"Honey," my grandmother would scold me after I'd calmed, "you have to pray to God for more self-control." She might as well have warned, "Your fortifications have been breached, add more guards. Tell them they must shoot to kill." Make your shell *more* impermeable.

Then I hit on the magic words. "I have a headache," I'd mutter softly, with just enough theatrical strain. My grandmother would melt; my mother would melt.

"Maybe you shouldn't go to school today. I'll call Mrs. Page and cancel your violin lesson," my mother would offer before she headed out the door to her music-teaching job, leaving me with my grandparents and many happy, solitary hours. Their easy acquiescence mystified me until years later, when I discovered they'd both suffered as girls from "the sick headache"—debilitating migraines.

My body collaborated to bolster my credibility as a delicate child: I suffered actual asthma attacks, wheezing through long nights, the vaporizer steaming away, pillows propped behind me, my mother listening to my breathing in the low glow of the night-light. Not only food dangerously crossed the barrier between inside and outside, but also air, with every breath.

But I'm convinced my picky eating and ailments, real and not real, saved my sanity. I had no other effective source of power as an only child among four doting adults. In some deep recess of my child wisdom, I knew that although my literal sphere of influence stopped at my skin, with cunning I could extend it outward. Of course, the emotionally entangled quartet I grew up with meant the best for their golden girl, wanting to guide me well with their intense love. But blinded by their own hopes, they couldn't recognize the collateral damage they were causing.

I'm not proud of my concocted ailments, nor am I ashamed, though back then I felt like a major-league liar. I knew I would not stop. Nor confess. When I was about ten, after one of many throat infections, I manufactured credible symptoms of rheumatic fever, keeping the doctors hopping for some weeks. At a loss, they finally gave up. I recovered.

I'm not proud, exactly, but I am grateful. My body remained my ally and found for me the way through the strangling labyrinth and finally out, with my essential self intact.

Food held no interest for me at all until my sophomore year in college, when I fell in love. With my virginity gone, my appetite accelerated from zero to infinity in two days flat. The sensual waves flooding my suddenly messy, gooey, inner landscape opened me, apparently, to everything. My body again had come to my rescue, in a new way.

"What's happened to you?" my roommate teased in the dining hall as she eyed my plate piled high for the third time. And she laughed like a daikini, those wild Tibetan forest spirits, causing well-coifed heads to turn and stare at us. I just grinned. We both knew what had happened and relished the unexpected sideshow: my ravenous hunger.

I fell for my first love partly because a character in one of his short stories could have been me: she negotiated her world in a submarine. She wasn't even underwater. But she had a well-cared-for shell that rivaled my own rigid vessel, protecting her from everything. Or so we both believed. How could he know? I didn't ask him; I just abandoned ship.

Now I'll eat anything except sheep's brains, haggis, tripe soup, menudo, sweetbreads, or what I once choked down in Istanbul: a rich and probably very nourishing delicacy made from fresh congealed blood.

But food still carried one odd burden and made me worry about fasting for four days. If my blood sugar dropped below a certain level, I first morphed into a cranky Chihuahua, then into a rabid wolverine. I've companionably called that wired, combative state the Grumpy Hungries. Officially it's called hypoglycemia. I liked the idea of revisiting my old food/no food ghost thirty years after my appetite kicked in, but neither my childhood semistarvation nor the Grumpy Hungries hinted at any trances or dreamlike altered states.

Kit had made it clear the quest relied on ritual and ceremony, but my experiences with ritual weren't promising.

At thirteen, I'd been baptized into a somewhat fundamentalist church. Draped in a thin white gown over my bathing suit, I waded into the baptismal font at the front of the church to meet the minister in his dark, wet robes. He intoned some words, now long gone, put one hand over my nose and mouth, held my upper back with his other, and dunked me backward into the cool water.

Not a moment of confirmation class has stuck with me, not a look or gesture from any of my insistently religious family. But I needed none of that. I needed only my bare feet leaving the smooth, marble floor of the pool, only the stained-glass windows and carved stonework swinging past my eyes as I sank to horizontal. No man had touched me so intimately before, stopping my breath, submerging me. And I remember what it meant to me in that dim cavernous sanctuary: Nothing. A big zero. I simply followed directions. I was ice. The whole thing just seemed weird. Empty ritual. Still, the memory remains, vivid. Had I not been so good at keeping my distance, it might have worked: I might have been initiated.

I never did well with church, the most obvious spot for ritual in my religious family. But any set forms made me squirm, struck me as efforts to make me conform to a shape I didn't want.

I retreated from religion, eventually fled my family's chilling control. I abandoned other things, too. But as I lit my afterburners to make my escapes from trap after trap, I knew the cages always included my own familiar sense of distance, even though my distance had also been part of my armor and my lifeline out, self-protection from real and imagined threats.

Jill Ker Conway's description of the way agency can go underground and become coercive matched the passive-aggressive way I'd survived my childhood. I hoped I'd outgrown my well-honed guerrilla tactics in most of my life, but I still planned to join the vision quest in camouflage.

It didn't even seem odd, only a way to satisfy my curiosity without much risk. But in order to discover as much as I could, I decided to *try* to play by the rules.

🍃

Here were the rules:

1. Write Sparrow a "letter of intent" outlining why I wanted to do a vision quest, including a concise sentence or two specifying my "intention."

2. Read *The Book of the Vision Quest*, by Sparrow's teachers, Steven Foster and Meredith Little.

3. Do a day-long fast in nature a month before the quest, following not trails, but intuition, and further clarify my "intention." This was called a "medicine walk." *Medicine*, in Sparrow's language, meant "anything that brings you to wholeness."

4. Appear at the appointed time and place, ready for the adventure. The quest itself lasted ten days with the guide and the other questers. Four days of preparation (van Gennep's *severance*), four days fasting alone in the wild (*threshold*), then two days of deconstruction with the guide and the group (*incorporation*).

🍃

As I drove north toward Colorado from Albuquerque for my day of not eating, the land opened up to high rolling hills with few trees. Ten miles south of the border, I turned west onto a graded dirt road that curved around the base of a single mountain, as regularly conical as a child's drawing. The road dropped down to cross a narrow bridge over a stream that fed a lush meadow filled with drifts of egg-yolk yellow chamisa, low scarlet paintbrush, and high sunflowers. I stopped by the bridge to take in the wild garden and to think quietly. I needed to work on my intention.

I'd written my letter of intent in mid-July, dutifully exposing some of my most tender innards as if I were being graded for completeness and accuracy. But I wanted to be thorough, not skimping on anything, since I still clung to the idea that I intended simply to see what happened if I kept up my part of the bargain. And to me, my part of the bargain required I be thorough and honest, if not entirely open. I left out my skepticism. "Transformation" wasn't on my agenda either: I'd finally managed to get my life into a shape I liked. Not perfect, but largely satisfying, in a landscape I loved. I wrote to Sparrow, "Daily I'm grateful that so much of my life is running as smoothly as a wide, deep river in flood."

True, some days seemed that way, but not always. From my journal entry, August 18: "I feel out of rhythm with my life, disjointed and inharmonious, beats constantly interrupting each other. I'm jangled, always wanting to get out from under the confusion. No one would claim Joni Mitchell, The Police, Edgar Varèse, and Brahms can easily be played at the same time. What to do?" And "Pressure—as in a balloon or behind a dam—needs to be released, popped, burst. The pressure is as bad as the lack of flow."

I couldn't find any certain place to lay blame.

But standing on the bridge over the small creek, I suddenly condensed my ten-page letter to one coherent nugget, grounded in elemental metaphor: *May all my energies flow with as much grace, ease, and power as water.*

The desire was general enough to fit most parts of my life, but I meant it mainly to refer to my work. I made my living from satisfying clients with paintings of neotropical migrants or cut-away beaver dams complete with beaver families, and through my projects helped others understand more about the natural world. But my voice concerned me more. It had been largely quiet so long, and I wanted it released. I could have rephrased my intent: *May my words flow with as much grace, ease, and power as water.*

I turned onto a four-wheel-drive road and followed it to the end. But when I rounded the last bend I found two hunters' camps: bow hunting season had just started. No humans, but under one stretched blue tarp a bulky bag hung heavy from a line. The hunter had already gotten his elk. By the door to the silent camper sat a worn, overstuffed easy chair, empty under the tarp's protection.

I backtracked up the road and camped next to a tilted outcrop of pinkish rocks whose fractured shelves stepped up to the highest meadows.

After I'd made camp and eaten dinner, I sat with a cup of tea in the late light, watching bright ripples on the stock pond across the road, listening to a distant woodpecker, and thought more about my letter of intent to Sparrow.

"Monsters?" he'd asked in his directions, and I'd answered:

My monsters are mostly abstract: gender roles, social roles, dominant culture, Christianity. I can turn them into images most easily by naming places and situations:

> I am in a motel room that smells of new carpets and tasteful cleaning fluids. Prints of Hallmark-card art hang on the walls.

> I'm in a small-town sitting room overstuffed with dark furniture and Hummel figurines. In the compulsively clean and neat room, six judgmental older women focus on Lawrence Welk on the TV. I'm a child, with no chance of escape.

> I've just come out of a dance when a pert, blond, female twenty-year-old Christian proselytizer shrilly rails at me, "You're going to hell! Dancing is the Devil's work!"

> I am locked in a small room that smells of mildew and has

limp elevator music playing loudly. A couple are arguing with each other about their appearances. I am unable to say a word.

I am mired in mud; the air resists movement, like honey. I have no idea how to get out.

I'm starving, seated at a turquoise Formica table under jittery fluorescent lights, with a thin paper plate and a flimsy plastic fork. On the plate is a Wonder bread and Velveeta sandwich surrounded by cold, overcooked peas.

I'd had to stop there, feeling my solar plexus tightening like a fist. "Fears?" he'd asked, and I'd answered:

I fear losing control over my own life.
I fear ceasing to grow.
I fear being manipulated.

The line between guiding and manipulating flickered in my brainpan. Where did the division fall between loosening your grip, so you could become open and vulnerable, and letting yourself in for some version of tyranny? Perhaps choosing the situation made the difference, or the trustworthiness of the guide offered safety. Perhaps an inner strength provided assurance that you could release into uncertainty and confusion, abandon all control, and still regain your footing.

Did my answers to Sparrow's simple questions come so easily because they were old answers? The fears I offered him had shaped me in the past, but now they had faded to minor warning signs, analogous to knowing the symptoms of heat exhaustion. By drinking enough water, getting enough electrolytes, I could avoid heat exhaustion altogether. I didn't really fear being manipulated: I knew the signs and wouldn't play. And I still hovered at a distance.

Then, briefly, one more detail popped up: in my letter I'd also mentioned a crucial fact that qualified me for a real rite of passage, the midlife somersault of all women who live past a certain age: menopause, that still mildly taboo word. I'd feared it for years (Ah! "What are your fears?"), terrified my hormonal acrobatics would make me crazy. They hadn't yet, but I couldn't ignore the literal, physical transition.

Dawn, 6 a.m. Frost flecked the grasses. At ten thousand feet, September nights were cold. I layered a fuzzy top, down jacket, and shell over my turtleneck and marked the start of the walk by burning a scrap of paper on which I'd written, "the medicine walk begins." Ceremonial minimalism. I climbed up past the pink rocky outcrop to the edge of the mesa's broad expanse, high enough for unimpeded views. Seventy miles east, the sun topped the Sangre de Cristos, and its first crescent brightness flashed through every tiny liquid lens on every spruce needle, every blade of grass, every seed head, every anchored spider's silk. I watched the growing light as it melted the frost, then evaporated the dew into dry air. Downhill from my perch, an old grown-over road crossed into shade where the still-frosted grasses looked like pale velvet, then it disappeared into the trees.

I turned uphill away from the old track and moved farther onto the mesa, where isolated aspens stood like sentinels above the tawny grasses. For half an hour I strolled over the uneven ground, reminding myself to let go completely my planning urges and just wander. And watch who snuck into awareness, vying for the badge of "spirit guide." I continued to try to follow directions. Sparrow had instructed: "Note what animals you encounter and what people appear in your inner landscape. These might be spirit guides."

On one east-facing slope an old aspen had fallen, and I propped myself against the smooth white hardness and contemplated my empty stomach. Two hours in and already I felt ravenous and missed my morning tea. Trying to get my psyche on track and away from toasted English muffins, I concentrated on northern flickers looping from aspen to aspen, white rumps winking. But by nine, lounging and flickers had lost their appeal. I needed to get on with it.

With a certain hopefulness, I stood, swallowed a mouthful of water, and aimed up to slightly higher ground. I'd gone no more than a dozen steps when I saw movement directly in front of me, about a quarter mile away. Through my binoculars I could see a small elk herd, running from right to left. Almost at once a spruce seemed to swallow them, but they'd only disappeared into a dip on the mesa. I walked a dozen more steps, and the herd reappeared to my left, closer, angling toward me on higher ground, skirting a conifer stand on a low ridge, their brown bodies strung out in a clear line in front of the dark trees.

Again they disappeared behind a near spruce; I stood, watching the wide tree. The wind blew directly into my face, carrying a faint forest scent mixed with the dustiness grasses give off in the fall's hot sun. In a small explosion, a flock of bluebirds erupted from a lone aspen, and immediately afterward, one, then two elk reappeared in the open, closer and facing me. With one foot awkwardly forward, I froze, right hand on my walking stick, coat blazing red. I had no idea if elk could see red. The wind from behind them erased my scent, though I couldn't smell them on the air with my pathetic human nose.

The whole herd materialized and came toward me, slowly at first, then running, running, directly at me, not pausing, not wavering. They kept on course, locked on me as if on a beacon. A robust female led them, her head tilted up and back, mouth open, sampling the air for the enemy: any human. How could she not know she ran directly toward me? Couldn't she see me, even if she couldn't smell me? Would they run right over me? Not likely, but they weren't slowing, and the barely audible rumble of their hooves had reached my ears. Finally, at twenty feet, she jolted in alarm, sidestepping out of her easy run, showing the whites of her eyes and nearly stopping. In a moment, she skipped to her left and led her band past me in loping single file, wary but not terrified. In the basin below, hunters stalked elk, but the elk were up here with me. I attached no meaning to it, no spirit guide significance. They were, after all, real elk out on their morning jaunt. But no mature males, no trophy heads. They passed in parade formation, fifteen feet away, elk muscle bunching and stretching under their smooth brown skins. Eighteen. The last two young males paused to stare at me for several long minutes, mystified, their short, blunt antlers in velvet. I still stood motionless. When the pair had finished their inspection, they cantered off after the others just vanishing over a gilded hillside. I pivoted to watch them go, then stared at the empty curve of ground.

The high, bright mesa hadn't changed. In substance it tilted and dipped exactly as before, with the same trees and grasses, the same distant grazing cows. I stood exactly where I had ten minutes before, but something had happened: a movement, unique and dramatic in my experience, though not in the daily life of the mesa.

I walked on, all thoughts of food forgotten.

As I pushed my way through the meadow's knee-high September grasses, they sang with insect exuberance, buzzing and humming. I aimed north, in this drainage the same way the water flowed. Slowly the land sloped downward until it fell off steeply into lower-level aspens. I half slid down forty feet of steep hillside into an open forest. A hundred years' accumulation of decomposing leaves cushioned my steps, and quivering light illuminated sparse underbrush growing from black ground. The trees were a foot in diameter, but groves of skinny, young aspens sometimes interrupted the mature trees. On most trunks, elk nibbles had healed over into dark grey quotation marks inside sharp parentheses. Fresh gashes oozed transparent sap the color of blood. The longer I wandered across the spongy ground, gazing at fragmented sun leap and shiver over white trunks, the more I felt I'd been transported into someone else's dream. Battalions of indefinable presences seemed to watch me with singular curiosity, their murmuring covered by the sound of the wind.

At noon I reached the small creek that marked the eastern edge of the aspen forest. Here, near the top of the watershed, water trickled over rocks in a flow barely a foot wide. Looking across the creek, I could make out a rough path leading up the sunny hillside. The leaves shimmered. I felt lightheaded and dizzy, though not hungry. I lounged beside the gentle water, not thinking about much. I lay quietly, watching the breeze stir the aspens. Light. Wind. Movement. Succulence. I didn't sleep and finally sat up, relaxed and happy.

I turned back into the aspens and their glittering, glittering leaves. I'd been afraid the day would be a bust. Seven hours in and nothing odd but a herd of elk running straight at me. And a great hike. But something could yet happen: six more hours to go.

The next several hours, I followed game trails as they disappeared and reappeared and disappeared again; I stepped through oval patches of flattened plants where elk had bedded down; I recognized maidenhair fern, osha; I turned 360 degrees as I walked, so the changing patterns of sun began to pulse. The pale, mottled trunks slid by each other far into the forest. My dizziness only added to a luscious, hallucinatory disorientation.

Still no spirit guides, though. My naturalist's logic remained intact: these high open hills were remote enough to shelter herds of game. Aspen stands grew as clones from a single root system, all variations on a single theme, and their fallen or undeveloped branches left behind dark eye-shapes. This forest had grown as a result of a fire that had wiped out the conifers in the late 1800s. I wasn't about to concoct any imagined visitations. As if I were watching a play, I'd suspend disbelief, but the performance still had to deliver more than an elk show or an aspen tableaux, no matter how uncommonly rich.

I'd stopped craving food, but my hunger had migrated to my head, which had begun to feel constricted with tight bands of a migraine, or worse, food poisoning. The Grumpy Hungries, I thought, annoyed. I found a sunny patch where some old aspens had fallen, and I lay down again until I felt revived enough to move on. I turned back up toward the mesa, aware of the time. Not a hundred steps farther, I ran into the steep hillside that separated the forest from higher open ground. But before I switchbacked up, I followed a well-traveled game trail along its base. With a bratty cheekiness, I sang out loud, "OK, spirit guides! I'm ready! I'm open! I'm available! Where are you, spirit guides?" Rude, I knew, but I hadn't spoken since I'd set out, and bellowing those words in a chant timed to my steps seemed to quiet my headache.

But my forehead still crimped itself into unnatural folds, and I wanted to get to the top of the rise, stretch out in the sun, and maybe nap. Maybe dream.

As I climbed out of the aspens, I rested my hand on their hard, waxy trunks. A fine white powder rubbed off on my palm. At the top, winded and weak from not eating, I collapsed. Immediately the resident squirrel started fussing. I stared straight up at her furry underbelly. She balanced on the lowest aspen branch, then skittered up to the next one, then the next. At each stop she settled herself and wrapped her dark tail around her body, peered down at me, and spit out her high-pitched staccato rattles. Around her sex, dark hair outlined a narrow slit, contrasting with her pale underside.

Instead of dreaming, I mulled over my intention, the sound bite distilled from my letter of intent. I'd found in the quest an opportunity to chew more on my old friend, my silence. Or rather, my voice. Finding voice: an issue nearly every woman gets to eventually, but the whiff of cliché couldn't drain its potency. Now that I'd broken the sound barrier by chiding my spirit guides, I said out loud into the cloudless sky, "May my energies flow with as much grace, ease, and power as water."

While I lay sensing the aspen shadows dance over my closed eyelids, I pictured breaking waves, rocky streams, hurricanes, quiet ponds, gushing faucets, and the contraption at the Co-op that dispensed water cleansed of Giardia and the bad taste of Albuquerque's municipal supply.

Suddenly a firm thought plopped in the middle of all that mental wetness: Of course, who wouldn't want to flow? Go with it, it's a hot topic.
The real issue is *how*. Ah, I thought, now I'm getting somewhere.

And immediately I saw the face.

In my inner vision, to my right and a little behind me, the face
appeared as real as the fussing squirrel over my head. Just a face—
life-sized, with no neck, no ears, no hair, not even eyebrows. At first it
seemed androgynous, but then I saw it more as a young, ruddy Irish fellow with largish features. As if in response to my "how," his lips folded
in between his teeth, and he kept them tightly together while the rest
of his face moved in animated expressions, almost contortions, as he
stared at me. His nose scrunched up, his cheeks pouched and released,
his forehead wrinkled up and down, his eyes, always watching me with
focused intensity, narrowed and widened. I saw the hovering face clearly
for two minutes or more and tried to fix it in memory. Simultaneously I
flipped through my Rolodex of possible meanings, potential references:
A friend who made odd cat faces with his mouth? My younger, non-
speaking self? A mask, even a humanly mobile mask? An "answer" from
somewhere—the spirit guides?—to *how*: we can't tell you, or we aren't
going to tell you, or we aren't going to tell you now?

It—he—disappeared. I hadn't ever had such a clear waking dream:
floating cinema, a holographic portrait. Despite my spirit-guide joking,
I'd not expected anything so dramatic—something outside myself, yet
something that couldn't have been anything but an image created by my
brain. And I'd been decisively awake.

The peculiar image might have held my attention longer except the
metal bands around my forehead had tightened another notch. Before
sunset I had to walk several miles back to my truck; the chilly wind had
picked up; and the intense high sun had begun to wring my optic nerves
like an overly enthusiastic washerwoman.

I felt like hell. Forget the apparition. Forget the golden hills sprinkled
with aspens and spruce and livened by a hovering kestrel, the raven that

did a somersault in midair, and the flocks of flashing mountain blue-birds. Forget the hulking peaks of the San Juans visible far to the north. The Grumpy Hungries had taken over. Muted gunshots drifted up from the basin below, and I vaguely wondered what that might mean during bow-hunting season. According to instructions, I wasn't supposed to return to my camp—and its apples and crackers—before sunset, at 7 p.m. It was only four.

Stopping often to lean on my walking stick and close my tense, aching eyes, I walked back slowly, feeling worse at every step. Even the distant herd of twenty-two pronghorns that gazed at me with hair-trigger focus like a four-footed audience couldn't counteract my body's revolt. Nor did the late sun bathing the land in a crystalline light give me any solace. Another flock of bluebirds startled from an aspen right over my head at the same moment a wave of diarrhea shook me. I squatted where I was—in the open—then dug through dense roots with my orange plastic trowel to bury my watery poop as well as I could.

I meant to rest at the rocky outcrop above my camp until dark. But nauseated, stumbling with head pain, and cold despite my down and polypro, I gave up and returned to my truck an hour shy of sunset. I'd left a second scrap of paper on the driver's seat: "the medicine walk ends." I burned it before I choked down half an apple and one cracker in the truck's protected cab. I'd thought food would fix me, but I slipped another rung lower on the misery ladder. I crawled into my tent but continued to shiver and throb, immobilized, only halfway in my sleeping bag, more worried than I'd ever been camped alone. I felt I couldn't take care of myself: hypothermia was a real danger in a night that had been forecast to fall into the twenties.

"Please help me," I begged out loud to the quiet night. I wanted someone to bring me hot chocolate and hold me. No luck. About eight o'clock, I leaned six inches out of the tent and threw up the few bites of apple and cracker; not long after, I found the energy to pull off my fuzzy pants and zip myself into my bag properly, still shivering. Finally

I warmed enough to fall asleep, but not before I thought of Kit lying in a fetal position, following juniper shade around his clearing. And I resolved, "No way am I going to fast for *four* days. My metabolism is screwy. I will not put myself through this again. It's too terrible. I'll be a wimp and bail out."

At midnight I woke. Nothing hurt. Not my head, not my gut. I felt buoyant and expansive, exceptionally happy under my relief. I got up to pee, then strolled around in the silver silence sipping a box of apple juice, as delicious as anything I could imagine. I wondered about my body and fasting. I hadn't been in an altered state—at least not that I'd recognized—just physically trashed. Awake in the freezing starlit night, I felt exultant.

I didn't know what to make of it.

The next day and for days afterward, my euphoria remained. I couldn't put together the day walk with my life—the crash at the end demanded all my attention and anxiety. The crash, and the face hovering in the windy air. In the next weeks, I scoured the library's ethnography shelves for masks that looked like the face apparition, with little success. I checked out Iroquois masks, sometimes carved on living trees. That appealed to me, but they were too exaggerated, too demonlike and terrifying. Only a pair of nearly identical masks from King Island in the Bering Strait came close, but they were dark wood and much too stylized: Good Shaman and Bad Shaman.

When I e-mailed Sparrow and Kit asking for answers, they didn't know either. Altitude, maybe? I'd been at ten thousand feet. But I lived at five thousand. My period had started the day before; maybe it was a combination of things. Kit reassured me nothing sounded dramatically askew. "Go ahead," he e-mailed me, "I'm thrilled you're doing it!"

I wouldn't bail out after all.

🍃

I went over my notes about fasting and pieced together a plausible

explanation for my misery. When we don't eat, our livers release
their limited stored glycogen as glucose for metabolism. Once that's
depleted—usually in about a day—our bodies switch to ketone metabolism, a different energy-producing pathway that burns stored fat and
protein. My switch-over mechanism apparently didn't work well at all.
When I woke feeling euphoric at midnight, I must have finally made the
change to ketone metabolism, with my happiness simply an odd bonus.
I also discovered that when blood sugar drops below a certain level,
the adrenal glands release extra adrenaline. Sunlight on the Grumpy
Hungries at last! I reasoned that once the alternative ketone pathway
kicked in, blood sugar would recover, and any headaches and aggressive
ill humor would abate, even without food.

But the neurophysiology of non-ordinary consciousness was a more
complex matter.

The more I read, the more I wanted to read. Every reference added
new pieces to the engrossing puzzle, though not necessarily clarifying
much about altered states or vision quests. A real explanation of consciousness remains elusive for philosophers and scientists, even after
great elaboration of the physiological underpinnings. Even though those
underpinnings included some wonderful details, what they really meant
in terms of consciousness seemed mostly up for grabs.

Two main observations about altered states described aspects of the
phenomenon, but didn't go much further.

Electroencephalograms (EEGs) measure brain waves as cycles of
electrical charge per second (cps). Normal consciousness sends out
alpha waves (8–13 cps) or beta waves (14–30 cps). Non-ordinary consciousness sends out much slower theta waves (4–7 cps). These long
slow pulses, unlike "normal" waves, are also synchronized in both left
and right cerebral hemispheres. But what these waves represent in brain
function isn't known.

Our autonomic nervous systems regulate involuntary activities—such as digestion, heart rate, blood pressure—with two body-wide neural networks. These roughly oppose each other, working together to balance "go faster" with "slow down." The sympathetic system is the accelerator; the parasympathetic, the brakes. When we're awake, the parasympathetic system dominates in only two situations: after an orgasm and when we're in an altered state.

Other aspects of our nervous systems seemed relevant.

There is no central control. The brain—itself no simple "thing," as William James observed—doesn't act as director but is part of an overwhelmingly complex neural grid. For example, we each have between 10,000,000,000 and 14,000,000,000 neurons in our bodies. These neurons pass messages to each other at synapses, where one dendrite (the receiving end) can be connected to as many as 100,000 axons (the sending end). Though each neuron "fires" electrically, chemicals that regulate the firing pass signals across the connecting synapses. Researchers have identified about 250 of these neurotransmitters. Perhaps the most famous one is serotonin; Prozac blocks serotonin's reuptake, improving symptoms of depression.

The most familiar triggers of altered states—drugs such as opiates, LSD, mescaline, psilocybin, cocaine—all mimic naturally occurring neurotransmitters. One notable exception is alcohol.

Our nervous system is not "hardware," but "wetware." It's fluid. Our neurons can—and do—grow new connections throughout life. Old connections not used wither away. New growing pathways and abandoned tracks offer the certainty of literal, physiological transformation. When we learn anything, from how to put up a new tent to how to speak in public, our neural pathways change.

Anatomically, our brains consist roughly of three parts.

First, the "reptilian" brain, also called the brain stem, sits just at the top of the spinal column and helps regulate basic life activities such as breathing, swallowing, digestion, mating, aggression, and defending territory. We share these activities with all animals, from snakes to ospreys to pocket gophers.

Second, the limbic system cups over the older brainstem. It's considered our primary emotional center. Not until the limbic brain developed in early mammals did mothers hang around to care for their offspring. Bonding requires communication: vocalization, singing, physical affection, responsiveness, passion. Memory. Also play. Someone once said playing is like poetry: it offers a chance to say one thing and mean another. In other words, all-important metaphor.

Third, the neocortex largely surrounds the limbic structures in two lobes. It's evolutionarily the newest brain part, but not the most advanced. Its textbook functions are reason, abstraction, will. But it also deserves credit for voice (written and spoken language), for dance (conscious motor control), and for sorting through how a vision quest might work (symbolic representation and problem solving).

This triune brain theory hasn't won universal acceptance largely because it oversimplifies. For example, not all emotional activity takes place in the limbic system.

Throughout the brain, particular structures seem dedicated to specific functions. For example, in the neocortex's left lobe, two areas oversee and decipher the *meaning* of incoming and outgoing speech. In the right lobe, their mirror images deal with the *emotional content* of speech. Depending on inflection, "Would you like some dessert?" could imply anything from "You're an insensitive boor!" to "Do you want to go to bed with me?" The synchronized waves in altered states suggest an unusually close connection between literal meaning and emotional resonance.

A small seahorse-shaped structure in the limbic system called the hippocampus seems to have multiple crucial functions. It plays an important role in the interactions among emotions and motivation, visceral responses, and learning and memory. The synchronized cortical waves of altered states apparently originate in the hippocampus. This suggests a dramatic physical integration in non-ordinary consciousness.

⟡

Recent research about body-wide learning surprised me. When we learn, our bodies also program our emotional chemistry, the hormones and neuropeptides that course through our blood and wash tissues outside our veins and arteries. If we learn something when we're angry, for example, we can better remember it when we're angry. If we learned certain critical life lessons in childhood when we were depressed, we have an easier time accessing that information when we're depressed. Some people spend much time in their adult lives orchestrating depression simply so they can survive. I considered my own childhood learning: much of it had taken place while I had been working hard to hide myself, trying to avoid my family's traps.

These can be disheartening closed loops until a major shift happens in experience. Conscious will can't affect those loops directly—neuropeptides operate in a different system—but conscious will can arrange *conditions* for change. Getting to that major shift totally alone, however, can be difficult. One obvious way to break a neurochemical loop is with chemistry: the drugs of psychiatry, like Prozac. But given an understanding of the body-electrochemical, other possibilities become clear: changing motor tone so fluids move more efficiently, acting out feelings, or practicing accessing information in an unfamiliar chemical state. Even modifying diet can have an effect. Clearly, non-ordinary consciousness could modify those loops, too.

⟡

These clues all suggested an altered state would cause a mild inner unhinging. Slowed, synchronous electrical discharges originating from an area awash with memory and emotion combine with the loose but alert flow of parasympathetic dominance. Pick up a tangled skein of rope to untie, and the first thing you do is shake it gently and rhythmically, loosening the strands. Your intention would front-load your internal vulnerability; telling your story to others would externalize it and establish it in a different way. I'd already experienced the effect of fasting, with the Grumpy Hungries and the euphoria after my day walk. Fasting in the wild, in a ritual-rich situation with strangers must go one step further. An altered state seemed likely to ease old patterns and allow them to become unusually available to change. In an environment filled with potential metaphors, your complex neural network would begin to reconfigure, informed by your conscious intentions. Then, as importantly, when you emerged from your altered state, you finally reinforced the newly growing neural patterns and revised emotional chemistry with other people. Perhaps you *could literally* change your life.

Of course, no one needed to know any of this to go on a vision quest, or to pursue any spiritual discipline, or even to make life changes. But it all gave me a greater ease with the whole idea.

∇

I'd gotten to a comfortable place with physiology, but I saw two other issues associated not with science, but with mystery.

First, I carried deep suspicions of locating extraordinary power in something less grounded than the breath of bats, especially while the constricting associations—church, dogma, narrow laws about behavior—overwhelmed that very mystery. Yet when I equated spirit with other nonrational phenomena like intuition, inspiration, or love, my resistance and hostility began to dissolve.

Second, mystical experiences—which must be altered states—and spiritual quests had a long history in religious literature and practice. Yet according to many spiritual teachers, such dramatic non-ordinary states served mainly to distract from living a compassionate life, their highs becoming sources of pride or goals in themselves.

As Sparrow presented the vision quest, it bypassed both conflicts: spirit came without dogma or structured religion; and altered states weren't an end in themselves, but tools to use in a journey back to daily life.

One October afternoon, sixteen hours early for my rendezvous with Sparrow and the unknown others, I gazed east from Emory Pass in southwest New Mexico over a desiccated world. From the cool heights of the pass, the Rio Grande hid in the brown, undulating rhythms of land, and the distant Jornada del Muerto angled up starkly. Could any other geography be named Journey of the Dead? On their terrible trek through the desert, the Spanish had missed the lusher land west of Emory Pass, in the Gila River drainage. The Gila Wilderness remained an isolated and relatively unknown area.

Years before, the Gila had won my heart when I'd discovered Mimbres pots. The Mimbres themselves had disappeared from the Gila by the time the Spanish struggled through the Jornada, but on broken pots they left behind countless rabbits and snakes, dragonflies and beetles, lizards and trout, cranes and quail, bats and bobcats, antelopes and bighorns. All painted and geometric, but all quirky and alive. I thought they were better with a brush than I was. And they surely knew their world more intimately.

At our appointed meeting place not far below the pass, I made dinner alone and bedded down. After dark two more cars appeared and turned to the campground's other end. Then at 3 a.m., another car woke me with its headlights.

During breakfast the next morning, I watched five people accumulate by one picnic table fifty yards away. I waited until nine thirty, the designated hour, to make my way up the short rise as the group focused on my progress. I stuck out my hand to the person who looked most like he might be Sparrow.

"I'm Mary." I smiled. In the nippy morning air, he wore a dark, bulky fuzzy hat and a loose, navy neck gaiter, but his face glowed sunburn red. Though he didn't match my grin of greeting, he met my eyes with a gaze that lasted a little too long and had a little too much focus for a casual introduction and confirmed, "I'm Sparrow."

He stood about my height, in practical gear: black Gore-Tex pants long enough to just trail on the ground, and a short dark jacket. "We wondered if that was you over there. Welcome. You could have come over earlier, if you'd wanted. I'll let everyone introduce themselves." He returned to his stove, puttered around, and made another cup of coffee. Easy, not seeming at all in charge.

The only other woman introduced herself immediately, "I'm Jenny. I'm from Rhode Island."

"Ah," I said, "I used to live in Providence, but now I'm from Albuquerque."

"I once spent a year outside Santa Fe. I love the desert. Now I live in Warwick." Her abundant dark-blond hair crowded her face, which carried a look of deep tiredness, dark circles wreathing her eyes.

The others made no move to introduce themselves yet, so I went on, "What do you do in the world?"

She responded a little shyly, "I'm a hospice nurse." Then, with more enthusiasm, as if to counteract a job that might seem dull, she said, "But I just finished my certification in holistic medicine." Then, more quietly, "I'm so glad there's another woman here."

She'd driven down in the dark from the Albuquerque airport with Vern, a building contractor in his late forties who lived near Ithaca in upstate New York. He had a reserved manner and an elegant bushy moustache, which seemed at odds with a Patagonia shirt the color of an emergency flare. Only when we pulled out the New Mexico road atlas did he join the wider conversation. "So where are we now? And where are we going?" he asked Sparrow, who obligingly moved his finger over the map and ignored the irony.

Doug, who had arrived with Sparrow after dark the night before, was tall, lean, and tough, but had the same tired eyes as Jenny. He lived in Wellfleet on Cape Cod, where he owned a landscaping business. Later I discovered his hotshot education and voracious reading habits. He wore his first morning's T-shirt all week.

Chuck was about six foot two, solid but not overweight. He wore jeans, a flannel shirt, and the bubbly talkativeness of a teenager. "So, luckily when I was working on that project for the Department of Defense, they pulled the plug on the funding. It was making me really nervous because we were getting close to the solution, and it would have upset the nuclear balance of power." We nodded, at a loss about how to respond. Currently he spent his days as a computer researcher at Yale. Like Jenny and Doug, he seemed sheathed in exhaustion, but on Chuck, the dark eye circles combined with pale skin and a bald head to give him a cadaverous look. "Did you see that movie—" he began again with no prompting and took off into some complicated plot. After a while, he rattled on without much response from his audience—by then only me and Jenny—and I reminded myself his verbal flood must come from unease.

Except for me, all lived in New England. Looking for transformation? Go west, of course. I'd done it myself.

And how did I seem to them? Tall, thin, in Tevas and hiking socks, shorts and two sweaters, a khaki bill cap over short hair—almost a New Mexican uniform at certain times of the year. And probably a little too perky for the occasion. But my social skills had been hard won, and I did my best to be actively not shy.

I knew something about who they were, but not yet why they had come to the Gila with Sparrow.

We bumped down dirt road after dirt road rimmed with forests of piñon and juniper, then ponderosas. At the edge of the Gila Wilderness proper, we forded the tiny Mimbres River and parked a hundred paces from a grassy open area. After we'd set up our tents, we gathered into a circle on the ground in dappled light under huge sheltering cottonwoods. Their narrow leaves didn't match the cottonwood leaves in my front yard, which were broad green hearts cut out with pinking shears. As much as I itched to take notes, no one else had a notebook, so I left mine untouched on the grass.

Across from me, Sparrow opened a Ziploc bag and took out a blackened abalone shell and a small clot of pulverized sage that he nestled under the shell's lip. He asked, "Does everyone know about smudging?"

Someone said no, and he explained, "It's a way of marking sacred space, time for stories. It's a way of purifying our interactions, of driving away distractions. It's thanking Spirit and asking for blessings. We'll smudge at the start of all our circles and try to speak from our hearts." He lit the sage, and as it sent up its white smoke, he cradled the shell in both hands and spoke into it, "Thank you Father Sun, Mother Earth, the four directions . . . " and continued for several minutes. And handed the shell to me. I knew the drill. I knew the smudge would make its way around the circle, but I hated the awkwardness of being put on the spot, expected to be heartfelt and reverent on demand. In a group of strangers. But I'd always loved the smell of burning sage, and I inhaled the drift of smoke, paused, and said the minimal, "Many thanks."

I meant it, despite my awareness of acting a part that didn't fit me. Nothing to be done. I'd joined Sparrow's show. I handed the smudge to Chuck, on my left, who blew on it, then passed it around his back in a hotshot basketball move, and came out with a short poetic prayer that caused Sparrow to nod at him and say, "Nice." Later Chuck confessed he'd memorized the inscription on the bronze statue in Albuquerque's airport—a nearly airborne Native American man holding on to a soaring eagle's talons. He'd *prepared* his first lines. Jenny, Vern, and Doug mumbled their thanks as briefly as I had. But short and self-conscious still counted—no one graded us for elegance—and we were off and running in sacred space.

Sparrow started by speaking Mary Oliver's "Wild Geese" with an easy, friendly expression, moving his gaze around the circle. Perhaps because I counted Mary Oliver as a member of my culture, or because her language had inherent power, or because the poem expressed a complicated but familiar emotion, for the first time I began to believe Sparrow might be solid enough, literate enough, and insightful enough to offer us the guidance he'd claimed.

"The 'harsh and exciting' call of the wild geese," he repeated. "It's not important for you to have a 'good quest' as such. We're not all Black Elk. This isn't meant to be easy, and it's taken courage for all of you to come this far. Mary Oliver also says, 'You don't have to walk on your knees through the desert—' But I do encourage you to address the darkness and difficulty." He went on much longer, every sentence reeling me in further.

"The writer Chellis Glendenning talks about the three qualities of a whole person. One, safety: 'I'm comfortable here. In this place, in my body.' Two, mastery: 'I have something I can do well. I believe in my capacities.' Three: connection to something bigger than ourselves. One of the reasons to go on a quest is to bring ourselves to wholeness. But we all have our own stories, and there are many ways to do that." He spoke easily, the beginning of another quest. He'd led them for thirteen years.

"You've all sent me letters of intent, explaining why you've come on this quest, but I'd like each of you to tell the group your intention, with some background. Community is very important here. Speak at whatever length you feel easy with, but don't be so brief you gloss over important details."

And he looked over at me. "Mary, would you start?"

I'd sat in the wrong spot. I felt like a sacrificial lamb. The only guidance I had was Kit's description of the first stories. They'd gone on an hour, an hour and a half, and he'd promised everyone would hang on every word. Beside us, the shallow Mimbres gurgled over its stones, surrounding us with a constant watery sound. So off I went, trying to behave, strip-teasing off layers of psyche, in the end having almost too much fun fingering the details.

I accounted for my younger shyness and silence with the overpowering presences of my mother and grandmother. Because I was a beloved only child of a beloved only child, I told the group, they'd wanted me to be their golden girl. I passed up the tales of my food oddness and my concocted illnesses. I described the slow transformation that had loosened my tongue, but emphasized the tenacious inner knot I still felt. And I repeated my intention for the small audience: *May my energies flow with as much grace, ease, and power as water.*

When I finally finished shedding after forty-five minutes, I nodded to Sparrow, and he said, "Would you like to say something about Spirit? There was a part in your letter of intent . . . ?" He wasn't letting me off easily no matter how much I'd flung into the air.

"Spirit's a problem for me because of childhood religion, but I'd be happy if I could figure out a way to have a more workable relationship with the irrational, or spirit, or whatever you call it." Despite my camouflage, I really did want to experience something I couldn't describe and follow an inner drive I couldn't explain even to myself, much less to my companions under the cottonwoods. I felt coerced, but I said, looking at him, "Thank you, Sparrow." I guessed that in this group, I was the most skeptical of the spiritual element, and though I hadn't owned up to it clearly, I had at least claimed my uneasiness.

I looked over to Chuck as I passed him the abalone shell.

"Like you," he moved out easily, "I had a domineering mother, and like you, I went into biology. But I kept at it until long after graduate school." I glanced away, up past the hillside back from the river to an open patch of sky where a vulture circled slowly, not very high. Chuck had followed a path I might have followed if I'd been a more obedient daughter and had become a research biologist. Caught up in the challenges to his mind, he'd barricaded himself against the contradictions: Find an engaging problem in the living world, track down some critters who might help you solve it, and kill them.

After leaving thousands of dead mice and lab rats in his wake, he'd eventually migrated to bloodless computers, but his barricades had stubbornly remained. I knew how bizarre this whole enterprise would seem to his lab mates if he'd confessed, and I admired the guts it had taken to throw over his rationality so completely. I had my skepticism; but he had a lifetime of "objective" observations under his belt, although they'd ultimately proven unsatisfying to him as a human being. I'd at least abandoned traditional science before I'd sunk past my knees.

"I'm not sure why I'm here," he went on. "I haven't done much preparation. I went on a quest with Sparrow in Vermont last year, and the feeling of belonging was so wonderful I wanted to find it again. When I got home after that last quest, I realized the only people I could tell about it were my twelve-year-old daughter and my quasi-wife. We've split up, but we're still legally married. For the health insurance. But I had to make an appointment with her."

"I've almost become human, but not quite." What? I thought, he's sure hard on himself. "I guess I want to finish the job."

He turned to Jenny, extending the abalone shell. She took it and placed it on the grass in front of her, then began softly, folded into a patterned wrap skirt and a loose shirt. She kept one hand at her stomach, the other on the ground supporting her. "I really want this to be a good experience for me, and I really want you all to have good experiences, too." She paused. "But I'm having a lot of trouble listening. I'm fading in and out of the stories and my stomach's boiling. I think I got your kernel," she said, looking at Chuck, then turned apologetically to me, "but I couldn't quite catch yours, I'm afraid."

Addressing herself to Sparrow in what sounded like unfocused rambling, she went on. I listened hard, but couldn't pick up anything specific about what brought her here, though from our first talk I could have made up an intention for her. She didn't mention anything about her family, her nursing work, or her holistic training, nothing I'd expected. Again I looked up into the sky, but the vulture had disappeared, leaving only deep, cloudless blue.

"I'm feeling very inadequate," she said, and stopped abruptly.

Sparrow met her. "I honor your expression of being in the moment." Good, I thought, she needs reassurance. In two hours I'd already realized that of all these sincere folks, she made me the most uncomfortable. For a nurse, she was alarmingly ungrounded and abstract. And so humorless the weight almost suffocated me. Compassion, Mary, I warned myself.

Later I asked about her notebook, which had two covers rather than a front and back. "Day" had a bright sun; flip it, and you got "Night" with a dim candle among stars. She used the "Night" cover and identified with literal and metaphorical darkness.

Dark/light: always the danger was getting stuck in rigid categories. But over and over in our circles and in less formal conversations, she mentioned chaos, her urge for inclusiveness, her recognition of her own subjectivity. Chuck admitted finding her direct, insistent eye contact unnerving: science meets universal solvent. I'd come focused on water's fluidity; in Jenny I encountered nothing less than the archetypal ocean. But oceans also have shores, the rich territory that harbors a spectacular world of particulars, from anemones to zebra perch. Jenny seemed to have not yet discovered she need not abandon the embracing sea to make forays on shore to identify orienting landmarks.

Vern took the shell, the sage still sending up a whiff of white smoke. He leaned against a wide trunk whose bark had fractured into deeply scored patterns, nearly geometrical. Alligator juniper.

"Let's see." He cleared his throat. "For about ten years I've been troubled by some dissatisfaction I can't pin down, exactly. Partly it took the form of looking at lots of travel books, fantasizing about getting away."

Vern's body moved with few excess gestures, like a giraffe grazing through tall trees. That physical economy could have come from years working as a builder, where repeated actions taught him not to waste energy, or from a natural quiet, or—my best guess—from limiting what he allowed his body to express.

"Then last month I took a course in 'proprioceptive writing' at the Omega Institute. And it was like somebody turned on a light bulb. It was very exciting. I went home, separated from my wife, finished all my half-done contracting jobs, canceled all the rest, and closed my business."

The power of words. The power of words bubbling up from body.

"You must change your life!" My college writing teacher, Reynolds Price, had quoted Rilke to me, his eyes fixed on mine like an itinerant preacher's. He'd quoted that line to everyone, but it didn't matter.

"Vern," something had whispered, "you must change your life!"

He continued, "But I don't really know what to do next. I grew up as a Lutheran—Missouri Synod—and I've been praying again lately."

"For what?" interrupted Sparrow.

"For clarity, for wisdom, the strength to keep to this new path," though the path was about as clear as pineapple tapioca pudding. "But I don't know how I'll make a living. I'm afraid I'll end up on the street, without any good CDs, you know." He drifted off.

"On the street with only *bad* CDs?" I asked. Something about Vern's innocent directness made it OK to tease him.

Vern laughed, and Sparrow added, "Only bad fifties compilations—" Then he said, "I just flashed on the Wizard of Oz and what he told Dorothy: 'Kill the wicked witch.' Once the crew had a definite task, everyone found they'd gotten what they needed and desired. Maybe you need a task?" In other words, get grounded. Earlier Sparrow had said, "If it has no practical use, I'm not interested in it."

Doug seemed more familiar with this format. He stared for a long moment into the smudge, then began.

"One morning this summer when I was walking out to my shop, I heard a voice say, 'Are you going to waste your life?' And I got really upset. I mean, landscaping pays the bills, but it's not very satisfying and doesn't help anybody." Later he told us he'd started speaking with no notion of what would come out, and his own voice had taken him into unexpected emotional territory.

He rocked back in his Therm-a-Rest chair.

"My father's always been really disappointed in me, and I was reminded of that all over again when he came to visit this summer. He's recently given up drinking, so we had a good visit for a change. But my wife and I aren't getting along that well. It's gone sort of stale. We've been married twenty years and have two kids." He paused. I watched Doug across a strangely lush lawn, evenly short, as if it had been mowed.

"When my parents got divorced, it was a big shock to me. I'd just gone off to boarding school. I was fourteen. When I went home for Christmas, on Christmas Day they told me they were splitting up." He teared slightly. "I'm not sure I've ever gotten over it. Our son has just gone off to school; he's fourteen now, and I will *not* do that to him. I'll do anything to stay married. I will." We all sat silently while he struggled against tears.

"Whew. So, there's that," he finally said, "but I'm here mostly hoping Spirit will give me a sign whether I'm suited or ready to become a ceremonialist." A ceremonialist? I wondered. I decided he meant to do what Sparrow did, or some approximation. "Whew," he said again, "I don't know where that came from."

After a moment, Sparrow said gently, "I want to point out that the hurt your parents caused you wasn't from the announcement—though their timing was abysmal—but from their silence. With you and with each other. By sticking, you might well be doing more damage than by opening up to your wife and son. In fact, maybe the same damage." I was surprised by such an instant and specific response. But Doug had done an earlier quest with Sparrow, and this time he was an official apprentice. He'd also been part of Sparrow's men's workshops for a year. They weren't strangers.

Around the fire that night, Doug told me about his trip to Ellesmere Island, its summer tundra overflowing with wildlife. No trees grow above the Arctic Circle, but tundra always reminds me of the edges where trees stop. The longer I knew Doug, the more I thought he resembled the flagged trees that grow at those margins, sculpted by prevailing winds. He seemed to stand with unwavering tenacity as he faced powerful inner winds. The wind and his tenacity had shaped him. He and I shared a fondness for books and ideas, and that gave me a clue to how he approached his world. I knew books were effective to a point, but they could offer a self-limiting detour around human messiness. They could bolster the barrier between inner and outer. Books, like maps, were useful, but in the end their brittle two-dimensionality had to be wedded to landscape, outer or inner.

"So, me," Sparrow said. "What would you like to know?" He wasn't going to keep his guide's distance but would flay back his skin with the rest of us. But I bet he'd flayed it back so often he'd installed a latch and hinge. Practice makes perfect storytelling. Past him and to the right, I could see one giant downed cottonwood spanning the Mimbres's diminutive canyon. Its bark had all fallen away, leaving wood weathered white, exposing its human contours, elegantly smooth, inviting, and hard.

"Tell us about your first vision quest," Chuck said. "The one you told us about last year."

"Oh yeah." Sparrow smiled. "This is how not to do a vision quest. I was thirty-one and living in a commune in Vermont, and one day I read *Black Elk Speaks*. I decided I had to do a vision quest on Harney Peak—never mind that Black Elk's vision was when he was nine years old and very sick, and that it wasn't on Harney Peak at all. I'd gotten it in my head, and I had to do it. So out I went to South Dakota and found Harney Peak and started hiking up it late in the afternoon. I had on jeans and a sweatshirt, no food, no water, no rain gear. It took me six hours to get to the top, plus it rained. It was very cold that night, and

I stayed awake shivering. Luckily it was August, and the sun dried me off the next day. I'd done no preparation—I just thought I was supposed to cry for a vision, and that's what I did—all day and all the next night, which was also very cold. I still can't believe I did it." I couldn't fathom such nuttiness.

"The third day," he went on, "I did a breathing thing that jolted me into a full-blown altered state. My consciousness was embodied in the mountain. I became the mountain. My skin felt like the surface of rock. I'd feel something on my shoulder and look over, and there'd be a squirrel running across the ground.

"Good thing something happened, or I'd still be up there." He laughed again. "Anyway, then I could hike down. And that's when I got my name, too. I was lying on the ground and a flock of sparrows kept circling right over my head for a long time. So on the way down, I decided to change my name."

He looked over at Chuck. "Thanks for asking." And went on.

"But that was the start of what I call my crazy period. Altered state after altered state, fasts on mountaintops in Mexico and Guatemala. All sorts of nutty stuff. I say now 'higher power' was my addiction. But I wasn't getting anywhere. Finally, after five years, I went to Steven and Meredith and apprenticed with them and got straightened out and finally grew up, I think, and was able to begin my real work."

He gazed at the now cold abalone shell in the middle of our circle. "Oh, yeah. Charlotte. Oh, Charlotte. Thank you, Charlotte!" And he shook his head, looking up toward the treetops, and grinned. "Before I worked with Steven and Meredith I was in a terrible relationship with this woman named Charlotte. She was beautiful, though. I'll give her that. When it ended, I hit bottom. Really terrible. And I swore I'd never feel that bad again. I didn't care what it took, what I had to do; I'd do anything. Finally I started going to ACOA—Adult Children of Alcoholics. My father wasn't alcoholic, just abusive. He beat me a lot when I was a child. Working with ACOA, I figured out I'd internalized the shaming father. So one of the things I did was inner-child dialogues—I wrote them an hour a day for a year, every day. My right hand was my adult; my left hand was my kid. Only after I'd managed to make my inner parent more loving and accepting could I get on with what I felt was my life's work."

Smiling again, he looked around at us, relaxed about stories he'd told many times. The grimness and confusion of the life they described hadn't pulverized him. He was a wounded healer. "Here," he seemed to say, "I came out the other end of the convoluted chamber of horrors. Trust me. I know."

"So, that's me. Thank you all. Time for dinner?"

🪶

That night I slept in long grasses by the gurgling Mimbres. Pine needles fell around me with the light ping of raindrops. At two I woke chilled from dew on my bag, pulled on a fuzzy jacket, and sank back into this dream:

> The room is bare and large. Bright. Two other people, but far away, small. Through a side door a javelina rushes in, snarling, aggressive, its hooves clattering on the stone floor. Once before I'd fought the creature with a huge knife, and I worry it will remember me, remember I'd fought hard and wounded it. As I run, I call for help, see its grey ruff flare, its yellow stiletto teeth lap each other. It leaps on me and knocks me into the sunken fire pit. No fire. Will I die? I struggle, but its dense weight keeps me down, its musk overpowering. I expect its teeth in my jugular and scream for help again. Panic. But it only nibbles on my glasses leash. Delicately. Its fur brushes my cheek as it chews. My friends pull it off.
>
> I escape through a side door, but circle around to the back, wanting to return. On the fire escape, I run into a dozen commandos, dressed in black, with machine guns. We talk. They're

not a threat to me, but I don't want to be part of their fight. I climb back down.

The stairs lead to a high school music room, deserted but for the stored French horns, clarinets, battered drum sets. Music stands crowd one side. I'm not supposed to be there. Through the dim corridors I slip away, avoiding the kids I hear around corners. I find the front door.

Outside, the traffic's terrible. How will I ever get home?

Back in the circle after breakfast, morning light.

"Anyone have any dreams?" Sparrow asked.

I rolled my eyes, dismayed. No one else said a word.

"And she rolls her eyes." Sparrow laughed. "OK, let's smudge first."

The smoking sage made its way to everyone again; we said our thanks, and I tried not to hear the leaden tones of a prayer before a Rotary Club meeting.

Sparrow began, "In this culture, we treat dreams as personal events. Some other cultures have a more communal idea of self and understand dreams as dreams of the group. We're partly going to do that here. The dreamer will tell the dream, then we'll go around and explain it as if we'd each had the dream." He looked at me. "Mary?"

No way out. I told them about the javelina, the commandos, the music room, the traffic.

Sparrow said, "Awesome!" and grinned at me. "Ideas?"

"I don't know," I said lamely. "Except the threats get progressively less dangerous. From javelina to traffic." I turned to Chuck next to me.

"Since I had this dream," he said, "I noticed the commandos were on the fire escape, and that says to me I'm threatened but trying to get away from a fire, or something else dangerous. And the javelina— what's a javelina?" He paused and looked at me, his pale eyes friendly.

He'd been on a quest the year before and knew the routine, but didn't mind breaking form.

I smiled. "A kind of wild boar that lives in the Southwest. They're about two and a half feet tall with coarse hair and a big ruff, and they have very sharp canines."

"Ah, gotcha," said Chuck. "The javelina was attacking me because I'd chased it before with a butcher knife. But it doesn't really hurt me even after it gets me down. Maybe what I fear isn't as dangerous as I think." Chuck nodded that he'd finished and looked toward Doug, next around the circle, who picked up. "When I woke up with this dream—" He echoed Chuck's response in his own words.

Sparrow slid into my dream more pointedly than the others. "The javelina seems like a part of me I'm trying to avoid. Maybe something like anger." He looked quizzically at me. I raised my eyebrows and offered him no confirmation. "Since it isn't harming me, but just eating my glasses, maybe I need to change the lenses I use to see the world. I seem to be avoiding these threats and finally just sneak out into traffic. The other thing that struck me was that I did these things alone. There's something about aloneness."

No judgment, I thought, though I didn't think I avoided anger. But aloneness: it pricked an inner tender spot. The strength of independence: self-reliance. The weakness of independence: distance.

Doug also had a dream for us to dissect, and the next morning Chuck and Vern gave us their own dream fodder.

As we stepped for each other through our sleeping adventures, we practiced storytelling, the dreams themselves doing part of the construction work. Rationality carried little weight. And none of us could quite see what secrets we might be revealing. Because we each in turn needed to inhabit another's dream, we focused more carefully on the telling and on the teller, and our listening to each other sharpened. When we spoke in first person, we offered interpretation to the dreamer, but by the back door we also revealed ourselves. And, just as importantly, we not only expressed content but we each became more available to the small community: with voice, body, and a palpable vibration of self. Each level provided a way to bond a little; each level let us relax into unguarded, honestly felt expression, something that has also been called authenticity. All good skills for our real lives.

In my dream I may have been alone, but by the Mimbres none of us could claim solitude. Though we were still nearly strangers, for hours we exchanged crucial, worrisome details of our lives, shifting back and forth between performer and attentive audience, with an unusual openness. Even I, in mild camouflage, tried to be accurate.

We were four men, two women, all between forty-two and fifty-two. We sat in the thick of midlife. Crisis or not, we'd lived enough since puberty to have histories and identities. We weren't a men's group drumming in the forest hoping to reclaim our masculinity or a women's group invoking the goddess under a full moon. We were here as humans, but our humanness included our gender. How could masculine/feminine issues not pop up?

I couldn't have invented a woman more opposite from me than Jenny. She took care of people for a living, worried about getting lost in the wild, seemed uncomfortable in her body, felt incompetent building things, and hated math. Her understandings were broad and nonspecific. Though her enthusiasm and warmth had won me over the first morning, she embodied a feminine I'd actively avoided for myself. She admitted to me she felt intimidated in our circles. "They're so male, so dominated by logos," she said with distaste, as if talking resembled an unruly, slimy fungus.

From my silent childhood on, I'd been more comfortable with guys: as sandbox playmates, tennis partners, poker buddies, confidantes, work colleagues, and lovers. I liked men a great deal. As equals. In my kid-life, I sometimes did have trouble with boys who wanted to help the girl (surely what I was, with my long hair and delicate bones, despite my height). How many hammers had I forcibly hung on to when some klutzy boy wanted to take it and hammer for me? I guess they'd learned at home that girls couldn't hammer. But I could hammer as well as any of them.

My taste in toys went to erector sets, with their intricate instructions—the more complicated the better—and their pierced girders, pulleys, and tiny engines. Dolls never held the least bit of appeal until that magical age of fluid child/adult fantasy, when my friend Pam and I discovered Barbie and Ken could have sex. Sort of.

My pants pockets kept stones and pencil stubs and scraps of paper and shells and feathers and seed pods. I hated pocketless skirts. I hated all skirts. Trees gave me the chance to climb into escape, temporary and terrifying, but still expansive. Math gave me clean logic and arcane but easily decipherable language.

I didn't like the obligatory mother-daughter talk when I was twelve. Neither did my mother. She copped out by reading me sheets she'd snagged from church. When she got to the chapter "Masturbation," she said, "Oh, we don't need to get into that," and skipped ahead to "Sanctity of Marriage."

By the spring when I fell for my first love, I'd had enough dates and enough boyfriends to know another assembly-line female imperative. As a kid, I was supposed to play with dolls in mother-training; as a lean teenager with a sweet veneer, I was supposed to apply the sexual brakes, paradoxically alert to finding a way into blissful wifedom. But wife and charming helper didn't match my aspirations. Still, not until I fell in love did it occur to me that always being the one to say no might have some unintended consequences in the complicated dances of love and power. Though not completely aware of the ramifications, I finally understood I could choose *yes* as legitimately as I could choose *no*. In the end, yes and no mattered less than that the choice could be mine. And *yes*, from a position of choice when an attraction had gone past a certain point, gave me more strength. And I didn't always wait to be asked. With my first love, I'd never hinted at *no*, and not until months later did I admit I'd been a virgin. As Jill Ker Conway would say, I operated with *agency*.

That first morning under tall narrowleaf cottonwoods and alligator junipers, Sparrow had set the tone for the rest of our ten days. In a spot closer to the narrow Mimbres, we ate and socialized around a campfire, drifting in and out of easy conversations, speaking loudly to be heard over Doug's deafening Primus stove, Sparrow wisecracking at every opportunity. But our circles concentrated our attention as if it had been passed through a purifying fire: almost everything extraneous burned off. But Sparrow knew what truly serious required—not the ponderous seriousness that kills liveliness, but a seriousness real enough to include laughter and lightness. "I'm not interested in anything that doesn't have practical value," he'd said. The lightness broke down the barriers of taking ourselves so seriously the seriousness itself became like iron bands interfering with movement. Moses wasn't bringing down the tablets from the mountaintop.

In the circle, we finished with dreams for the day.

All of us had spent time hiking and camping, but this adventure had more than tents and camp stoves; it had an agenda of intuitive knowing, mediated by language, in an environment mostly cleared of modern distractions. This conscious preparation before an altered fasting state jibed with what I'd come to in my summer research. But another part of the agenda became increasingly obvious. We dealt not only with our individual minds but also with the Mind of Nature in an embodied, palpable way. Even sitting by the Mimbres under junipers and cottonwoods in the light breezes, with owls hooting in the night, offered us more than simply an isolated stage set for the dream. The land's richness gave us ready metaphors and a groundedness impossible to ignore. Slowly I began to sense how primal the experience could become.

Academics have used the phrase *re-enchantment of the world* to talk about counteracting the Enlightenment split between mind and body, the split that afflicts us like crypto bacteria. We *were* talking, as Jenny noted with such distaste, but not about those abstract concepts. We addressed our real lives, ways to conceive of nature and modify conditions so we could trigger our own re-enchantment: mind with Mind, body with Nature, mind with Nature, body with Mind. Was such re-enchantment, the expanding of possible connections, *spirit*?

Something indefinable had kicked in, and I became more and more receptive.

Eating had long before lost its position as gatekeeper between my self and the outer flux; and my voice, while not as fluid as I'd like, also rarely played a part—even by its absence—in propping up my walls. But my preconceived notions, often bolstered by childhood artifacts, my scientific training, an ex-New Yorker's sophistication, and perhaps an excessive groundedness, had partly taken their places. I'd begun to see that my skepticism was not only an outgrowth of my dismissive rationality but also a protection against fear. I feared being a credulous fool, despite my own experience. I feared public exposure, of letting something that mattered to me be seen or heard. I'd protected myself at a crucial time in my past, and self-protection stuck like bubble gum to my shoe. Beside the tumbling Mimbres, light filtering down to the smooth stones along its shallow bottom, I felt all that begin to dissolve.

We wandered for ten minutes, peeling off layers and snacking. We each picked up a rock from the stream, as Sparrow had requested. As I returned from my stroll in the cool water with a loaf-sized grey stone, Jenny stopped me on the path.

"I just wanted to check that we're doing OK." She gazed at me with a look of concern.

"Oh yes," I said, not wanting to admit my unease with her. She'd clearly caught it.

"It's so male here; I'm more uncomfortable than usual. I'm so glad you're here too." And she reached forward and hugged me. "I'm usually

really touchy-feely, hanging off my women friends, but that's hard here."
I nodded without speaking and smiled, easy in my camouflage.

We returned to the circle together. Chuck nudged his Therm-a-Rest
into new shade, still in long jeans, not wanting to toast his pale skin.
Vern stayed close to the downed trunk, leaning against it in his mirrored sunglasses. Jenny had put on a short-sleeved T-shirt but kept her
legs wrapped in her voluminous cotton print skirt, staying in cool
shade, too. Doug, like me, had changed into shorts and crimped himself back into his Therm-a-Rest chair. Sparrow wore cream-colored
cotton shorts, and an open khaki fisherman's vest over his bare chest.
His canvas cap shaded his sun-reddened face, which matched his arms
and legs, their pale hair glowing in a golden aura. He looked up at the
sky through tree limbs and angled his own Therm-a-Rest chair back
into the sun.

On the grass, four stones we'd gathered from the stream lay in their
own tight circle, surrounding the blackened abalone shell with its burnt
sage. Sparrow swallowed his last bite of apple and began again.

"This is an official 'teaching.' I learned it from Steven and Meredith
in the mid-eighties, and it's been really helpful to me. The stones are
aligned to the four directions, but they also make both a circle and a
cross. This cross has equal arms. Native Americans say Christians have
made their cross with way too long a vertical axis: too much Father Sun,
not enough Mother Earth." We laughed. "The circle divided this way
is a symbol for many things: a year, a day, a human life. It's called the
Shields of the Four Directions: the four seasons, a metaphor for our lives.

"We need the lessons from each season in order to move on. It's like
a stool with four legs: one's missing and—." He frowned and shook his
head. "Shields are modes of expression, shields to take into battle. But if
you can't take the shield off, it turns into a mask, a defense system. Each
shield has lessons you need to learn to be whole, but each one also has
a shadow." He looked around at us. The wind ruffled the long grasses
behind him.

We'd moved straight into the margins of therapy. This was a developmental model, but easy to remember, easy to relate to, grounded in its particulars.

"East is yellow: spring, entrance, exit, birth, death." He pointed to each rock in turn. "South is red: summer, childhood. West is black: fall, adolescence, inwardness and introspection. North is white, the time of winter, adulthood, when we live on what we have harvested."

He laid his tanned right hand on the red rock's jagged bulk and kept it there while he talked, sometimes rubbing the stone with his fingers. "The two lessons from childhood are trust and innocence. Trust: Enough that you can say to yourself, 'This is a great place to be,' both your location and your body. 'I'm easy and comfortable here.'" In the filtered light, going over material he'd covered countless times with others, he seemed comfortable exactly where he was, a poster boy for trust. "Innocence is a belief that at your core you are good. Your unmediated impulses are basically all right. It's the story of the Garden of Eden. Before the Fall.

"Now, if we learn those lessons of trust and innocence, many gifts come to us." He counted them off on his free hand. "Emotion: expression that's not considered beforehand; it just comes out. Children don't feel anger; they *are* anger. And then it's gone. Next, curiosity: a passionate, active engagement in the world. A love of exploring. Last, the senses, sensuality, eroticism: ease and delight in the body, the physical world. When you put those things together—emotion, curiosity, sensuality— it's the basic passion of life. But it's also very centered in the self.

"When you're stuck in the South, you can't take the shield down. Typically for men in this culture, it's materialism—little boys in men's bodies, lots of toys. For women, it's Barbie doll stuff; you see yourself as a sex object. In this shield, the only kind of relationship is erotic. There's no connection to anything else. Just an affair of the organs."

He lifted his hand from the rock. "Most intentions to go on a quest have to do with the South Shield: with reclaiming and re-experiencing the delight and playfulness of childhood, reconnecting with deep emotions, rediscovering passion for life." He looked around the circle. "Questions?"

I couldn't resist. "I had a paradoxical childhood: much love, but also much control and judgment. I'm curious and I'm comfortable in my body, but my emotional side mostly stayed shut down when I was a kid. So the story seems more complicated. The shield divided up. Any thoughts?"

"The thing that comes to mind is that perhaps you were loved for your position in the family, not for who you were. So—mixed messages created a mixed reaction? That make sense?"

I nodded. It almost made sense.

He covered the smooth black stone I'd brought from the stream with his left hand. Its top had dried to pale grey, but its bottom remained wet and dark.

"West. Adolescence. The lesson here is mainly introspection, the way a plant's energy in the fall moves into its roots. Looking within develops a sense of self and self-consciousness, a way to determine what you value. It allows you to make bonds with others. The gifts here are self-awareness, self-love, empathy, forgiveness, and all the qualities of personal relationship. You go into the darkness of the personal unknown to seek self-knowledge. For example, dreams"—he paused— "or shamanic journeys. Most traditional psychotherapies are expressions of the West Shield."

I sensed Doug stir beside me. This relegated psychotherapy to only a quarter of the circle.

"The shadow? Self-criticism. An overemphasis on symbols and meaning and therefore an avoidance of the other shields, an avoidance of being in the world. There are lots of therapies for depression, and none are as effective as exercise, an activity from the South Shield. Meaning is fluid. There's a brief story Joseph Campbell tells. A fox eats a chicken. What's the meaning of that? It depends on whether you are the fox or the chicken. Or the farmer. Hmmm?" He looked around. Everyone looked up as he paused. "Meaning is in the head, but people sometimes believe they're after meaning when they're really after experience."

This time Vern moved as if to say something but remained quiet.

"The cultural gender stereotypes of the West Shield are: Men don't go there. Women get stuck there."

He paused again. "Questions?" No one had any, but we were deep into note-taking.

He moved his hand to the white stone. "North. In some sense, this is associated with mind. It sees the bones, the structure of things. The lessons here are wisdom and the giveaway.

"By wisdom, I mean several things. You understand that you can't change the past—your parents and childhood—with all its liabilities and resources. In the North, you look around and see what the situation is, then ask the adult question, 'What are we going to do?' That requires determination. First to make a determination, then to have determination to act. If you're in the North Shield, you have no problem with acting."

Jenny rearranged her legs under her skirt. An empty horse trailer rattled down the road.

"The second lesson is the giveaway—gifts to others, to your people. After you've discovered who you are, after the full development of your South and West Shields, the North is an expansion of your identity. It's not about martyrdom, but about fully embodying yourself, whoever you are. And it's a recognition of interdependence.

"Sometimes a quest from the North is to find the answer to the question, Who are my people?

"Being stuck in the North? Talking heads. It's being stuck in your head, a common place to get mired down in this culture."

He took a swig of water from his water bottle, letting us catch up with our notes. He rested his left hand on the lumpy yellow stone.

"East. Springtime, sunrise, the doorway in the tomb. The

transformative doorway. Here's where spirit comes into form from nothing." He stopped abruptly. One of the orange butterflies flashing through
the clearing had landed on the tip of his bill. He froze and looked up
at it, moving only his eyes. It took off. He shook his head as he glanced
around at us, then continued.

"The lesson? Illumination. But the East is also the land of paradox.
What we're searching for is beyond what we know. The last impediment
to enlightenment is the desire for it. Paradox.

"Here—and on your fast—it's important to release your intention.
You can't get there without it. But you also can't get there with it.

"Qualities or metaphors? Inspiration, imagination, creativity, the
muses, prayer, the circle, ritual—ritual where we use the known to
pluck a chord that resonates beyond the known. Into deep brain structures, or wherever."

I nodded. It was the best explanation of ritual I'd heard.

"The South, West, and North are ways of accumulating and developing wisdom. In the East, let it all go wild. Do you all know the Tibetan
forest spirits? They're called daikini—literally, wisdom that's gone wild.
It's important to learn the lessons and the forms, but the point is to let it
grow beyond itself. The point is to let it all go wild.

"East is the opposite of West—going beyond the self to find your
self's essence. It's the force, practice, methods, and experience of the
walls coming down. Getting out of the box. Way out."

I loved his paradoxes. I loved that he nearly tossed out his whole
system.

"And the shadow? It's got one, too. It's avoidance or lacking access.
Or seeing everything as god. Like certain elements of the New Age
think, 'High, high, happy, happy.' It's a refusal to recognize that sometimes life sucks.

"Often people come on a quest wanting to experience the East, but
they really need to consider and work on South and West issues. Some
people use the shields as a way to structure their fasts. On the first day,

they concentrate on experiencing the South and childhood: they play in the river, cover themselves with mud and wash it off, and so on; second day, the West and introspection, et cetera."

He stopped, glanced around the circle, then, as he had many times before, let his eyes rest on mine. I figured I just offered encouraging eye contact.

I liked the system, its acknowledgment of shadows, of paradox, of synergy. I thought again of the flow between inside and outside. The shadow for each shield meant a gripping, a movement stopped by some invisible force—the way I'd once been silenced by a steel trap slammed shut on my vocal cords. The shields' shadows described four ways to be stuck: stuck in your genitals and your hungry reptilian brain; stuck in your dark, swirling psyche, neural net sparking along the same old patterns, driven solely by a search for meaning, for memory; stuck in your stunning mind, your cerebral cortex always hot on the trail of logical solutions, linearity; stuck in the outer ozone with everything fading in and out of angelic splendor, all butterfly, no tomato hornworm chowing down the harvest.

Though Sparrow had added many details, his lesson for me seemed to confirm what I knew already and wanted more of: be light, don't grip, keep it all moving.

Lunch between my truck and Sparrow's rental car. The others had collected by the cold fire ring, thirty yards away. He mixed up some hummus, spread it on a tortilla, and added chopped tomatoes, green peppers, red onion, and canned black olives. Much better than my peanut butter, jelly, tortillas, and chips.

"So," Sparrow asked, shedding his guide's tone from the circle, "do you have a writing practice?" After Vern's reference to his recent writing epiphany, both Sparrow and I had mentioned we also wrote.

"I do," I said, glad to have an answer. "Effulgences."

"Which are?"

"First thing when I get up, I have tea, sit down at my table, and write whatever comes into my head. One page in a six-by-nine notebook. They're more poems than anything. Then I close the book and sometimes don't read them for days."

"Is effulgence a real word?" He chewed away.

"Yup. But I had to look it up to make sure. It means radiant splendor." I cleared my throat. "But I named them before I found out exactly what it meant. Wishful thinking."

"Maybe not," he said. "Have you done them for long?"

"About a year. Mostly they pop out as complete and finished things. It's stunning. It's the first time I've consistently made things that seem to come from beyond myself." This was true. I'd left my camouflage elsewhere.

He listened carefully.

"How about you?" I asked.

"Yeah. I try to write every day. A couple years ago while I was out leading a quest, I sat down with a pad. And nothing happened. Nada. I have such trouble with authority, I couldn't get out one word. But then, because I was sitting by a river, I thought to write the river a letter. I wrote 'Dear River,' and the words just flowed. I've been writing letters to the river ever since."

At first light that morning, Sparrow had folded himself under one of the cottonwood bridges with a yellow legal pad and sat writing until our meeting time.

"So those letters to the river are a little like your effulgences, but mostly I write them while I'm leading quests. I have hundreds now." He made a face of inundation. The accretion of the radiant East. "Sometimes I write them at home, but it's easier when I'm sitting by a real river."

After lunch, Doug the apprentice relayed information about practical matters: tying up our tarps, drinking enough water, using sunscreen. All matters, I thought, of the North Shield, though Sparrow labeled them "the physical plane."

On the third morning, Sparrow sat grinning at us, holding up a brown rattle, shaking it lightly. "This is ritual." He looked around at us. "It can move you into an altered state."

"Not ceremony?" I asked while everyone else stayed obediently quiet.

"Ritual and ceremony catalyze consciousness," he said. "Ritual changes it. Ceremony celebrates what already exists. It's confirmatory. Sometimes they overlap."

Smudging with sage, a plant that had been with humans since the Pleistocene, was ritual. It moved us into the circle's tone of engagement—sacred space, maybe, but without question our encounters expanded after the fragrant, sage-filled shell had been passed around the circle. We spoke more openly, listened more attentively.

My medicine walk, with its luscious but confusing neutrality followed by feeling like hell, had been ritual. I'd bookended it with small ceremonies—words on paper burned, turned to ash.

I thought again of my baptism ritual. My immersion in the marble pool hadn't meant what everyone intended it to mean; my belief in Christian doctrine had not been confirmed. Afterward, the Welch's grape juice and crumbled saltines making the rounds in heavy polished silver did nothing for me, despite their obscure conversion into Body and Blood. But the ritual hadn't been wasted. For nearly forty years, the sensations have remained, robust and engulfing. I'd been part of— no, the *focus* of—a public activity that resembled nothing I'd ever seen adults do, and that severely disrupted my categories. The preacher preached from the pulpit, shook hands after the service, behaved in an unshakably moral way, and consoled his flock. Yet for an hour, with witnesses silently cheering, he'd acted out with me and a dozen other nubile children a deeply erotic set piece. It had been wildly at odds with everything I thought I knew about religion. I'd thought religion dealt with some nearly inaccessible disembodied ether knotted tightly with unending instructions about being good. Period. That day I glimpsed something else: not the suddenly revealed hidden power of a system that could churn out such treacly magazines as *Ideals*, but the potential power of *doing*, of disrupting categories, of my own capacity to feel, of my ability to define my own experience. It hadn't been a big zero. Ritual. It had made me feel a hunger for something different, something more.

I turned my attention back to Sparrow, who had begun to describe traditional rituals and well-known ceremonies—so he said—that would be of use to us on our fasts. He reserved the afternoon for a discussion of self-generated ceremony.

"One way to look at it," he said, "is that rituals activate or rely on the old brain, what some call the reptilian brain. They bypass our cognitive filters, so we understand with a broader self. Changed consciousness changes our filters for experiencing a world much more complex than the one where we think we live. You can also consider what the Mayans say: gods don't care about humans at all. But they're a lot like bears. When humans create great beauty and wonder, it's like honey. The gods can't stay away."

In front of me, an inch-long caterpillar crept across the grassy landscape. Its main fuzziness shone pale gold, but down the center of its back ran an irregular dotted black line. At its front and back, long ebony antennae extended like thin horns, and at one end, white whiskers quivered. I put my pen down in front of it, and it crawled up the barrel, exploring its new situation as I continued carefully to take notes.

"Medicine," Sparrow repeated, "is anything that brings us to wholeness. It's important to see and acknowledge the kind of medicine we receive. Medicine is a gift from Spirit."

I raised my head and looked at him across the circle. At once, with a start, I saw him clearly as the mask vision that had hovered beside me as I lay tired and headachy on my medicine walk. My god, I thought, What's going on?

He had the red-blond coloring of many Scots with Viking blood and loved the sun. His eyebrows, fine eyelashes, and moustache had bleached as his skin had darkened, so his face had become mono-chrome. His ears lay close to his head; and for the first time he'd removed his bill cap, and I could see his head was entirely bald. His features were largish, and his face enormously expressive. His lower lip was broad and full and had reacted to the sun, so it matched his skin. Together, his moustache and lower lip gave the impression his lips were turned in between his teeth. From the first, his eye contact with me had been so concentrated that I'd been uneasy, though I'd gotten used to it. I knew no one else who looked remotely like the mask vision, but Sparrow himself could have been with me on that high open mesa. I stared hard at him. Why hadn't I noticed before?

"There's no better or worse medicine," Sparrow continued, unaware of the jolt that had just hit me. "In dreaming consciousness, 'I' isn't sepa-rate from 'it.' A caterpillar's world is as complex in its own realm as ours is." The caterpillar still crawled slowly up my pen.

Vern asked, "What's the difference between medicine and medicine animal?"

Sparrow answered, "Here's an analogy. Say you go to a party and have a great connection with someone. That's like an animal giving you medicine. Insight, whatever. But a medicine animal is different. It's like having a relationship with someone over time. And there's reciprocity." I took notes, but I hardly heard what he said. I couldn't possibly be imag-ining it, could I?

If Sparrow was the face, maybe he had the answer to "how," though that made no rational sense. Categories dissolving like crazy. Sparrow talked to each of us individually before our fasts. Doug, as apprentice, joined him. I thought I'd better ask them about my medicine walk. I doubted I'd confess I'd seen Sparrow's face.

We'd sat in our circle again way past lunch. Time for a break.

"Who wants to go for a walk with us after lunch?" Sparrow asked.

"I really want to talk to you," I said, laughing, jumping on the chance, "But I also really want to take a nap."

"Take a nap until three, and we'll see you then," said Doug, who kept track of clock time. That gave us an hour until we reconvened at four.

From the back of my truck, I gobbled peanut butter on a tortilla with some corn chips and headed to the deep grass next to my tent. Held half awake between breezy light and the melodious Mimbres, I dozed for an hour, then joined Sparrow and Doug at the fire ring.

We didn't go for a walk, but only stepped to the river's gravel edge. I rested my upper back against the smooth, pale, downed cottonwood; Doug leaned on it to my right; and Sparrow stood to my left, ankle deep in the cool water, hands on hips, shirtless in the sun, listening to me intently.

"I want to talk to you about my medicine walk," I began, and told my tale: the elk, the aspen, my intense headache, the face, and the question "how." "It looked like a mask," I said, not admitting it looked like Sparrow. I didn't think they'd believe me. I hardly believed it myself. "And the closest I came to finding a mask like it was a pair of Inuit shaman's masks from an island in the Bering Strait."

"Let me get the timing clear," said Sparrow. "A herd of magnificent animals runs straight at you, you're treated to hours in a gorgeous, hallucinatory aspen forest that seems to watch you, and then you wonder where your spirit guides are? And then you get a headache and see a face that won't talk to you?" He cocked his head at me.

"Yeah, I know. But I'd chosen where to hike. I knew lots of wildlife was up there. And the aspens, too."

"But you always choose where to hike, don't you?" asked Doug.

"Right. And a herd of elk has never run toward me before."
He nodded.

"And you want to know what the face was saying?" Sparrow asked and looked at me hard. "I think it was saying 'How? Mary, you know how already.'" That had never occurred to me. He continued, "On the first day I heard you say your voice was blocked and then I see you interact with people in the circle and you're perceptive and articulate and lively and not at all blocked. You're already as fluid as water." He paused again, clearly not finished. "And you've majored in being out of the corral."

I stared at him a moment. I felt like I'd been caught with my hand in the cookie jar. I'd come on this quest largely to research a piece of writing: not a serious sin and the kind of thing many others had done, but I still knew I was a spy. I'd not been dishonest, exactly, but perhaps I'd settled on something too familiar in order to seem like I was with the program.

I said, "I don't feel blocked, exactly, but I can feel an internal knot—" I touched my hands to my stomach. It was true.

"Maybe so. But it's small." Sparrow's voice had an edge it hadn't had in our group circles. "There are two reasons to go on a hero's journey. The first is the most common: something is wrong, out of kilter, and the hero goes on the journey in order to fix it. The other reason is to celebrate. I think that's your reason. I think you need to go out there and celebrate your gifts, not ask for more, and maybe then you'll get something else. Maybe." He'd nailed me.

Doug said, "Maybe the answer is in images, not words?" A good thought. He went on, "And you might think about sacrifice. Sparrow's implying you're being a little greedy." Doug wasn't skilled yet at not provoking defensiveness.

I nodded, but sacrifice reminded me too much of childhood churchy lectures. And it fit more with a view of a world filled with limited commodities: give up x to get y. The either/or view. So much in real life grew

when you gave it away. Love, for example. Love was not barter. You
didn't have to choose between having love and giving it away.

"Maybe I'm projecting," Sparrow said. "I keep doing all sorts of
workshops when people tell me I don't need any more training—and
I think you're in the same place. Claim who you are and go for it." He
shifted in the stream and stepped a little closer. "Let me ask you this.
What if you accepted that you're the 'golden girl'?"

My face scrunched up as if I'd just bitten an unripe persimmon. "Ugh."

He laughed. "You should see how you look."

I frowned, wondering if he'd understood after all. "Golden chains
are still chains," I said, not willing to abandon my restraints.

But I'd unexpectedly passed an internal gate. It didn't matter just
then whether the face I'd seen on the medicine walk had looked like
Sparrow. Back here on the decidedly grounded plane, the goal was
to understand myself as accurately as possible and move from there.
The guide had functioned as guide. Without knowing how much skepticism I still harbored, he'd told me to get serious. I'd already chewed
long on my lack of voice, but he'd seen me—heard me—clearly: I no
longer lacked a voice. Whatever the next step, I had to take it and stop
being so calculating. Really stop. This quest, this impending fast, was
about something different than my stated intention and even about
something different than my hidden agenda. Another layer peeled
away, but I couldn't see what lay beneath it.

A palpable shift. The charged part of our talk was winding down.

Sparrow said, "I really want to give you a hug." I smiled and put my
arms around his bare, warm back as he reached around my shoulders.

I hugged Doug, too. He needed to practice hugging: he'd not quite
learned how to relax into a nonsexual physical encounter.

"So how do you know Kit?" Sparrow asked, and I explained.

Doug said, "Think I'll go change." And Sparrow wailed after him as
he climbed the bank, "Don't ever change!" Doug laughed weakly. Old
joke, I guessed.

I asked Sparrow, "Do you guide lots of quests during the year?"

He said, "Yes, but mostly in the summer and fall. This is the last one this year. Then I can rest for the winter, except for one weekend workshop a month I do with men."

"It must be hard. It's so emotional. Do you get burned-out?"

He said, "It is hard, but not in the way you'd think. I love being out; I don't get drained at all on the quests themselves. But this year I had things scheduled so tight. I'd get home, throw my clothes in the washer, answer a million e-mails, and head out almost immediately. I only had a day or two between. That's what was hard."

We could see everyone else had gathered.

Sparrow looked at his watch. "Oops. Late again."

Sparrow cruised through our many options for personal ceremony, which we could mix and match to fit our needs, a little like building Mr. Potato Head, but much more gutsy.

"For severance," he said, "you can bury, smash, burn. A retired principal once buried the brass nameplate from his desk. You can symbolically vomit something out of yourself—dig a hole, vomit your life's poisons, bury them. Wash off in the river, take off a piece of clothing or a ring."

He'd left off his bill cap, and with his bald head, his red skin, bleached eyebrows and moustache, and his mobile expressions, the resemblance to the image from my medicine walk became more and more striking.

He went on. "For incorporation, you take on. Ingest, carry, put on. Decorate your body—it's not as lightweight as it sounds. You can use ashes, mud, crushed berries. One guy painted himself as a warrior and ran through the forest naked and howling. Then he decided he needed a task. He snuck into base camp and stole half of my water." He laughed. "Of course I didn't even notice. I just figured I'd forgotten how much I'd brought.

"All kinds of movement. For example, transforming from old life to new life." He stood up and curled into himself, arms crossed, crouching, head down and muttered, "Old life." Then he leaped to the side, expanded and said, "New life! Make it as elaborate as you want. It may seem simple, but acting it out has a strong effect.

"Ritual scarring. I don't recommend this, though I have had some people who have done it. I don't want to feed any subconscious wish to harm yourself. One guy changed his name to Two Crows and made a design on his shoulder, upper arm. He burned it in with a buck knife heated in the fire. Two crows facing each other." We all groaned faintly. "It was nicely done," he said, as if that made it more palatable. "Malidoma Somé says, 'It's not pain that kills you, it's meaningless pain.'

"Then many possibilities for your threshold time. The threshold is just hanging out, entering mystery, getting in tune with where you are. It's about presence. Prayer—speaking from the known to the unknown. You let go lists and agendas and step into sacred space. You could yell your prayer." Tilting his head back, he bellowed at the top of his lungs, "You're so beautiful, I want to eat you up!" The stone wall across the road sent back an echo, and a pair of small birds started from the branch over his head. We laughed.

"You can rattle, chant, dance, dance like the Dervishes, gaze with soft focus, blindfold yourself and experience the world in a new way." He gave us more examples from his past quests.

"There's also value in just hanging out. When you're in nature, you're in a world humans didn't create. It created you. Expand yourself to meet it." He paused, looked around the circle, and waited.

I said, "I thought I'd do a ceremony for each element. Gaston Bachelard says, 'The elements are the hormones of the imagination.'"

Sparrow's eyebrows shot up. "Bachelard? I thought I was the only one who'd heard of him. I was reading him and Castaneda when I got kicked out of grad school!" I was equally surprised. Most people I knew had heard of Bachelard.

Vern asked, "Who?" He still had on his reflective sunglasses, and his bushy moustache barely moved when he spoke.

I answered, "French philosopher of science from the thirties. But he went past science. He wrote a series of books about the metaphysical aspects of the elements. *Water and Dreams* was one. That's where that quote came from. *The Poetics of Space* is best known, probably." I looked at Sparrow, who nodded. "A good read."

I explained my elemental ceremonies. Jenny spoke up after a moment, startling me she'd been so quiet. Yet another patterned skirt, this one purplish, covered her legs and a blousy sage top covered her arms. Its scooped neck revealed a delicate gold chain with a small owl pendant. "That sounds a little heady. Maybe you could be more physically involved?" Right. She was right.

"Ah," I said, and smiled at her. "Good idea."

Chuck said, "I want to do a piercing ceremony, but I haven't quite figured it out. I want to break through the shell around my heart. I was thinking maybe some cuts on my forearm. I'm open to suggestions." He still hadn't changed out of his long jeans, but his feet rested bare in the grass in front of him. His white T-shirt had a colorful mandala on its front with the words "Free Tibet" under it.

Sparrow said, "You want to cut yourself literally?"

I piped up. "Shall we wait while you go call your lawyer?"

He laughed and remained focused on Chuck. "Maybe you could do it symbolically? Did you bring any extra clothes you could sacrifice? Make a stand-in for yourself and pierce that?"

Chuck shook his pale head. "No."

We all sat and thought for a while, not wanting Chuck to hurt himself.

Finally I said, "I don't know if this resonates, but you could trace yourself on the ground, maybe with rocks around your silhouette, and then stab the ground inside?"

He nodded a little. "That's a possibility."

If Jenny, Vern, and Doug had planned their ceremonies, they kept quiet about it.

The next morning we packed up and drove fifty miles from the quiet Mimbres to the canyon the Gila River had cut into the rock mountains. The road curved briefly along one rim, then widened to a small parking area. Below us, a thousand feet down, the river's dark blue curves reflected the ever-cloudless sky. Along one side of the broad canyon, meadows alternated with airy stands of trees, and inside the current's gentle curves, wide gravel bars opened the vistas. During the short spring runoff, the river covered the bars, but in October a quarter mile of smooth stones and pale sand separated the trail from the water in many places. Except for the deep pools that sheltered Gila trout, the river ran shallow enough to wade, twenty to forty feet across. Through golden grass and scattered piñons, we hiked down to the shady groves along the river.

Sparrow admonished us, "You're looking for more than a campsite. Be a little practical, but find a spot that feels right. Use your intuition. Your spot will feed you while you're fasting. Hunt from your heart."

Jenny and Chuck didn't wade the river, but followed Sparrow so he could show them the freshwater spring. Jenny also wanted Sparrow to point out the caves above the river for something she had in mind. Vern, Doug, and I stepped through the ford to the path on the other side. In a couple hundred yards, Doug peeled off, climbing up the hillside to the right. About a mile farther, when the trail first skirted a gravel bar, I left Vern for the river. Almost immediately I saw a grove of trees downstream, at the end of the raised bank that supported the long strip of meadows and trees. The grove sat isolated from the upstream trees by a small treeless expanse. I angled toward it, stepping carefully across rocks and through dried plants whose seed heads resembled tiny medieval torture implements and stung my feet when they caught under the straps of my Tevas.

A foot below the cool water's surface, the stony bottom glistened and wavered under the quick current as I waded across. Just downstream from the grove, I scrambled up an eight-foot bank, dislodging sand and loosely anchored roots. Directly below the bank, an unmoving backwash supported dense stands of cattails and hollow reeds higher than my head; on the water's surface, duckweed had collected next to thick watercress along the edges. The quiet water gave off a faint swampy smell, damp and fecund, and mingled with the sharp aroma of grass and soil baking in the sun. The grove itself grew on a flat area paralleling the river for about sixty feet. Fifty feet back from the bank's edge, lichen-covered boulders marked the beginning of the canyon's steep ascent. A few young ponderosas and junipers stood shoulder-high, interspersed with older trees.

Two old trees dominated the grove.

Nearly in the middle, a rangy alligator juniper curved and bent its trunk high overhead, one large branch hanging dead to the ground.

The other venerable tree spread at the grove's back corner, next to the open upstream meadow whose grasses hid a subterranean pocket-gopher playground. About four feet up, this tree's wide trunk split into three equal branches, each meandering up in gentle contortions to the expansive crown. Green and grey lichen spotted its mottled bark, and except for its leaves, I'd have called it an oak. But its leaves didn't resemble any oak I knew. They were smooth, two-inch-long ovals with a point at each end, almost the color of sage. And no acorns littered the ground.

I didn't know how to label it, but something besides its name stopped me. About two feet from the ground, the main trunk dipped inward before it split into its branches. Spanning that indentation, lost in the bark on either side, was an old piece of barbed wire. The wire had surely been part of a corral from the days when cattle once grazed this canyon. The tree had grown around it, flourishing. Though the rusty wire still lay embedded, it made no difference to the tree, which had grown magnificently. I felt a tingling on the back of my neck as the hair stood up. I shivered. I had walked from base camp directly to a living footnote to my talk with Sparrow the day before. More articulately than words, the tree said, "You may still have a knot inside from your past, but you've healed over it. There's no need to try to rip it out, or even untie it; it's part of you now. Learn from me. Just be what you are and grow."

"Oh dear," I said aloud, flummoxed in spite of myself. I stared, not quite believing what I saw. I hadn't made this up. It had come to me in nearly as much of a jolt as when I'd recognized Sparrow's face from my medicine walk.

Finally I turned around. From the grove I could see far up and down the river, thanks to the gravel bars on both sides. Directly across the river, cottonwoods and willows leaped and turned in the wind. Behind them the canyon showed off yellow and orange rocky outcrops, the far wall rising grey. And always the river's murmuring washed over me.

Whether I knew how or still needed to learn, whether I had an inner knot or no inner knot, whether I accepted spirit guides or kept myself aloof, I wasn't cheeky enough to dismiss the force of the river's metaphor. Or dense enough to ignore the literal river, noisy and fresh, clear and moving.

Here's Gaston Bachelard, in a passage at the end of his book *Water and Dreams* I'd copied in my journal the week before.

Where is our first suffering? We have hesitated to say . . . It was born in the hours when we have hoarded within us things left unsaid. Even so, the stream will teach you to speak; in spite of the pain and the memories, it will teach you euphoria through euphuism, energy through poems. Not a moment will pass without repeating some lovely round word that rolls over the stones.

I'd found my spot, but for the sake of thoroughness, I thought I should at least make some attempt at comparison. I crossed the gopher field, breaking through into excavated passageways every yard, and took a look at the group of trees just upstream: not flat, restricted views, and no venerable trees.

Done.

🍃

That night, after we'd all told our stories about finding our places to fast—all surprisingly appropriate—and had a communal meal, Sparrow said, "While you all are out there fasting, I'll be here, in case anyone needs to come in. I'll also pray for each of you in the morning and evening. And you might want also to pray for each other." I clenched a little inside, as uncomfortable with the word *pray* as with *sacrifice*.

"What would each of you like the rest of us to pray for?" The answers came randomly from around the circle: "loving support, like a lullaby," "to feel less alone," "open path to spirit." I heard myself say, "I'd like to ask for balance: between directed focus and play, between inner and outer." From the corner of my eye I saw Sparrow smile and nod. Inside. Outside. Tenacious polestars.

"And what would you like, Sparrow?" Jenny asked, ever concerned, ever trying to be inclusive.

"Please let there be some brownies left over . . ."

🍃

From the air along the gentle river, in some antechamber of shadowy dream, a whispered idea woke me. The idea seemed to come half from my mind, half from the wind itself, hissing warmly through swaying oak branches over my head. I lay awake in my sleeping bag close to the river and couldn't hear the five others breathing their own dreams. One o'clock, ten million stars. I worried about the next four days, but the idea had nothing to do with food. The thought came partly from the poet Octavio Paz, but I felt I'd known it all along.

The creative, the erotic, and the spiritual spring from the same source; the experience of each is similar. They're simply different manifestations of the same mysterious energy. I understood this as three kinds of openness: to one's self, to another, and to the universe. I knew it ran counter to many traditions: set spirit against body, and don't even mention the creative.

But it fit the last several days.

I'd come to the Gila curious, alert to others' stories that had been raw but carefully told, alert to Sparrow's shaping of our days and our expectations: creative energies on overdrive. And I'd always been alert to my own tink-tinking construction projects.

I'd felt an openness unfold in everyone, a vulnerability and connectedness that was erotic but not sexual.

I'd come curious to see if spirit in this form could convince me of its presence, of its usefulness, of anything at all. I had to admit my narrow experience and long-standing resistance to "spirit" made the grouping more hopeful than certain.

Like any parsing out of the human realm meant to rescue experience from the chaotic, this triad seemed a tad heady, as Jenny might say. But then, Sparrow's Shields of the Four Directions did much the same thing. I also remembered his reference to Chellis Glendenning's description of "wholeness": a sense of safety, a belief in personal mastery, and a connection to something larger. An abstract system with practical applications.

When I thought of the creative/the erotic/the spiritual in terms of openness, I knew it to be an antidote to distance, to the barrier between inner and outer.

For two hours I lay awake, bare arms folded under my head, the river's musty smell swirling around me. Inside/outside. Art/eros/spirit.

Under both lay the luscious particularity that such broad concepts require to exist at all. *This* star-filled night, *this* warm wind, *this* damp ground, *this* river, *this* canyon, *this* mind, *this* body.

Soon after dawn, we all began wedging gear into our packs with great concentration. In silence. Not enforced, not even suggested, but we each faced an unknown and a personal trial that had no analogue in the larger culture. We'd chosen and prepared, but that only took us so far. I knew everyone's cerebral cortex was sparking away. But our boundaries had also grown more permeable. The physiology of permeability, however, eluded me.

After we'd all tightened the straps on our full packs, the six of us stood evenly spaced around the circle of stones Sparrow had laid on the sandy ground. One at a time we stepped into its center to be sent on our way with proper ceremony. With a pair of banded hawk wing feathers held crossed in one hand, Sparrow wafted sage smoke from the smudge in his blackened abalone shell and sang. Front, side, back, side, front, ending face-to-face, blessing us with words to reflect each of our intentions. My curiosity overwhelmed me. Sparrow's eyes stayed open, and mine, but no one else watched the ceremony. (Or was it a ritual? I couldn't keep them straight.) And Sparrow's irises, unaccountably, had become yellow-brown. "How the devil did he do that?" I asked myself silently. Yellow was the color of the East. East signified entrance, exit, the place of spirit, where all bets were off. For four days his eyes had been brown shading into green, but this morning, with the sun just cresting the ridge to the east, they'd turned pale gold.

When only Doug and I remained, I stepped into the circle for my own blessing, acutely aware how little it resembled any event termed sacred I'd ever encountered. I had no resistance, no judgment, no feeling of anything imposed on me. No barriers to whatever the moment became, unless curiosity itself could be understood as barrier.

Soft drafts of feather-blown air on my bare arms and legs, sage smoke and song rising around me. Not English words. Enveloped in voice and sharp fragrance. I closed my eyes briefly, caressed, as everyone had been caressed, with careful attention. Then Sparrow stood before me, our eyes level, his hand with the shell and smoldering sage swinging back and forth in front of my breast bone, the smoke still drifting up. We both smiled.

I've forgotten almost all his words, though he spoke at length and to the point. Finally he wound down, "May that small knot inside unbind . . . And may you find a fruitful relationship with Spirit. May you walk with Spirit hand in hand for the rest of your life." He stopped, moved back, and nodded, still smiling.

"Thank you," I said. I did feel blessed. I stepped out of the circle, then slipped into my pack and headed toward the river. Sparrow's voice faded behind me as he sang to Doug.

Stopping just before the shady path entered the flow, I drew a single line in the sand in front of me with my walking stick. Across the river, past the flood-arranged limbs and trunks high on the bank, the cottonwoods caught the first sun of their day. The night's wind had moderated but still lifted the late summer leaves in mesmerizing masses. They glistened with freshness.

I'd marked my own threshold, my own passage into a waking dream, and I spoke out loud, as if to friends.

"Thank you, river; thank you, trees and everything around me. Thank you, spirits, embodied or not, and though I still hesitate to say, 'I believe,' I hope you'll understand and not take offense when I ask your blessing anyway. And thanks for all my gifts. I ask your guidance and support in seeing my place in the world differently." And I crossed my line in the sand, then waded through the chilly river. I didn't quite believe, but having a conversational interchange with the river, the trees, and whatever invisible forces surrounded me—whether photosynthesis or gravity or anything else—felt as companionable as splitting a morning bagel with a lover. Relaxed and available. And I hadn't felt as if I'd started the conversation. Rather, I'd just kept up my end.

Almost immediately I ran into Vern climbing out of a pile of river detritus where he'd gone to find a walking stick. Vern and I were "stone-pile buddies." We'd separately rearrange stones once a day at a location between our fasting spots. A small element of safety. We hiked together the two miles to our stone pile, first along the trail, then waded in the shallow river.

"Good luck!" we said in unison as we turned in opposite directions.

Calf-deep in the clear water, I sloshed back upstream, past white-barked sycamores with enormous trunks; past banks overgrown with virgin's bower, a tangled vine covered with white flowers; past a gravel bar split into four parts by the river. Something odd had caught my eye earlier, but I hadn't wanted to stop then. Where the river made a bend just up from the bar, its curving force had eroded the sand-and-gravel bank into a clean vertical wall, about fifteen feet high. A canyon opened above. I knew a huge flood two weeks before had likely rearranged the river. An indentation about eight feet across and four feet in cut the bank's nearly smooth side as cleanly as if earth-moving equipment had excavated it. Just to the left of center, a delicate cascade of water trickled from the small side canyon. Somewhere above, perhaps in one of the old mines, the water had picked up iron. In its course to the river, the flow had slowly dropped its load, staining the sand deep red all along its path. But the stained sand showed through the water, and the rivulet itself still carried plenty of dissolved ore. This water looked more like blood than any water I'd ever seen.

A vertical red slit in a beige indentation. No earthwork artist could have constructed a more blatant, sexual representation of femaleness, complete with flowing blood. I'd never seen anything like it anywhere.

At the foot of the flow, a small delta fanned out into the river, creating a red shelf just above the water. I stood on it, staring.

"What?" I asked it sharply. I was primed for portents, but this seemed so heavy-handed I half expected to find a label from an LA gallery. But what? Gender issues? Sex hooked to Spirit? And the most obvious: something to do with menopause? Yes. All of the above. But what? The earthwork's opacity rivaled its drama, but this waking dream had wasted no time trotting out a potent symbol, as solid as the canyon's rocky cliffs.

The quest had swallowed me whole. I'd abandoned all hesitations.

I waded back up to my grove of junipers, young ponderosas, the venerable old oak.

As much for protocol as anything, I needed to tie up the unwieldy blue plastic tarp. No rain likely. One end of the main line I looped over an arm of the ancient oak. As I tied off the other end, I kicked up a tiny Swiss Army knife out of the sand. Red and sharp. I slid it into my shorts pocket. Using the Sparrow tarp-tying methodology, I secured the tarp to a stretched line, then began to support the corners with sticks. I propped one corner but couldn't find another loose stick long and straight enough to prop the other. But at one side of the grove I spotted a still-attached dead branch about shoulder height. I braced it with my left hand and pulled it down with my right until it snapped. As it broke, it whacked into the base of my left thumb.

"Oh, shit," I blurted, pissed. "What a dope. I didn't even need another stick. Compulsive." Quickly I looked down—no blood—and started back across the grove, remembering Chuck's obsession with piercing to release his inner bottleneck. This isn't even my imagery, I thought cheerily and glanced down at my hand again. Blood covered my thumb and forefinger and was dripping onto the ground in a steady stream.

I let go the stick, pulled my first aid kit from my pack, and walked to the edge of the grove where an old stump stood about table-high. Deal with it. I rinsed off my hand with water from my water bottle and doused some hydrogen peroxide on the two gouges before I looked over into the meadow's golden grasses. With an alarming brightness, they pulsed as if the meadow's gophers were setting off rafts of flashbulbs. My head no longer sat on my neck exactly right, and my left middle finger had begun to tingle. At the core of my pelvis, a hot wave formed and began to move up my spine.

"I'm about to faint. I really don't want to faint." Before the hot wave rose past my ribs, I pulled my bandanna off my neck, clamped it with my right hand on the still gushing gouges, slid to the ground, and leaned back against the stump. Eyes closed.

"I've never cut myself badly hiking alone." My inner dialogue tried to distract my fainting instinct. "And I'm not squeamish. I've never fainted. It hurts, but not that much. What's going on?" Even sitting didn't settle my head correctly back onto the top of my spine.

"Breathe," I told myself. "Deep. Slow. One, two, three, four . . ."

Ten minutes passed. I opened my eyes to check out the flashing meadow. Still flashing. Ten more minutes. Still flashing. I sat until the meadow had reconfigured itself from pure light back into dried grasses, and I could stand without wavering. I finished bandaging my hand. The deep cut on my thumb's lower knuckle must have nicked a blood vessel.

Half a day into the waking dream: a sexual earthwork with a small river of blood; a bloody libation spilled in a river grove presided over by an ancient oak; the oak itself healed gracefully over a piece of barbed wire embedded in its youth; my left thumb cut badly enough to nearly jolt me out of consciousness; a small, sharp, red knife. Good material for dream analysis. Except none of this had come from inside. Outside, all the way.

🐟

I'd concocted a simple set of ceremonies for the four elements, more related to the world than to any personal issue. But then, when Sparrow had busted me, he'd suggested I celebrate, and that's what I meant to do.

For each element the pattern was the same: I rang a small bell, thanked the element out loud, performed one symbolic act, then danced. I'd heeded Jenny too—I didn't want to be too heady.

Air: the front moving through; soft breath on your cheek; wind riffling a pond's still surface, invisible made visible; gusts combing thick grasses; the air hanging heavy and still before a storm; space unfolding and unfolding across transparent, dry distance. Fast for four days and you'll survive; stop breathing and you won't last long. I knew the relief of being able to breathe at all: growing up, I'd wheezed through many asthma-gripped nights. Breathe in the world; breathe out your self. Repeat.

I blew up a cerulean balloon I'd brought along and popped it, mingling my breath with the larger breath. "Pressure," I'd written months before in my journal, "needs to be released."

And after such formality, I let loose and danced. I danced as wind, mimicking the willows and cottonwoods across the river, my arms and body swaying and tossing, my movements light and buoyant. And I sang wordless songs with no melodies, my voice high and breathy. At first, self-consciousness danced with me, though I had no audience but trees and grasses. I'd spent countless hours in modern dance classes exploring imagery just this way. But being out with the wind put me in a forum with no human intermediaries, no history, no preexisting categories, no distance. Dancing for a nonhuman audience bore no resemblance to any dance class. As I moved through the afternoon light, I gradually relaxed. In unguarded solitude, I became human wind.

I spun and laughed, throwing my energies out beyond my fingertips, past my toes, off the top of my head, out my elbows and knees, filling my lungs, sucking air through my pores, spewing it out again—always feeling the touch of the wind on my skin, lifting all my tiny body hairs. My arms circled over my head and through dappled sun and shade. I pirouetted across the grove and back, scooping the air into my arms, kicking it away with my legs, letting it tumble around my body, gradually sensing the space around me expand and expand to fill the entire airy canyon, from rock wall to rock wall, open wide to the heavens.

My energy lifted and lifted, then slowly eased, like a long sigh.

"Wow," I said, surprised. I sat, still breathing hard, at the edge of the bank. And instantly, above the river in front of me, an osprey appeared, hunting for dinner. Facing the up-canyon wind, she hovered in one place, vibrating her wings slightly to stay balanced, now and then tilting to one side and recovering, using the moving air to stabilize herself. I could see her pale head and underside, her black mask. Once, she threw back her wings and plunged into the river, but caught no fish and returned to hovering. She vibrated. Once, she sailed downstream into a wide loop, circling back to the same spot. She vibrated. At last, with long wing beats, she traced the river's path at an airy distance and disappeared, still hungry, straight into the wind.

I hadn't eaten for twenty-four hours but felt no hunger. I felt only relaxed astonishment.

🐦

But the day hadn't finished.

Sparrow was a practical guy, more eager to help people become better parents or find more satisfying work than to hook them into some fiery current of universal energy. "Non-ordinary ways to deal with the ordinary," emphasis on *ordinary*.

In some traditional cultures, a person who feels death approaching will go to a special house. That's a sign it's time to tie up loose ends, to die to one's old life. And move on. He called it the Death Lodge.

"You say, 'The Death Lodge is now open,'" Sparrow told us, "then sit quietly, look around, watch the wind in the cottonwoods, let your mind drift, and in a while, you'll notice you start thinking about someone from your life. Speak to that person."

"The Death Lodge is now open," I said aloud, and watched the last warm light stream across the canyon and glow in the swirling cottonwoods, the willows beside them baring their silver backsides. I watched the wind in the cottonwoods, the mullein spikes on the gravel bar separating me from the river, the cattails swaying up from the quiet backwash, the duckweed on its surface. I smelled the moist, fecund but not unpleasant reek rising from the still water as the day cooled.

Impatience began to get the better of me.

"Hi, Mary Lib," my mother said. She spoke with no sound.

I saw how the flowers on the mullein spikes had opened progressively up their stalks, the uppermost ones blooming still.

"Hi," I said out loud, uneasy to have even her image join me in this canyon. I readily admitted to anyone except her that she was the most problematic person in my life. We had our long, tense mother-daughter history, but we also kept up the ongoing secret war: the War of the Hallmark Card. According to her, all emotions, all sentiments, all human complexity could and should be reduced to six lines inside a greeting card with a nicely printed bouquet of roses on the front. If possible, six *rhyming* lines. This assessment was no doubt unfair, but the muffling effect of her neutralizing attitude had been palpable, from my childhood rejection of strong tastes through my recent sense of rebuff after her flat phone response to some excitement of mine: "That's interesting." Dismissed. Clunk. I believed she meant well. She didn't mean to disempower me (did she?), but to keep everything at a manageable level. Just in case.

Knowing that even a whiff of her well-meaning censorship could infect me with the dread Hallmark virus, I sent her no writing. But she and my stepfather, a Baptist minister, couldn't help nipping at me. "We'd love to read what you're working on. Why don't you send us something?" they'd kept on in one phone call the previous spring. I'd slithered away once again, well-trained in deflection, but that night I'd suddenly sat up in bed in a fury—luckily alone and still in weather cold enough to have the windows closed—and let loose.

"No!" I screamed into my dark bedroom. "You will not turn me into something acceptable. You will not stop me. I will not write sanitized drivel." And I pounded the bed over and over. I kept on with my solitary fury for half an hour or more, amazed but loving my anger. I was aware of what I did, but it was no performance. After I'd wound down, I thought I'd at least get up and write about it, but at my table my pen skittered across the page. I whacked the table so hard my palm stung, and I took off again for another screaming round.

"I do not care what you think. I will not do what you want. I will not cave in. You will not stop me." The next day, I could only whisper in a hoarse croak.

Back in the canyon, she said, "I'm glad you've found such a nice spot."

"Yeah, well, it was easy. This whole canyon is gorgeous."

"Are we really supposed to say good-bye for good?" she asked silently.

"That's the idea." Out loud.

"Well, OK." She seemed to collect herself. "I *am* proud of you. I like who you've become. Your life is so interesting and different, and you make such beautiful work." She meant the posters and other projects that rolled off my drawing table and drained my heat like vampires.

I'd heard her proper praise a million times. My turn.

"Thanks for everything you've given me—for all your love and attention when I was growing up. For being such a strong independent woman, a good role model, a good person. For being a musician, for giving me music. For always trying to help people, for always looking for transcendence." I trailed off. The sun had set. I paused to crawl into my sleeping bag.

"But you know, Mary Lib," she said, this time out loud, through my voice, "you're so smart and well educated. Your life is interesting, but your father and I really hoped you'd go further."

She'd never admitted this before, at least to me.

"And it's too bad you never had children. And I worry about you not being married." She paused. "And I wish you'd find a good church to attend."

We had been over this ground, though not often.

"I'm proud of what you've done, but I really wish you'd turned out a little more . . . well . . . more regular."

Another admission I'd never heard.

"I figured you felt that way," I said. "Thanks for finally telling me. It would probably have been easier if I'd had a sibling who was more normal. You know, I'm still really mad at all kinds of things from when I was growing up. There was so much collateral damage you never noticed; and all of you except Daddy were so controlling, but so obviously good." I went on with my litany of unintended consequences, my tiresome complaints. But I couldn't muster much fire. No screaming, no tears, no drama. We'd come to a familiar impasse. No Primal Scream here.

But before she could answer, I felt a strange disturbance outside the Death Lodge's imaginary door. Someone wanting to come in.

"Good-bye," I said to her, a little short.

"Good-bye," she said. "I love you." Almost an afterthought. And out the side door. Unceremonious.

"I'm so happy to see you," I said to my father, who had taken her place. I nestled deeper in my warm sleeping bag for a long conversation. My father had been dead for eighteen years. Like my mother, he wasn't a visual hallucination, only a presence speaking with my voice, but no less himself.

"I'm glad I'm finally getting to talk to you again. It's been a long time," he seemed to say as I gazed over my head into open branches creaking slightly in the night wind.

My father had been a gentle, shy man, literate and funny, but prone to brooding. When I'd known him, he'd been a government antitrust lawyer, but he'd started out working as a writer. Before I'd been born (when he was forty-five), he'd abandoned writing and gone to law school. I'd always believed that his dislike of my first love sprang from his own rejection of writing as a viable life. And here I was. Writing.

I wanted to ask him so much about who he'd been when I was growing up, how he'd felt, what had happened in all those years. But after a few minutes, I also realized I wanted his blessing. Desperately.

I'd always been more like him than my mother—physically, intellectually, emotionally—and I knew he'd at least understand the difficulties. And the inner drive. He'd grown up in Nebraska, just west of the hundredth meridian, where the West began. I'd not only reversed his path and begun writing in my forties, but I'd reversed his path geographically and moved to New Mexico from the East Coast. His dreams had been transplanted in me.

"Can you see what I'm trying to do? Can you give me your blessing? It would really help, I think," I begged. Nothing quite so direct had ever passed between us in life.

"Well," he said, musing, careful and considered as usual, "I'm not sure I can give you my blessing. It's a tough road. I was sure you'd be a scientist. Or marry one."

"Oh, yeah," I shot back, "I always thought you were on my side. It made me feel like hell when I found out you'd be just as happy if I married a scientist instead of being one. Did you dislike Peter so much because he was a writer?"

"Well. I know I have to be honest."

"You do."

"Yes," he said. "But I just wanted the best for you. I would have been happier if you'd gone on in zoology. It was a big blow to us when you went to art school."

"I know," I said, a little chastened. "But the whole scientific enterprise was so limiting. Couldn't you see that?"

"Of course, but I thought you'd be able to get around it somehow."

"I wanted more of the world. I still do."

As we talked on and on, tears slid down my cheeks in the chilly night. We talked about the tensions he felt living with my mother and her parents, about growing up in his father's hotel along the North Platte River, about the famous outsized "folk hero" he'd invented, about being at Columbia in the Depression and failing his comps, about his other lovers, about his sister Helen (a woman we'd both dearly loved), about Helen's Missouri farm, about his dreams and why he'd really stopped writing, about his breakdown when I was two, about his last unhappiness in his Florida banishment, about the diary my mother had found after he'd died.

One thing led to another, and my years of silent curiosity spilled over for hours.

We talked about how I'd come to be fasting along the Gila River.

"Do I have it right?" he asked. "You're out here partly just to see what happens and partly to find some sort of answer?"

"To see what happens, yes, but not really to find an answer. To find a more expansive way of being."

"Tell me more."

"I've so often found myself in vessels that feel too small. Like zoology. Like illustration. Like being a sweet girl. It's why I'm not married with a husband and kids. I'm claustrophobic. I feel the walls. That's why I'm writing."

"Ah," he said. "Walls. And distance, too, I'll bet. Like me. I'm sorry I couldn't be closer to you. But I couldn't." And finally he sighed. "Well, OK, I can see that it makes sense. You have my blessing."

I felt enormous relief. But we kept talking. He wouldn't leave. I didn't want him to leave. Against all of Sparrow's instructions ("You need to finish business") we agreed we'd had such a terrific time that we'd meet again for another conversation later. We set no date. And he swept on out of hearing range.

I'd spent three hours in that emotional reverie and felt drained. I didn't have energy for another charged encounter and considered closing down the Death Lodge. But as I shifted my weight and tightened the drawstring around my mummy bag against the cooling night, my first love unexpectedly spoke from the same silhouetted branches my father had just vacated.

"Are you really not eating for four days?" he asked, incredulous. "What about the Grumpy Hungries?"

"Oh, I'm happy you're here," I said. "But what a surprise. How are you? I've missed being in touch."

"Well, I'm in touch now. What on earth are you doing out here?"

"You always accused me of being too reality-bound. I'm breaking free."

"Good. It's about time."

"Don't be snotty."

"I'm not being snotty. I always thought you needed a lot more experience of the sacred. Divine. Mysterious. Unknowable. Whatever."

"Yeah. You were always better at that. But even you didn't become a Sufi when you had the chance in Turkey."

"No, that's true. I was tempted, though. You remember I didn't do it mostly because they treated women so shitty. You'd never have stood for it."

I laughed. "Tell me about your life now." He didn't answer.

In college he'd been wild and confident, reading the *Mabinogion* and the *Mahabharata*, writing like a maniac, winning awards, winning grants. Together we'd become adults, breezing through our independent lives. Along with my appetite, my sense of self had grown with him. I owed a lot to him We'd agreed sex could be one way to explore the world, with lovers besides each other. Originally I'd understood I could only hold him with open hands, but as the years passed, I'd found the arrangement more congenial than he had. Such openness was in the air then. We'd read Simone de Beauvoir's *The Mandarins* and hoped to emulate her freedom—Sartre's freedom—and we'd mostly made it work for many years.

In those days, he did words, I did visuals. And we both struggled in the marketplace. Though he'd had many more dramatic successes than I had, they hadn't been enough for him. For sixteen years we'd stuck together while I'd watched his certainty fade, his sense of failure grow.

"I'm still sorry I lost my desire for you," I said. This was the Death Lodge. Finish business. "But I never thought you'd failed me."

"But that's the way you acted."

"This is old territory. You know I just really wanted to talk to you more."

He couldn't help chuckling. "After all that time, it was so ironic our differences came down to that."

"Yeah," I said, "girl wants talk first, guy wants sex first."

"It was more than that," he said.

He'd wanted children, but I'd insisted at least one of us must have a stable career before we could even consider kids. I didn't want to be the focus of his certain resentment when he stopped writing to support his family. We'd finally split, sadly but amicably. Afterward I'd become much happier. Eventually he'd moved back to our college town, gotten married, and had a son. No one knew if he still wrote, and everyone I heard from had gotten too embarrassed to ask.

"And are you writing?" I asked.

"Am *I* writing?" He laughed again. "The real question is, Are *you* writing?"

Like the old days, we joked around, rooting up our life together like two pigs sampling the compost. We revisited our group house in Providence, our adventures in Turkey, our hiking trips, our time on the beaches of the Outer Banks, our New York struggles. I hardly noticed I still lay next to the Gila River's gentle rush, with frost beginning to collect on my sleeping bag on a moonless night. Unlike my parents, Peter had known me as myself. We had much less unfinished business, much less unexplored emotional territory.

"And Mary," he said suddenly, "do you really think it's a good idea to get tangled up with Sparrow? I thought you might have outgrown that stuff."

"I'm *not* tangled up with Sparrow," I said defensively. He had a certain—perspective—on my sexual history. "And I don't think anyone ever outgrows it. If you're lucky."

"Sex and spirit and creativity aren't the same, no matter what you claim." He'd taken on a stubborn tone I knew and still disliked.

I said, "But the energies are the same. And even the experience of losing control, of being possessed, almost. And they inform each other."

He stayed silent. Back to the agenda of the Death Lodge. Finish business.

"You were so important to me, to who I am," I said. "Thanks. I hope you're happy." I still worried about him.

"Sometimes, yeah, I am. It's great having a kid. You shouldn't worry."

"And *are* you writing?" I asked again, more insistent.

"Not much, but some. I hope it won't be so hard for you." He paused as an owl hooted from the forest up the hillside. "Now you'll probably want my blessing."

"Yup."

"You have my blessing."

For a while we talked on, but I'd reached the bottom of that day's energy well, and I could feel sleep tugging on me. In friendship and in love we said good-bye. For a short time I tried to stay open for another farewell visit, but after a few minutes, I gazed blearily through the dark branches to the stars and mumbled, "The Death Lodge is now closed."

I sank like a stone.

🍃

Fasting, day two.

Morning. The sun had already begun warming the other side of the canyon, but I still snuggled in my bag in damp cold shade. I thought about the Death Lodge. I didn't make a habit of talking things over with people who weren't there. Or who were dead.

My encounters had been much realer than I'd expected or could explain, even though I could see how the process worked. Inner had become outer. My memories, with lives of their own in my complicated neural net, had been allowed to move again. As I spoke out loud—and that seemed crucial—my voice, with its physical vibrations, with its cognitive requirement to choose specific words, had opened the internal pathways and added a legitimate layer to my history, shooting it all out into the night air. Several things seemed important. I'd not only tried to speak truthfully without censoring myself, but I'd been diligent in trying to enter into the inner realities of three important people in my life. The activity resembled mirroring the dreams of my questing friends.

In creative work, much happens that can't be explained. That's the ultimate charge. Something emerges from nothing. Neither my folks nor my old true love were with me in the night, but I'd been open to myself, where a small part of each of them lived. I didn't need to explain what had happened by believing in their disembodied presences, nor even in an official psychological unconscious. The unconscious itself seemed most likely a cognitive unconscious, as grounded in the physicality of our cells as our need to breathe. The Death Lodge had been unexpectedly strange and affecting. At the least it had made clear that two men in my life—men who wrote, but who had both been beaten down—were as much an issue as my mother, or perhaps their memories were allies in my struggle to escape the muffling parts of her influence. I didn't know.

Still, the Death Lodge fit more comfortably with my understandings of the world than the primal, outer events of the day before. The land seemed to know at least as much about me as I knew about myself.

I checked in with my body: no visions of eggs-over-easy with home fries, no crushing headache, no craving for Irish Breakfast tea. But I did crave some warmth. The night's chill had pooled on my side of the canyon, as damp and penetrating as a winter day on the coast of Maine. Or a lemon ice. From across the canyon the sun crept toward me with all the speed of cheddar cheese aging. Slower. When it finally began to thaw patches of the gopher meadow, I zipped out of my bag with a buzz on to move. After hours in my Death Lodge, then hours in dreamless sleep, I felt not dead, but cooked to a juicy medium rare. Still, I couldn't face wading through the refrigerated Gila to the stone pile. I needed an overland trail.

On the grove's downstream side, I found a faint path winding up into ponderosa forest. Almost at once it looked out over the river where I'd splashed alongside the small gravel islands the day before. In the shallow water, four ducks stood washing and preening like a quartet of girls getting ready for a fancy dinner party. Their elegant attire matched: pale grey bodies with white chins and breasts blushing into faint pink at their bellies, thin poppy-red bills, rust-red heads with feathers swept back into distinctive, wind-blown 'dos.

In the field-guide version of nature, names rule. My shelves were crammed with Audubon and Peterson guides that I used nonstop to pin names on birds, plants, tracks, scat. Identification: the list obsession. But from names, you could leap to something else. Names mattered. The river's osprey had been fishing for trout, but not just any trout. Here native Gila trout lived their bug-nabbing lives: highly local, officially endangered, a sign of this canyon's isolation, a warning of imminent threat to the entire ecosystem. Reams of nature detail crowded my brain, and I had no trouble labeling the ducks common mergansers on a break from their fall migration. And they were all *female* common mergansers.

But in the strange territory I'd entered, scientific nomenclature took second place to symbol, where neither neatness nor accuracy counted. The birds were called common mergansers, but on that sunny morning, something else mattered more: gliding across the deep pool, sipping its clear water, four female birds decided their next moves with heads like red flames. I'd been swallowed whole by symbolism's whirlpool. The Charybdis of circumstance.

When I started walking again, they splashed up together and disappeared downstream.

Well. The merganser messengers didn't offer any more clarity than the sexual earthwork did, but I added them to my list of portents, free floating and affecting.

Through the pines. Through fragrant needle-bake I followed the trail, then half slid into the small canyon. Flattened with crusty, cream-colored sand, the arroyo's floor contrasted nicely with the trickling blood-red stain that split it down the middle. On the slower flow, a filmy surface luminesced blue-green, magenta, purple. Psychedelic blood. I shook my head again, no longer surprised but still feeling an unsettling but magical kinship. I stepped across the stream and climbed up to more forest. Angling back to the river, the game trail led down a steep incline to a sandy strand of large cottonwoods and sycamores tangled with underbrush and downed trees. My mind wandered as I retraced my steps back and forth, looking for a way through the thicket.

This archetypal male story—and I was convinced that's what we were living—had more than enough female imagery. Of course, if I were a guy, I could interpret it all differently. Idly I wondered what Sparrow did in his men's workshops. Male, female, I thought. We're all part male, part female. Anyone who's not doesn't do well in the world. Archetypes are one thing, life another. Jim Harrison, novelist and poet, had written somewhere, "Gods laugh at the fiction of gender." And at that moment, I startled a snake. It slipped quickly across a sunny hollow and disappeared under exposed roots. Not a rattler: a pale stripe extended the length of its back.

OK, I thought, symbols everywhere, why not snake? Why not in the middle of thinking about maleness, femaleness?

At the stone pile I rearranged the rocks into an undulating line, ending with a flat triangular stone with two stony eyes. In the matted flood detritus I found a bleached bird's sternum, two holes on one side evidence of the hawk that had been its end. I picked it up to take back to Chuck and hoped he'd found a way to pierce himself without drawing much blood. Male blood.

The day had warmed, and I waded back upstream to the mergansers' low islands. The island farthest downstream had grown in the current, like a narrow lozenge, about twelve feet long and seven feet wide, barely above the water. At its upstream end, a woven mat of branches, grasses, leaves, roots, and the odd bone had been leached by sun and river to a uniform grey. Cobbles covered most of the bar, but at its widest part and nearest the main current, a deposit of sand made a soft spot, body-size. I arranged my fuzzy jacket and vest over the smoothness, took off the rest of my clothes, and lay with my feet upstream, bare in the sun next to the Gila's chill tumble.

By turning my head to the left, I could look directly into the riffling water, umber and brilliant blue, flecked with foam, shadowed by wavering rocks darkly visible; above that moving pattern stretched the opposite bank, pale with sand and faded grasses. Directly above the low flaxen wall, a wider band of distant ponderosas and rocky outcrops led to the overarching, deep ultramarine. At water level, the river's gentle rush overpowered even the sound of wind, and the cool wetness smelled of mint and winter. Like a stone sinking in a still pool, like a slow-motion waterfall, my weight melted into the sand.

But before my mind could lay claim to any idea, I felt the flow of the river pass through my body in quivering, moving vibrations. First I shuddered slightly at the strange sensation, then stretched out my legs and arms and focused on the flow—what else to call it? sheer energy—entering me, then racing unencumbered through legs, through torso, inside my arms and out my fingertips, in gushing ease. I hadn't ever imagined the river inside me, speeding past circulating blood in a straight shot, ignoring the logic of skin and the laws of physics. But this wasn't imagination. My living tissues shook. I thought briefly of the Egyptian goddess whose body was the Nile: I saw her but could not name her. Nameless then myself, I understood.

And what did I understand? Not the river's necessity, kept in its rocky bed; not Roman aqueducts, sturdy and arched; not a culvert's corrugated sides channeling irrigation water; not a tube worm's dinner plans, siphoning sea water; not a straw's utility, sucked on by some thirsty god.

Nothing so direct.

I didn't suddenly grasp hydraulics or how to capture energy as water flowed downhill through my body's spillway. I lay passive, unchanging, except for my awareness. Next to the river nothing happened. Except I understood something beyond my capacities with language.

The nonbeing of some disembodied energy passed through my solid body, my solid being. Revelation of bones and blood.

Is there any other kind?

I lay there until the sun moved me into shade, bathed in liquid grace.

I finally got up, chilled and needing to pee—a more down-to-earth version of liquid conductivity—and moved to the shore. I'd rarely felt so completely content, even foodless, and my pleasure asked to be shared, no matter how literally alone I was. I wondered how the others were faring on their fasts and sent them each in turn my "prayers": what they'd asked for, but also my own concerns for their welfare. I decided to take back presents: the pierced bird's sternum for Chuck; for Jenny, a basket woven from willow branches and whatever else I could find. The others I'd figure out later.

When I waded on upstream to my grove, I nodded to the female earthwork. But we didn't speak.

In the warm afternoon sun, I sat on the bank overlooking the cattails and mullein spikes, views upriver, downriver, across the canyon. I worked on Jenny's small basket, weaving the willows with long grasses and some hand-spun wool I'd brought along for a knot ceremony that I'd abandoned. No knot destruction: instead, a woven nest.

"Earth," I called, still under Sparrow's language influence, "thank you for your stability, your richness, and your fecundity." In my hand lay a bleached moon shell I'd brought with me. Its spirals had originally grown in Cape Cod Bay or in Nantucket Harbor or on the Outer Banks. Some distant seacoast part of my life.

I stood with it at the western edge of a huge anthill at the back of the gopher meadow.

"Ants," I said to the tiny, pheromone-besotted insects hurrying to take care of business, "you're the guiding image for community, the quintessential living neural net, the answer to one or many?, a reminder that I wouldn't want to build a bonfire alone, the proof that synergy works."

I buried the shell a couple inches down. "Keep me honest, ants: everything's not connected to everything else, but almost. And there's always some way to understand the complex maze."

I began to dance, rhythmically growling low tones that vibrated in my bones. Heavy. Energy downward through my feet under the oak, under the alligator juniper. Weighted and rooted. No self-consciousness. Step, hold. Gravity like flypaper. Body wide and sonorous hollow. Run down imagined row on row of plowed dark soil. Stand upright like the rock ramparts, solid and still; make the wind whistle by. Tectonic plates fracture: quick sharp changes of direction. The curves of silt-carved sandstone canyons: follow them with shoulder, arm, cheek. A round, smooth stone: shape it. Many round smooth stones: form them with hands, cup them, hold them. Reach around a boulder rolled from the canyon's top. Be the boulder rolling from the canyon's top. Throw yourself facedown, arms outstretched, legs outstretched. Feel the curve of ground, the curve into blue distance, from horizon to horizon. Feel the slow, slow spinning through blackest, deepest space.

I lay still. The earth spun very slowly.

Down-canyon the low sun caught the air's hidden density and made it visible. Layer after layer of bright specks milled around in kinetic complexity, tiny wings propelled by tiny muscles; and interspersed with the insect multitudes, long silken threads bowed and drifted in the breezes, silver filaments aloft in the canyon's windy sleeve. At the end of each gossamer strand a young spider rode, trusting and ready. Trusting? They had no choice but to trust. Nor did I.

That night I dreamed for the first time since the javelina had chewed on my glasses.

> The stoneware bowls are rich with earthy slip glazes and flare marks from reduction firing. But I need to clean them up, get them to pristine whiteness. With some magical potion and sandpaper, I work and work to scour off the sienna and chestnut and black. I want to get rid of all the "imperfections." Finally I succeed. They shine white like the finest porcelain. But no! All their life has evaporated. They sit inert and mute.
>
> My mother enters. She says, with a tone of concern, "Oh! They were better when they were messier! I liked them more irregular."

Fasting, day three.

Swim up from sleep into river sounds; step stone-by-stone out of darkness into shadow into light reflected, not yet bright. By my eyes two swaying grasses shone gold against morning blue. No hunger? Not possible. But no hunger.

Hermes, I thought.

"Hermes?" I said aloud, quizzical.

Of course, I thought again. Sparrow is a Hermes figure. Lively trickster, intuitive healer.

One of the Greek gods, Hermes had become an inner touchstone for me, not at all stuffy or dusty, but alive as a force. Although he's often been portrayed as the patron of liars and thieves, he's more an embodiment of movement itself—whether it's words ("liar"), goods ("thief"), thoughts, or emotions. He counters stagnation, opposes hoarding, loosens tongues tied too tight. Traditionally he's the messenger between humans and the spirit world; in representations he often carries his staff—the caduceus of twining snakes that's still used as a symbol for doctors. Kit's MasterCard even had a caduceus on it. The well-known image of St. Christopher ferrying the baby Jesus across a river derives directly from older depictions of Hermes with his caduceus. On his shoulder he carries the baby Dionysos, god of altered states.

"Life takes on a special flavor as soon as Hermes becomes your guide" wrote Carl Jung and Karl Kerényi, as the epigraph to *Le Divin Fripon*.

Hermes was a slippery character, and the original reason for his slipperiness had special meaning for me. In his myth, he'd been the child of all-powerful but randy Zeus and the nymph Maia. He'd used his wiliness to escape the label "bastard." A family trap, though a different family trap than mine. Eventually he'd tricked and charmed both Zeus and his own half brother Apollo into acknowledging him as a god.

Writer Lewis Hyde notes that most cultures have a trickster—a Hermes figure. These figures embody the crucial energy of escaping rigid social norms, adding lively, messy, disruptive life.

In my childhood, I'd felt pressed hard to be acceptable, but through my own mostly unconscious wiliness, I'd escaped, becoming a person who didn't fit any of my family's templates.

For centuries piles of stones at thresholds or crossroads have acknowledged transitions, quietly invoking protection. These stone piles are often called *herms* and are notably phallic.

All that familiar information flashed through my mind as I lay snuggled in my sleeping bag in the growing morning light. And I wondered, "Am I about to get into trouble? Peter had it right. I find Sparrow awfully appealing." With no conscious effort from me, my ur-male narrative had almost morphed into an erotic female one. But I knew I still retained my *agency*, my ability to act on my own behalf, heroine-like.

Although I wasn't experienced in vision quests, I had often been a member of temporary communities—summer classes at bucolic craft schools, river trips, summer jobs, writing workshops. When interesting and energetic people live closely together with a common focus and are outside their familiar social situations, romances often began quickly and unexpectedly. I considered those mostly temporary sexual adventures healthy, despite whatever distress might eventually result. It had happened to me more than once and had only added another layer to the larger experience. And gratefully I'd never felt any man had imposed his desires on me. We'd always been equal participants.

My long-term relationships, though crucial to my life, always had to accommodate my work, harmonize with my independence. Since I'd moved to New Mexico from New York, I'd happily lived alone. Sparrow had explained in one of our circles that he'd recently split amicably from his lover of some years. I also knew any teacher who slept with his or her students usually broke a code of ethics more valid than strictly sexual ones. Unequal power and violated trust could easily interfere with real human contact, or worse, cause substantial emotional damage. Still, I didn't rule anything out.

And then I remembered this detail about Hermes: he invented fire. Prometheus stole it, but Hermes invented it to save his skin.

Ah, fire. As fluid as water in its way. More transformative. The burning metabolic energy of life. Sparrow was right; I could already flow like water. Maybe I needed to claim more fire. I'd reverse the order of my last two elemental ceremonies: today, water; tomorrow, fire.

The sun had risen above the canyon's rim and warmed the grove enough for me to climb out of my sleeping bag. Not worrying about breakfast had its advantages. I pulled on shorts and took off again for the stone pile. When I crossed the small canyon, I stepped across the river of psychedelic blood and saw it with fresh eyes: water into blood into fire, fluidity into nerve. Again I picked my way through the sandy cottonwood thicket, following and retreating along the same dead-end paths as the day before. Slow learning curve. And at the same sandy depression, I startled the same snake whose same slithering length disappeared into the same exposed roots.

At the stone pile, Vern had rearranged the undulating rock snake into a bow with an arrow pulled back ready to let loose: Sparrow's image for our fast. After intense focus, release. But Vern had made the bow still aiming. Where was the release? Inside the bow, Vern had placed a piece of bear scat the size of a scone and a freshly cut branch with small tough leaves. I coiled the stones into a spiral, grading small stones at the center out to large, ending with three sharp yellow pebbles. I circled the bear scat with a ring of more yellow rocks and tucked the branch into my pack.

Back at the gravel island I barely noticed I had stopped eating, but my energy had slipped several notches. No food for sixty-six hours. Or sixty-eight? A long time. I drank as much water as I could and rested in the sun.

And then—how could I not?—I built a herm at the lower tip of the most upstream island.

I found another quote in my journal from *Water and Dreams*:

Liquidity is a principle of language; language must be filled with water. As soon as we are able to talk, then, as Tristan Tzara says, "a cloud of impetuous rivers fills the dry mouth."

I sat facing the small riffle by the island, bare feet in cool flow, and wrote in my journal a note to the river, to water:

As you never stop filling and moving on, singing, dancing, flying, seeping, dissolving, freezing, thawing, making clouds, raining, washing, cleansing, laughing, playing, reflecting, feeding metabolic fire, lapping, licking, cutting, shaping, replenishing, falling, splashing, softening, covering, smoothing, vibrating, quenching, changing shapes, moving, returning, combining, breaking apart, making waves, lying still, carrying iron, carrying earth, crashing, whispering, climbing up through stone to springs, ringing, shouting, flooding, moistening, threatening, saving, calling, cooling, curling, shaping, asking, answering, giving, receiving, offering solace or power.

May I take on your qualities as they are appropriate. May I always feel your fluidity and flow within me, through me.

I cast off these words, words of my mind and my heart, offering them in the spirit of gratitude and celebration for what you've already given me, and in the spirit of sending gifts on to others in the world. Thanks, river. Thanks, water.

From the flood tangle I gathered a handful of smooth twigs, each a quarter inch across and about ten inches long. I copied out my river message until black scribbles covered their river-polished surfaces. On three smaller sticks I wrote the three epigrams from the first page of each of my notebooks:

We work with being, but nonbeing is what we use.—*Tao Te Ching*

Write from the heart.

We make the road by walking.—Antonio Machado

I read my scripts out loud to my river audience and one at a time placed the wordy branchlets into the waves and watched them bob downstream and disappear.

With little juice for a full-blown dance, I began to weave my arms loosely, lightly, then lay back on the sand with my arms outstretched parallel to the river, feet still in water. With palms up, I bicycled my eight fingers like the upturned legs of a barnacle, a sequence from little finger to index finger. At the same time I began repeating a three-note descending phrase, wordless, chantlike, that gradually meshed with my hand dance and the splashing riffle until I felt myself slip again into the energy of the flow, continual, linear, circular, water moving through standing waves, spilling over smooth stones into small eddies, sinking into clear pools, swirling in submerged turbulence that echoed a thousand other fluid worlds in every river, every stream, every tumbling cataract, foam-flecked and melodious.

Back at the grove I made presents for Doug and Vern.

For Doug I tied together with wool and dental floss an embarrassingly funky cube of river twigs. A box with no walls. Structure with no barriers. For Vern I wrapped a symbolic bundle: the twig he'd left inside his stone bow, a willow sprig for flexibility, a polished river branch for flow, and a piece of rusted barbed wire to remind him of his own corral, perhaps now in his past.

For Sparrow I turned the canyon into a poem. It ended with these lines:

> . . . Waves stand in the river's center:
>> water fills them and moves on.
> Water is substance;
>> wave, movement and spirit of movement,
>> but they cannot be separated.

> The waves still stand,
>> flecked with foam and vibrating.
> I stand still.
> I vibrate.
> The canyon fills me and
>> flows like a bright,
>> dancing flame.

That night I dreamed about names.

I walk into the dorm office at college. The secretary says, "Oh good. There are some people here who would like to talk to you. They've been waiting."

She hands me a folder with my name and an unfamiliar name. A teenage girl and her mother step up. The girl wears a name tag with the first name *Reynolds*. She says, "I want to be a musician, but I'm worried about my name. Do you think such an odd name is a handicap?"

I say, "Oh no, not at all. It's worse to have a common name like mine." Her mother frets some more. I say, "You must remember the unusual is not a blemish, but an advantage, because it sets you apart."

Music had given my mother a way to escape her childhood in the coal-mining towns of eastern Kentucky. I knew my grandmother had been the force behind that plan for her only child, but I knew only a little more than that. She hadn't been asked to do household chores, only to practice. By the time she was a teenager, she was teaching piano, then church organ. Eventually she'd become a music teacher in the D.C. public schools. After I was born, she earned a degree in counseling and temporarily moved away from music. Whenever I asked about her early years, my ever-optimistic mother became quiet, almost embarrassed. Or ashamed. And her given name is unusual.

The only person I knew named Reynolds was Reynolds Price, a writer I'd worked with in college, who had also been my first love Peter's mentor. Reynolds shared his last name with a good friend of mine who was also a successful writer. Through the agency of names, two beaten-down writers in my life had been supplemented with—or perhaps transformed into—two fighters whose words had been unstoppable.

🍃

Fasting, day four.

My tissues felt like meringue, frothy and light, aerated so the spaces between my cells had cleared out. My brain tasted like icy sangria, fresh mint sliding into my mouth. My blood coursed like wind, no resistance. My torso resembled puff pastry filled with glazed blueberries. Across my synapses the crucial chemicals floated like milkweed fluff followed by foam blown from spent waves. A tune from a wooden flute echoed across inner space. I lay suspended in a warm sea, released from gravity. But the sea carried clouds and wheeling hawks, not reflected on the surface but moving all around me. Gravity had been replaced with electrostatic bursts, delicate and sweet, and they hit like light rain, like spray, like dissolved will.

Dissolved will, all right. Was spacey an altered state? I didn't know. But I did know that water was water, and I'd been drinking plenty of the Gila River, filtered through high-tech membranes. I'd grounded my spaciness once with electrolyte powder, absent the standard glucose content. Along my neurons, potassium, calcium, sodium ions replenished themselves. That influx of ions banished lethargy but did nothing to lessen my euphoria, my gaping transparency. Food had become an interesting concept, but I wasn't concerned with eating any. A touch of heartburn. I nibbled half a Tums, and my gut released its pain. Release. Every contracted muscle bundle got the message: shake out the kinks. Every obsessive neural pathway, I swear, heard the river's siren song: "Look for other ways, you're free to move on." Every question had five answers, and the answers swept from the trees and flew across the meadows. Every answer called a question from my limbic brain, so the questions became gestures, gestures became memories rearranging themselves, time turning back on itself in bright, spiraling ribbons.

🍃

I lay in my sleeping bag. Awake. No question. I didn't even feel stoned. A flicker worried a nearby ponderosa: rattling random rhythm. The canyon still embraced me, impressively impersonal when I thought about it, intimately available when I let go.

My ceremonies had been like conversations, richer than the one I'd had when I crossed my threshold on the first morning, but still easy, reciprocal talk. Not talk between strangers getting to know each other. I had often hiked alone for a week at a time without seeing another human, and I knew this territory, if not this exact canyon. But the ceremonial conversations, like talk between close friends, were a sign of something deeper. This vast knowing space outside my consciously crafted structures stunned me. Not that the ceremonial conversations were insignificant. But I'd come out to fast focused on a couple of things: loosening my voice, loosening the old knots I thought still held it enthralled, loosening enough to see if any of Sparrow's claims were real in order to write about the quest. And I'd encountered a different agenda, one that encompassed mine but cut closer to the bone: get nervier, ease tensions with your mother, contact some female vibe, explore an intimacy with the guide. And I still had one more day left.

Just the idea that another agenda existed, apparently outside my control, meant I had engaged something real beyond myself. Real and astonishingly responsive. Hermes? Spirit? I didn't know. I couldn't explain it. But I didn't mind. I didn't need to know its name.

🍂

But the day waited. As soon as I got up, I thought, Oops, my period's started. Completely out of its cycle. I slipped in one of the small sea sponges I use instead of Tampax. Always come prepared. And off again on the overland trail to the stone pile: follow the path through the pine forest, step over the psychedelic river of blood, negotiate the downed trunks and prickly brush. The trek itself had taken on the repetitive quality of myth. But I knew where the snake sunned in the sandy hollow—I'd startled her twice already—and I crept up slowly, ready with my binos.

She moved just far enough so I could take a good look at her head, a long dark triangle. At the triangle's base, the pale stripe extending the length of her backbone widened into a decisive orange end. In the sun, her round, black eyes glittered over white cheeks interrupted with black, angled stripes. She rested as immobile as the cottonwood branch next to her. Then, once, twice, three times, she flicked out her forked tongue. Three bright red licks. Testing the air for body warmth, for messages. I knew the explanations. But I saw not information gathering, but something laden with a message for me: fire emerging from fluidity's mouth. What else could I think after the last three days? Another sentence in the ongoing conversation.

I stood transfixed. She lay in her sandy bowl, curving sinuously under jumbled plants, her reptilian heart beating like my mammal's heart beat, her cells' oxidation cooking as surely as mine cooked, her nerves sending their impulses with exactly the same exchange of electrolytes as mine. She lived her own life of basking, swimming, sleeping, catching mice, yet our lives had intersected in such a way and at such a moment that she had transformed from snake into talisman. From crucial creature in the riparian ecosystem along the Gila River into embodied, symbolic message, straight to me. After three and a half days with no food, I might have been in an altered state, but the snake with her ruby tongue was no more hallucination than the sexual earthwork or the blood dripping off my own gouged thumb.

That morning she became Snake speaking to me in the same way the ancient oak with embedded barbed wire had spoken: in a language before words, but no less clear for its lack of explainable grammar. "Here I am," she said silently. "Ready to shed my skin; very male; the Devil in the Garden, tempting you; Kundalini coiled at the base of your spine. My sharp red tongue gives you permission—no, it goads you—to speak with burning words." From outside, she answered my inner world.

Finally I stirred. She flowed her way back into the exposed roots, getting on with her snake life.

❦

I got on with my fasting life, stepping through the sandy tangle to the stone pile. I rearranged Vern's rocky butterfly into a starburst and made my way back to the gravel island. Tiredness threatened to swamp me. Two quarts of water with dissolved electrolytes, and I revived enough to stop imagining Sparrow would have to hire a burro to carry me out. I didn't feel bad, just drained. But no immediate tasks. I lay by the water. And for once I simply lay by the water.

Back at the grove, I measured out my exhausted moves with care. After the snake's directive, fire deserved something dramatic, but my invocation was short.

"Fire," I said with as much juice as I could muster, sending words up into the bright sky, "thanks for my independence and drive. Thanks for the flame at my core. Guide me to work with your heat and light, your life and understanding, with the fleeting subtlety of desire. May I use you not instead of water, but as another element I've too long kept at a distance. Fire. Thanks."

I wrote on a single page the same three journal epigrams I'd sent down the river, then burned it next to the stump where I'd sat gripping my gouged thumb and trying not to faint. I danced, briefly and gently, like a votive candle's flame, contained and small. No great conflagration. Ceremony overwhelmed by body's needs.

Fire. Facing the sun, I swayed, eyes closed, then spun slowly, inner vision flashing like sheet lightning. I inhaled the gopher-meadow's heat, breathed out fire, hissing like a welding torch. Sit on baking ground, sit upright, feel the energy down your spine shoot into the earth, to the earth's burning core, ricochet back up into your tail bone, spiraling up your vertebrae and out the top of your head in a fountain of sparks, a blaze of lightning bugs in the night, an eruption of smoke and desire. Spontaneous combustion, pyromaniacal change, the igneous heart of matter.

I crawled back into the oak's dappled shade to cool off.

Fire. Looking up into the old oak's branches, I remembered no fires, only the welcoming, comforting trees of my childhood. I stood and leaned against the oak's trunk, covering the embedded barbed wire with my stomach, resting my cheek against rough bark.

"Oak," I said out loud, "I'm going to tell you tree stories." All rules were off. And all embarrassment. "Trees were my best friends once." And I told her stories: the particular trees I climbed barefoot so I could feel my way, gripping with my toes; the days I hung onto narrow limbs as the wind rocked us; my slide into reveries of escape as I flexed with the wood's rhythm, hiding from my world. "No wonder the druids worshipped oaks," I said. "You're a great listener." The oak didn't answer.

❦

I began concentrating on my last ritual: the Purpose Circle.

Besides its mellifluous sound, the Purpose Circle had other elements of good design: after four days with no food, place four stones on the ground at each of the four directions and fill in stones to trace a circle large enough to contain you. At sunset, repeat your intentions, step into the circle, stay awake through the night, and at dawn, step out. Hold strong to your hopes for your new self.

In my physiological understanding, as valid as ever, sleep deprivation on top of mild starvation could make your deep neural patterns even more vulnerable. Concentration from your cerebral cortex might nudge those neural pathways into something different.

In Sparrow's symbolic and mythic description, the ring of stones became what helped you in your life: your skills, your friends, members of your family, your abilities. You were free to throw out stones that served you poorly. The rocky circle also became your tomb, out of which you emerged at dawn, newly born.

I saw no contradiction in those two descriptions.

And I wish something dramatic had happened. Mostly I shivered and rearranged my legs over and over, stretched my back, tried to sing, and watched Orion turn slowly in the star-washed sky. At midnight I fetched my sleeping bag and draped it over me. At one, fully clothed, I crawled in and sank into the arms of Morpheus. But I never got warm, so I woke every hour, tried to climb up to alertness before I sank again. At six, when the sky still showed no hint of dawn, I stood and faced Venus to the east, where she peeked through the trees. A great horned owl—Athena's animal—hooted from the forest. Aphrodite and Athena. Love and wisdom: goals at least as important to me as Hermes' flow and fire.

As I stomped my feet and hopped around to keep warm, the sky lightened. Ice covered my sleeping bag, and the water in my Nalgene bottle had frozen solid. At seven fifteen, with relief, I declared dawn.

The Purpose Circle hadn't done much, but in the overall picture that seemed minor.

⮐

Monday morning. My last food had been on Wednesday evening. Did I mind? Not a bit. The slows of the day before had disappeared. I felt more energetic, able to stay out for another week. But even dreams had schedules: I needed to meet Vern at the stone pile. Slowly I stuffed and rolled and folded and rearranged and got my gear back in my pack. Ready to leave the sheltering grove.

And, in the way women have been tuned for eons, I remembered my period. My first day's flow was always light, but it had picked up. I squatted under the oak, retrieved my blood-soaked sponge, and rinsed it under a water bottle. As I watched the reddened water sink into the soil, the next jolt hit. I'd spilled blood from my hand at the fast's start; now, in eerie symmetry, I spilled menstrual blood. The shady river grove had begun to feel as sacred as any druid's haunt. I still couldn't pin down any meaning beyond loose symbolic associations, but I knew absolutely my conscious mind had nothing to do with either bloodletting.

As my very last act, I poured my extra water in a circle around the oak's broad trunk. "Thanks, again," I said to the ancient tree, which stood as implacable as ever.

Off to the stone pile again, this time fully loaded: follow the trail through the pine forest, slide into the sand canyon, step over the psychedelic river of blood, negotiate the downed trunks and prickly brush. Too early for Snake to be out sunning.

Nine o'clock. The stone pile had been transformed into an appealing rocky fish, but Vern was nowhere in sight.

Sparrow expected us all back between eight and ten.

By ten thirty, I decided I'd better climb up to check on Vern, when I heard him call from a ways up the hill, "Mary!"

"Oh good!" I shouted back.

He'd slept wrong on his arm and could hardly move it. "It took me forever to pack because I had to use my other hand." He held his walking stick on his left side; his right arm hung limply at his side. I suspected that some muscles had cramped and pinched one of his cervical nerves and in a while they'd loosen up.

"Did you stay up all night?" he asked.

"No. Too damn cold. You?"

"No. But I fell asleep on some rocks in my Purpose Circle. That's probably what happened to my arm."

We alternated tossing the stone-pile stones into the river before we set off along the official trail, with Vern in the lead. Despite his assurances, I wanted to keep an eye on him.

I knew the trail would open up to a river view when it skirted the wide gravel bar, and I could look back right to my fasting grove one last time. Spent sunflowers and prickly seed-heads crowded the path, and I focused on my Teva-clad feet until I felt the sunnier openness around me. I paused and, sensing someone had silently called my name, turned my head sharply right. And there, fifteen feet off the trail, grinning, with arms folded, stood Sparrow. A flesh-and-blood apparition. I stared with the same mix of recognition and disbelief as I'd stared at the embedded barbed wire, at the snake's flicking red tongue.

"I didn't think you both could just pass me by!" He laughed. "How are you?" He walked over and hugged me as well as he could with my pack on my back.

"I'm great. It was wonderful. I felt fabulous the whole time. I stopped to say good-bye to my spot. Vern slept wrong on his right arm and he doesn't have much feeling in it so it took him a long time to pack. I wondered how long it would take you to come looking for us. Is everyone else OK?" My words tumbled.

"They're good. I thought you'd have a fine time out here. Where was your spot?"

I pointed out the gopher meadow and the cattail backwash and the grove on the bank a quarter mile away. He stood silently a minute as if deciding whether to speak, then said, "That was my spot once. It was the best fast I ever had."

"Oh," I said, unsure if I'd bumped into another portent, and if I had, what it meant.

"I'd better go stop Vern before he gets too far." And he sped off down the trail.

Sparrow hurried back to let the others know we were all right, leaving us to make our way more slowly. On the river's bank I forgot to recross my threshold with any ceremony at all, but when we reached camp, Sparrow said, a little over dramatically I thought, "The Return." But who was I to judge drama anymore? He smudged each of us, and we moved on to the clearing to hug the others, who all fairly glowed. With transformation or relief, I couldn't tell.

At last Doug gave me a quick hug and backed off. "I don't want to get between you and food!" And someone handed me a large bowl of fruit: fresh apples, oranges, green grapes, and walnuts. Fresh fruit? The osprey must have airlifted it in. I didn't question. Nothing could have tasted better.

Two bowls of fruit and half an hour of relaxed chatter later, we began to hike out of the canyon: steep, but less steep than many mountain trails I climbed every summer. I've always hiked slowly and didn't mind bringing up the rear, but about two thirds of the way out, I began to flag. I could see Chuck weaving ahead of me. Sparrow appeared from up-trail, minus his pack, and took some of Chuck's load, then moved back to me and offered the same relief. He unstrapped my Therm-a-Rest and tarp from my pack's top—not much weight—and headed up. Twenty of my slow steps later, and he was back.

"I'll take your pack if you want, and you can carry these lighter things."

"I think I'm OK," I said. "I'll be slow, but I'll get there."

He glared at me. "This isn't a race."

"It's not that heavy."

"That's why long-distance runners carry backpacks—it's easier to run when you weigh 170 instead of 140."

My self-reliance gremlin rebelled at any offer of help, no matter how much I needed it. But I still didn't want to seem like a wimp.

"This is a gift." He glared some more.

I was pooped. Then I felt an inner release. "I'd love for you to take my pack. Thank you."

We exchanged loads, my pack needing substantial adjustment on his bare, tan torso. Off he went with my pack and my emergency energy bar, leaving me with my light load on a shoulder strap, my water bottle, and my walking stick. A quarter mile to go. Steep uphill. But I'd used up the fruit and nuts, and I had no reserves left. My quirky metabolism finally made an appearance. Way beyond the Grumpy Hungries. Less painful, but as debilitating as the Medicine Walk. Twenty-five steps. I began to feel nauseated and lightheaded. Just get to that patch of shade up there. Six more steps. Sit on that rock. Hat off.

Hold walking stick. Lean head on hands. Breathe. Five minutes. A sip of water. Get up. Better.

Twenty-five steps. The nausea and the fuzzy head returned. Just to that next patch of shade. Collapse. Five minutes. Seven. Up.

And so it went. I could see the glint of windshields at the top of the hill. I could go no faster. Twenty-five steps. Slow. Count them. Collapse. Rest. Get up. I could see Sparrow between two junipers, hands on hips, checking my progress. I could go no faster. I could hear laughter. I could go no faster. Twenty-five steps. Collapse. Rest. Get up. The trail would never end. Water almost gone.

The quarter mile took an hour, yet at the top I knew I only needed some sports drink. Not so dramatic. Glucose. Electrolytes. Water. Tend to the body.

"We were just taking bets," said Chuck, as I retrieved my extra water and an Endura packet from the back of my truck. My hands shook. "If someone offered you another fast, would you do it?" I took a sip. Whew.

"Absolutely. I'd do it next week." He didn't know I'd been in Nirvana for four days. And now, blood sugar restored, I felt great.

The plan had been to swing by a hot springs up-river, rinse off dust from our dreams. But it wasn't noon anymore; it was three thirty.

"Well, I'm still into it, but I'm the reason we're late," I said, feeling guilty but trying not to apologize. No one else seemed to mind my slow climb.

"But we're late because of me, too," Vern pointed out.

"Oh, yeah." Surprised and grateful, I looked at him. I'd already forgotten. "The dynamic duo." I laughed with everyone else.

We bagged the hot springs, but drove to the store at the settlement of Gila Hot Springs to make phone calls. And to get ice cream.

"Go slow!" warned Sparrow about our driving. "You're still in a strange state."

At Doc Campbell's Trading Post, a battered, brown Jeep with a power-ful sound system blared Hank Williams and Merle Haggard across the parking lot. The Jeep's owner, shirtless in jeans and a black Stetson, puttered around, drunk, waiting for UPS to bring him a part so he could head back out. Head out? Wherever. We gravitated to the freezer full of frozen treats.

On the store's wide front porch I savored plastic spoonfuls of butter-scotch ice cream from a Styrofoam cup while Sparrow and I traded stories.

"So," he asked, "were you ever a hippie?" I had no idea if it was a non sequitur or not. Did anything follow coherently from anything else?

"Yeah," I said, "for about two months the summer of 1970. I drove in a van with five guys from Seattle to San Francisco. One was my sweetie. When we got to San Francisco, we snuck into a vacant apartment to crash. How about you?"

"I lived in a Berkeley commune the last year I was in school, and when I got kicked out of grad school, I went hiking for five months. Then I joined another commune in Vermont. And I was a hippie for twelve years." He grinned as he munched a few more Doritos.

"Yikes," I said. "I guess I was also hippie-esque between Duke and art school. My honey and I lived in Istanbul for a year. The Turks sure thought I was a hippie. A tall blond American girl on the loose in a down jacket."

🍃

We all phoned home. Hank Williams took off on another song, wail-ing from the brown Jeep. Had I been forced at gunpoint, I couldn't have chosen the realer reality: Doc Campbell's parking lot or the Gila Canyon, filled with improbable portents.

"At least it's good country and western," said Vern, then smiled. He unfolded a Gila Wilderness map he'd just bought. "Where were we?" He laid the map on the porch floor at Sparrow's feet.

"Right in here," Sparrow said. "Here's the bridge we crossed; here's the parking area." He put his finger on the contour lines by the blue river.

Doug squatted next to the map and focused on the canyon's abstracted shape. "Have you been to these hot springs?" He pointed to a notation partway up the canyon's side.

"No," said Sparrow, "but I've spent lots of time looking for them."

"And our first camp . . . " Sparrow's finger moved east. "Ah—just off the map."

Next to Doug, Chuck stood peering down with mild interest.

As a questing buddy, he didn't match the digitized android he worried he'd become, but instead bore more resemblance to a panda in an overgrown armadillo suit. He just needed to find the zipper. And he'd been looking hard for it. His pale skin had reddened, too, and like everyone else, he seemed easier, his body perceptibly looser.

"What scale's that map?" he asked. "It looks like a mile's very small on it."

"Yeah," said Sparrow, "this is the whole Wilderness, or at least the south part." He turned the map over to find the scale bar.

Jenny sat a ways back on the next bench, silent, leaning with her elbows on knees covered with yet another lightweight wrap skirt (this one with small red circles on an orangy background), intently watching our map reading but not at all concerned with the particulars. I'd hear soon what had happened to her in the caves.

Vern folded the map.

The UPS truck pulled into Doc Campbell's parking lot and delivered the missing Jeep part. Doug looked at his watch. "It's easier to cook while it's still light. If we leave now, we'll get back to the Mimbres about half an hour before sunset."

We'd readjusted enough to the mechanized world to tackle the drive back. After the road curved down through the mountains, it skirted the flat fields of the Gila valley, their hay bales scattered in loose grids ready to be retrieved in rickety trucks. And like a gesture of grace, the warm

October light bathed the land, streaming across the fields, the mountains, and our small, speeding caravan.

Back by the familiar Mimbres, we cobbled together a jovial dinner, but not saying a word about what had happened on our fasts. Those tales required a more formal setting. We all understood each other's lives well enough to know how vulnerable we'd become. None of us had a good take on each other's day-to-day bustle, but we grasped a certain deep ground of individual distress. We'd tell our fasting stories, listen to each other's tales, and hope Confusion, that character in all our lives, would become like the backyard compost pile, a chaotic but nourishing ferment. I couldn't wait to hear what had happened to the others.

For my feast after the fast, I savored peanut butter and crackers and two cups of instant Nile Spice soup as if I were nibbling tasty canapés and fresh gazpacho. Someone once said, "There is no asceticism that fails to increase the capacity for pleasure."

After we'd finished eating, Sparrow said, "I know you're all tired, but I'd like to start with at least one story tonight." He went on, "In some ways the vision quest isn't a story, and in some ways it is. The experience exists somewhere, but the stories we tell almost become our experience. The story isn't just reporting, it's a creative act. Tell it in your own way, true to you."

"Any takers?" he asked and looked around at our firelit faces.

Doug said, "I'll go first." He was silent for a moment, collecting his thoughts.

"I'd gone out with some fear and trepidation," he started. "I feared if I had a vision, it would be terrifying. I was afraid of despondency, of the unknown." But for most of the four days, he'd felt a tone of peace and ease. I listened to Doug's story with growing relief. Of all my companions, he'd been the one I'd most worried about because he faced his inner winds with such grim determination.

On his first day, on a high ridge, he'd done something that for him was an act of bravery. First, he'd stripped except for his Tevas and sunglasses; then he walked away from his clothes. Walking away naked had been the real act of courage.

The second day, he started up a brushy, little-used trail, but abandoned the hike, deciding the psychic safety in exhausting time wasn't the best plan. He returned to the river, stripped again, then completely covered himself in mud and let it dry. "I even rubbed it in my beard, in my hair. It seemed reptilian when it dried. Like I had scales all over me." He smiled.

"Then I dove into the river and was surprised at how easy the caked mud washed away. I did a mud bath every day—encased myself in dirt, then whooshed clean. If I lived here, it would be a daily ritual." Not only wildly symbolic but, I thought happily, wildly childlike.

"On the fourth day, I started feeling some apprehension because I knew the Purpose Circle was coming. I got it all together and hoped for a powerful, overwhelming vision, but that didn't happen. I managed to stay up all night, mostly singing spirituals.

"Nothing abnormal happened, but about five thirty, I reached some peace with it. All my prayers had been honest, heartfelt prayers; the answers just didn't come. At least then. They will sometime. I'm confident about that. I think the experience was exactly what I needed." He paused. "I did realize I need to make my Purpose Circle bigger. I could barely walk around inside. And after a while I couldn't see it, so I ripped out pages from my journal and put them under the rocks." The image of glowing white pages in a circle struck me forcefully.

Doug nodded he'd finished. He sat bent into his Therm-a-Rest chair on the ground across the fire from me.

Sparrow lay to my left on his stomach. He smiled at Doug. "Thanks," he said, then looked at his watch. "It's ten thirty. Is everyone too tired for another story?"

We all wanted to crash. And I wanted to talk to Sparrow.

"Then let's reconvene at nine. Is that OK?"

The fire had burned to embers, and Doug lit one of the candle lanterns and set it on the standing log to my right. In the chilly darkness, the candle cast a cold, spectral light, like a tiny fluorescent bulb. Jenny and Chuck disappeared up the hill toward their separate tents. Doug sat awhile in silence, perhaps reliving more of his fast—the parts that hadn't made it into the story he'd told us, parts undigested even by a night's dreaming. Then he stood and said, "See you in the morning."

I kept my place, knowing Sparrow would stay by the fire as long as any of his charges wanted to talk. And I did. For a while Vern fidgeted across from us, chatting. Was it about Mormons? Or the osprey in the canyon? Or Nuevo Flamenco? I only half heard what he said, though I tilted my head toward him, smiling, and kept up my third of the loose talk. I had my agenda with Sparrow and knew this night was the only chance I had to talk to him alone. I didn't know if I would get where I wanted to go, but I trusted the lingering openness from my fast. On the other side of the dying fire, Vern lingered too, shifting on his feet.

"Well, think I'll turn in," he said finally.

"Good night," Sparrow and I answered together, and Vern made his way down the trampled path in the hip-high grass, his flashlight dimly lighting his way.

I stared into the remaining embers, poking them with a stick. We sat mute for some minutes.

"You're very good at this, you know," I said.

"At what?" he asked.

"Guiding quests," I said. "I wanted to confess something."

"Oh yeah?"

"Remember I saw a face on my medicine walk? What I didn't tell you was that while it wasn't an exact resemblance, it looked like you."

"Like me? From your description, I thought it was an old, wrinkled hag, without any teeth."

"Nope. It was a young, ruddy Irish guy. Some younger than you, but still very close. It seemed really weird to me, which is why I didn't tell you before."

"Yup, pretty weird." And apparently it didn't fit in any of his boxes. Just wait, I thought.

We both stayed quiet for a while longer. Get on it, Mary, you chicken. If you don't say anything, nothing will happen. I cleared my throat.

"I've decided I need to think about fire more," I said at last.

"In terms of . . . ?" Sparrow trailed off, the encouraging guide, not knowing where I was going.

"On my fast there was lots of fire imagery. Fire and blood. You'll hear about it tomorrow."

"Did that surprise you?"

"Um huh. I don't quite know what to do with it, but I have some ideas."

He said, "I just flashed on you writing raving pieces filled with fury and swear words." He laughed. "The javelina returns?"

I said, "No, I don't really have trouble with anger, with expressing it when it's appropriate. It doesn't seem quite like a need for more anger."

He waited patiently, but I wasn't going to pursue fire just then. At length he shifted his weight, began to stand and said, "Well, it's late, think I'll say good night."

I sat on my folded right leg, my left leg bent into my chest, my hand holding it to me, chin resting on my knee. I stared at the bare ground. "There is one more thing."

He reversed himself and settled back down.

"This may be an occupational hazard of yours," I said.

"Uh oh." He knew what was coming. I had no idea how he'd respond and was too blitzed to worry.

"Uh oh is right," I said and dived in. "I'm wildly attracted to you."

With my eyes I followed the gentle curves of the blackened stones in the fire ring, lit to grey chiaroscuro by the candle lantern. Around us the crickets creaked over a more uniform insect buzz, and just behind us the Mimbres kept up its gurgling laughter. One minute. Two.

"That was a conversation stopper," I said. I still hadn't looked at him. My courage didn't extend to eye contact. How old was I?

Immediately he answered from a foot away, laughing slightly. "But the thinking's going fast and furious."

One beat. I heard him take a breath.

"Two things. First, the attraction's mutual."

Oh good, I thought. I hadn't manufactured the spark. Now what?

"Second, I have my vision quest guide ethics to consider."

Of course. "I understand," I said, still not looking at him, in a voice that hit my ears like a dry wind. I was nothing if not reasonable. And what else could I say?

He stood up, as if sitting interfered with speaking, and went on. "Even when I got your letter of intent last summer,"—he mimed holding a paper—"I thought, 'Where did this woman come from?' I couldn't wait to meet you. And you haven't disappointed me." I didn't think the letter had been that interesting.

I waited, but he'd apparently reached the end of his encouragement.

"You're still coming off your fast," he said.

Right, I thought.

"Let's talk again in a month." He continued, "Two months." Perfect. I knew I wouldn't follow his instructions, but it was the honorable, concerned, I might even say loving, thing to say. And besides, the sexual logistics were impossible.

"Okey-doke." Pert Mary. And tongue-tied.

He sat back down.

Pause again. No lively verbal sparring here.

Later I heard from Sparrow himself what I couldn't have known: already that summer he'd violated those vision quest guide ethics twice, though for the first two times in all his years leading quests. I have no idea how many advances he'd successfully fended off. Sex with clients wasn't something he'd wanted for himself. In the early eighties, he'd apprenticed with Sun Bear, a well-known guru in some circles, and with distaste called Sun Bear's habit of sleeping with his students "sex addiction." Big disillusionment. Sparrow had seen the bad fallout in some of those women, and it didn't match his idea of helping people. But that summer, freshly out of a relationship, Sparrow had found himself eyeing the field, curious, a little hungry, a little lonely, and his vision quest guide ethics had given way to his impulse to explore what was presented to him. Neither of those encounters had lasted past a weekend, hard on the heels of each woman's quest, and he'd had some difficulty extracting himself from further entanglement. And he wasn't about to replicate those experiences with me.

I'd not arrived in the Gila on the prowl. I still don't know whether Sparrow had or not. And maybe he didn't know.

Never mind. That night Sparrow's complicated dances with women weren't apparent, and he'd not been prepared for such directness from me.

And the topic seemed closed, at least for the moment.

"Would you be interested in exchanging writing?" he asked. I looked full at him then, relieved to be back in less charged territory. But the door had opened.

"Oh yes. I'd like that a lot." Contact, after all.

"You can attach them to your e-mails, you know."

"But I don't know how to do that. I'm a technological dinosaur. I'm still into hard copy and the U.S. mails."

"I know what you mean. I'm a two-finger typist."

Default not to sex but to computer talk, where we were both at sea.

In a wave, my energy drained. "Gravity's just increased," I said. "I need to go to sleep." And I began gathering up my things.

"How about a hug?" he asked. The ambiguous hug. Maybe we'd not abandoned the whole idea of sex after all. At least a little necking.

We both stood and clutched. No quiverings in my second chakra, not much heavy breathing from either of us.

"Good thing hormones decrease some with age," I said past his ear. Then a momentary sinking sensation, and immediately he let go and leapt backward. My hand shifted to his chest, my palm flat against his navy sweater. As he fell away, I saw my fingers peel off, my hand gently pushing him away, open. I'd agreed to this, hadn't I? He seemed to jump far off and to become very small very quickly, the way a pier recedes as your boat drops its mooring lines and heads out, gaining speed. I thought, What a great move: instant distance.

I picked up my notebook, my flashlight, my sleeping pad, and said, "'Night," eager then to be gone. A little shaken. We'd veered far off the quest's agenda, and I knew it. And I had been without food for five days, except for a few mouthfuls of ice cream, some soup.

"Good night," he said, neutral.

Twenty steps away I realized I was not on the path to my tent, but to Vern's. I turned back and muttered, embarrassed, "I'm on the wrong path."

Sparrow still stood where I'd left him, illuminated by the candle lantern's burnished silver light, his hands hooked into the front pockets of his jeans, staring into the nearly cold fire. I corrected myself in the same soft voice, "No, I'm not on the wrong path," and found the smooth, downed cottonwood I needed to climb over to get to my own sleeping bag. I doubt he heard me.

I knew I wasn't on the wrong path, but I didn't know what path I was on. It seems safe to claim paths are multiple, though that feels like a cop-out. But in the Gila the paths *were* multiple, as they are in my life. I'll admit to it in one breath, a champion of braided rivers, of many watersheds, of species diversity, of overlapping ways to know, of simultaneous loyalties. But with the next breath, I'll be tempted to offer excuses for letting desire wiggle its way into an activity that had more of a spiritual dimension—more direct, confusing contact with the irrational—than anything I'd ever done. I didn't want to admit it, I don't even now want to admit it, because to say I fell for the guide threatens to pull the plug on what the guide was guiding. The focus moves away from the journey and its transformative intent, and toward a dime romance. Or that's my fear. I know it wasn't that way. So what way was it?

I understood the problem. I wasn't so befuddled by my fast or so naïve that I didn't grasp the inherent dangers in a sexual relationship between the guide and the guided. We were equals in most ways, but in this situation we weren't.

But the question didn't have a clear answer.

What to do with that craving to be connected, to gather in as much of the spinning exuberance as possible? What to make of the gratitude you feel for the person who's engineered an opening that momentarily feels like the deepest answer you've found? Is it just that the default position between men and women is sexual? Or that the sense of high energy expansion is so disturbing and frightening that grounding it sexually serves to defuse it? Sex makes it more manageable rather than less?

Or is the sexual an appropriate way to move forward, to grow? If the creative, the spiritual, and the sexual do spring from the same source, isn't the sexual inextricably linked to the other two? In the lush spring when I first fell in love, sex had carried me across my first frontier. I couldn't tease it apart from the love I'd fallen into, but the physical had been the primary revelation. I knew as well as anyone that different impulses and different agendas could be embraced by the same act. I'd always been alert to those varieties of motives, trying never to judge, trying always to move forward through desire to let the more complicated human possibilities find expression alongside the sexual. I'd also learned my attitudes were uncommon. But I'd not let Sparrow in on any of my faintly odd sexual perspective. It was territory where I expected always to be comfortable. However, that night I felt barely seventeen. Given my experiences, my awkwardness with Sparrow surprised me more than anything.

At dawn I sat up with my sleeping bag still warming my legs and made notes to use when I'd tell the story of my fast. Slowly the sky lightened, and I spotted Sparrow across the Mimbres, thirty feet away, resolutely striding from his own sleeping bag toward camp. He didn't glance over at me. I didn't mind. We'd returned to the proper agenda.

Post-fast sacred space, via blackened abalone shell with smoldering sage. It seemed about as necessary as chewing water before you swallowed it, or inviting ice to melt in the desert. For days I'd been in space vibrating with enough odd energies to sacralize a slug, and I wondered if I'd ever get out. Or if I ever wanted to get out.

But ritual was ritual, and I'd learned it put everyone onto the same page. In real time, we all told our stories the way Doug had told his beside the fire the night before. Our tales went on all day with pee breaks in the bushes and snack breaks by the Mimbres. In the late afternoon, we changed to our forest finery: clean T-shirts, deodorant, and fresh shaves for the men. Then we drove two hours to a café in Silver City for the celebratory meal. On the last day, we focused on one story at a time, reflecting to the tale tellers what we'd heard of their journeys into myth. How did the unexpected relate to lives, to tangled conundrums? What lessons had popped up? What echoes had we heard in curious portents, from their dreams?

But for this narrative, I've interrupted the flow so it's less confusing. Responses follow hard on the heels of stories.

Two people were most relevant for me: Jenny and Chuck. Jenny embodied a feminine I'd actively avoided. Chuck had followed the life of science I'd abandoned. Two lives I recognized: there, but for the grace of the everlasting mystery, go I. While Vern's and Doug's stories had their own quirks and extravagant details, they didn't resonate with me. I've given them less space.

"So," Sparrow said, repeating himself from the night before, "the story we tell almost becomes our experience." Jill Ker Conway and the ur-male and ur-female narratives intruded in my mind: I must be sliding back to analytical land. What if the stories we tell step mostly to the culture's expectations? Can't the wrong stories pulverize experience?

Sparrow went on. "Some people make real performances out of their stories, speaking of themselves in third person, or talking to drums and music."

I chased away my suspicions, because I knew we'd all been on an inner journey in an outer world rich with unpredictability: alive and surprisingly responsive, no matter how much we overlaid "inside" onto "outside," no matter how much scripted images threatened to shape what we'd lived. In such a place, fasting into an altered state, none of us could escape the flux across our boundaries, pierced or not, influenced by standard stories or not. As we selected details and shaped our narratives, we did it in a forum unusually free of judgment and restraints. We did what humans have done since the first words were spoken: after the adventure, bring back stories. This all had a certain comforting reasonableness. What continued to stun me was how my corner of the canyon had seemed to know me better than I knew myself. I wondered if anyone else had found themselves in the same weird world.

No one made any theatrical performance art, but as I listened to my friends' stories, the drama seemed powerful enough in the words themselves, spoken in unadorned voices. The day-by-day linearity provided plenty of undergirding structure for events as strange as any dream.

"And who would like to start?" Sparrow looked around the circle.

"I'd like to," said Jenny, and we all perked up in surprise. Except for her Sarah Bernhardt imitation describing her search for her fasting spot, she'd been remarkably quiet, especially since we'd returned from our fasts.

"Oh good," said Sparrow.

"Just before coming here," she began, "I'd been in a period of celebration, moving out of shame into lightness." For long stretches she read from her notebook, and she'd taken a microrecorder on her fast, so she had a more detailed record than anyone. But her stylized language sounded as if she'd taken it from an external source. She expressed herself almost in code, and though I could understand her, the rhythms and vocabulary seemed to put up a barrier to more personal expression, perhaps even to her understanding of herself.

"But even on the plane, I felt like Mouse. And when I got here, I entered a descent. I wanted to acknowledge my celebration, but from the first circle I felt afraid.

"I feel a strong masculine influence, and that has made me uncomfortable." Oops, I finally realized, it's not just these guys; it's me, too.

"I'm strong in other areas in ways that are from the dark and more intuitive. I feel it's still the way I need to be, but now I'm also wanting more communion. I have a strong sense of when there's a block and when I can move it. My intention was to find ways to integrate sky, sun, spirit as the other way, to give me what I need in my life's work. At my threshold, I saw Mouse and Snake as dark forces and a place I could go to transform. But I also had a sense of my isolation and narrow-mindedness. For me, the danger is seeing only the subjective, and I have shame and guilt around that. But I still need to bring that with me."

Whatever else had happened to her during those four days, she'd found the nerve to speak to us with astonishing candor, in her own language.

The first day, all day, she'd done a Death Lodge, starting under her black tarp. She'd set it up with great struggle.

"It seemed like a math problem, and I felt deep embarrassment and frustration. I kept hearing the voice of giving up. I started to cry and felt the woundedness of young girls in not believing they have that kind of competence."

Finally she'd gotten the tarp up. "My daughter came first and we talked long and wonderfully. Afterwards I felt exhausted, so I went down to the water."

At the river, her seventeen-year-old son appeared in his disembodied form. "That's the way he acts in real life. He has to choose the place and time," she said.

"Then I wandered through the trees and meadows while many people came to me, including my father. In real life, he's in a home and has dementia. But in the Death Lodge, he was pissed as hell that I wasn't staying home and taking care of my family."

She paused for a sip of water. "I energetically had the last day of my life," she said, "and decided I wanted to sleep in the meadow." Her dreams came fast and furious: about trying to find directions; about losing control; about a woman with a body like aerial photos of earth lying naked on the floor of a vegetarian restaurant; about a one-legged man in the grocery line, his chest skin flayed off. "I kept trying to help him. He obviously needed it, but he refused me over and over.

"Finally I woke up and prepared to die. I took down my tarp and hated it. I spun and spun until I fell down dizzy, a kind of symbolic death. Then I climbed up into one of the caves, to be reborn. I was an Rh-negative baby, and I think that's had a big effect on my life. So I wanted to go through my birth again, consciously."

Her cave was a mining passageway cut into the mountain's rock. According to Sparrow the walls showed swirls of psychedelic yellows and purples, a real geologic show, visible in flashlight beams. But the cave had a major downside: clouds of flies. When no one moved, they rested quietly on the walls; but when anyone stirred, the flies rose in agitated masses. I wondered that Jenny mentioned none of those details.

"I walked about sixty feet in to where it was nearly dark, and I settled down with my sleeping bag." She spent the rest of the day and her second night in her rock womb.

My fondness for caves barely extended past their mysterious openings, and I thought of the rippling meadows and dancing cottonwoods she'd forsaken for her psychic agenda.

"I wanted the cave to speak to me," she went on. "I wanted to know her, but in the end I couldn't bridge to truth, so I told Cave's story. But it wasn't Cave's story. I felt my limits."

Twice she felt intense, nauseating pain in her gut, but worked through it by concentrating on aligning her chakras. A bat came and went. Another bat. She had three more complicated dreams.

"I woke up when light came from the entrance again, and I saw my son leaving the cave. I said, 'I'm outta here, I'm going to the sacred mountain.'" I was as relieved as she'd been.

"I was born!" she crowed.

"But I needed a break. I needed to be loose and free." She'd told her tale for more than an hour already. We were still riveted.

Sparrow got up and disappeared behind a tree to pee. "Talk louder!" he called over his shoulder.

"I moved next to a pond with lots of frogs and lay on my stomach with my feet up behind me. I started to paint, but my judge and shame were still around. I pleaded for them to go away. Suddenly a bird came and landed on my foot!" Then it flitted to the ground in front of her and hung out for five minutes. "I don't know what it was," she said, "a dove, maybe.

"On my fourth day, I found a sandy, exposed area by the water and took off all my clothes. I bathed in the river, like I was getting ready for love. I basked in the sand; then I made love to myself, letting the sun guide me, wanting sky energies to impregnate me and grow in my life."

I remembered the river's flow racing through my own body, fluid and alive.

"Then I climbed the hill and laid out my Purpose Circle. But when I tried to go back to it later at dusk, I missed the landmarks and couldn't find it. So I just decided my Purpose Circle was right there. I shifted out of the place of form to hold essence."

Alas, I thought, she needs more form, less essence.

"I prayed. And prayed. Eventually I felt all prayed out, and I dozed. I woke up, and the tree next to me spoke. 'Be patient; great gifts await.'"

She felt open to the sky, but freezing and awake, and the night passed very quickly.

When she finally finished her two and a half hours of story, Sparrow asked, "Can you tell me more about the content of the bird interaction?" Besides the various cave bats, the bird had been the most concrete external detail in her whole narrative. And something she hadn't planned. The unexpected. A gift from Hermes. But her answer to Sparrow had nothing extraordinary. "It hopped around, looking interested." I marveled at how she'd woven four days around an urge to become less subjective, but had kept her subjectivity wound tightly around her, like a dark Muslim chador. But undeniably, she'd become more open and more confident and felt a pride of endurance and achievement.

Pee break for everyone.

Here I must make a small confession. My journal notes read, "It was touching almost beyond measure to see the considered, attentive, loving, and honest responses to the stories, images, conscious thoughts, events—to an extent I've never seen anywhere, under any circumstances." But though we said much, and everyone had an original take, I remember only a fraction of the actual words.

The energy lived in the moment, and the memory of that energy has stayed with me, rather than the language that generated it.

With some exceptions. I recall what I said to everyone, and the singular sensation of becoming a vibrating source in the midst of the vastness of the Gila Wilderness. I recall what everyone said to me about my fasting story, and the deep, humming pleasure I felt as the object of their focus. I recall a few other surprising comments, and some of what Sparrow reflected back to everyone.

Writer Susan Griffin says, in *A Chorus of Stones*, "It is perhaps a choice each of us makes over and over, even many times throughout one day, whether to use knowledge as power or intimacy."

I didn't know about anyone else, but despite the trust we'd developed, despite the practice we'd had with each other's dreams, I felt an enormous sense of impending judgment. My stomach clenched: not only would I be judged, but we'd all been given the task of speaking about others' most tender spots. It felt much worse than cheerleading tryouts in high school.

No cocktail conversation here. It didn't match the way we'd all been socialized to get along in the world. I'd spent many years avoiding exactly this kind of exchange, except with my lovers. Here, politeness didn't count. In fact, it was tacitly banned. Otherwise, what point could there be? Our unspoken directive: be as perceptive as you can, be loving, but do not flinch. As we moved through our stories, I became more and more aware that exactly this careful listening, these honest responses, were skills that would help each of us in our non-quest lives. Altered states, Death Lodges, inexplicable relationships with the natural world, and the non-ordinary realities we'd all encountered were the most obvious part of the show, but this utterly human, utterly mundane activity of exchanging meaningful words was equally important.

The circumstances helped: our fasts were mythic journeys, at some remove from our real lives; and despite our closeness, this community was temporary. We'd scatter in two days. We need never see each other again.

Sparrow said, "We'll use the deer antler Vern found as a talking stick. You can only say something while you hold the antler. OK?" We all nodded. "So you can really listen, someone else will take notes for you. We'll trade off so everyone will only have to take notes once. Does this all make sense?" We all nodded again.

"OK. Jenny."

We started leafing through our voluminous notes and when Sparrow said, "All right," Doug groaned. "I'm only on day two!" But Sparrow picked up the deer antler and began.

He didn't mince words, and I felt my own mild panic at knowing Jenny didn't welcome what he said. To do his job, he couldn't mince words. "I'm not even going to try to interpret your dreams. I think you could do that as well as me. You've done enough work with Snake. You understand the darkness. You need to move on. You were out there four days, and you spent two of them in the dark?" He shook his head. I remembered the canyon's swirling light.

"Your son wouldn't even come under your black tarp in your Death Lodge. He'd only appear at the river. Your son is one of your guides. Pay attention to that. The bird that landed on your foot is important. That happened when you were the loosest and most off your agenda." He looked at her a moment. I could sense her tautness next to me. He elaborated, but his meaning remained: let in the light. Let the unpredictable outwardness illuminate your inner darkness. Open. Inner and outer: tenacious polestars for others besides me. She had wanted to be praised, but Sparrow had told her she was stuck. Still stuck.

He handed Chuck the antler. Chuck looked directly at Jenny, not aggressively, but with no hint of uncertainty. "It's been interesting for me to be in such close quarters with your strongly female energy. On last year's quest there were only men, and I think it helped that there were both genders this time. I had a lot of trouble at first with your direct eye contact, which made me really uncomfortable, but with Sparrow's help I found a way to talk to you about it." I had sensed a mild tension between them, but hadn't realized it had been strong enough that they'd needed to discuss it. Now it was out in the open with all of us.

"I'm going to tell you a secret about men. Even it if seems like we know what we're doing, we don't. We just act that way." Doug nodded beside me. "When we start a project, we just barrel ahead because we figure we can improvise as we go." I smiled. I did things that way, too.

He told a story about rebuilding a carburetor with his engineer dad. "And when we had it all back together, I said I was glad he'd known what he was doing. And you know what he said? 'Oh I didn't have a clue, but that never matters.'" Chuck laughed.

"You really are in the grip of the darkness, almost loving your incompetence. I kind of think you just need to relax. But all that time in the cave really impressed me. You're much braver than me."

When my turn rolled around, I had to echo Chuck. "I appreciated living around such different female energy than mine. I don't get that opportunity very often." She smiled in gratitude. But I needed to address some of the crucial things I'd heard in her story.

"In many ways, I've always felt more male than female, and I'm very comfortable around men. So your uneasiness here probably hasn't been just these guys, but me, too." I looked at my notes.

"I was struck by your repeated worries about getting lost in the wild, about your self-judgment around setting up your tarp, about all your dreams around water. To me, that is about ignoring particulars." I wasn't into the dark and light stuff. It smacked of gender stereotypes.

"You're in the ocean, which has some great advantages, but you need to come in to shore to get your bearings. The settings you chose for your processes were wonderful, but the specifics kept getting drowned. I think you need to remember the tide pools at the edge of land and see the fabulous stuff that fills them. Pay attention to the details: the starfish and hermit crabs and periwinkles. You can go out to sea again when you need to. It doesn't mean you need always to be land bound." I had thought that when I'd first met her, and her story confirmed it.

I felt relieved to acknowledge her differences from me and to assuage some of my regret at not being able to bond with her more strongly. I knew she'd have been more comfortable if we had. Females together. Sisterhood is powerful. Not this time. I also felt an uneasiness that I'd been judging her because she embodied so dramatically what I'd always perceived as cultural gooiness: stereotypical female imprecision.

Maybe I had the same internalized images as the guys? I didn't quite know what was hers and what was mine.

When we'd all had our say, Jenny spoke with a small catch in her voice, "I appreciate your comments, but I still feel somewhat misunderstood."

All the guys had used the same paired dichotomies: dark/light, female/male. It was an old, old setup, but its tenacity proved neither its accuracy nor its personal usefulness, no matter how many religions had embraced it to order the cosmos. Ironically, Jenny seemed to be gripped by the same dualities, but she'd attributed more positive values both to dark and to female. In Jenny's story and in the group's responses, I could see the pitfalls of relying too much on mythological frameworks. I agreed with Sparrow in principle, "You've done enough work with Snake," and maybe that's what she needed to hear, but it also seemed to trigger her ingrained defenses.

🍃

Vern's story.

The afternoon before we'd gone out to our fasts, Vern had unpacked his two rattles. On his way through Albuquerque, he'd bought them at the Palms Trading Company, and they surpassed any rattles I'd ever seen. Each one had a substantial two-foot-long wooden handle, stained and wrapped, topped with a hollow leather head. Both heads had been painted with shiny black backgrounds, one with a howling coyote (I could forgive him—he didn't live in New Mexico), the other with a waterfall. Lustrous black feathers hung from the beaded wrapping, their cords first passing through slices of elk antlers.

"They told me they were filled with quartz crystals," Vern said as we each took turns trying them out. A little shake, one rattle at each ear, and you knew even Niagara Falls couldn't give you such an aural jolt.

Vern had a full set of props for a vision quest: not only rattles, but a pipe with an herb called kinnikinnick to smoke, a high dramatic rock with a great view, and most importantly, the enthusiasm of a beginner. His life had jumped the tracks, but he still expected the old wheels to work. He had the tools, and he expected if he followed the blueprint like a competent contractor, his house of spirit would rise, vision by vision. To his dismay, that wasn't the way it worked in this non-two-by-four territory, but he'd done his best. Consider the rattles.

"The first night, I used the rattles for the first time," he said, almost ruefully. "Across the way on the ridge, little white lights blinked on and off in the trees. That's all that happened. I had the feeling someone was behind me, but I walked in a circle, and no one was there. Sometimes it felt like the earth was moving a little.

"The next night when I started rattling again, the pinpoints of light were less distinct but flew up like embers from a fire. I rattled longer and harder, but it never got any better. After a few minutes, the crickets took up the rattling rhythm in unison.

"The third night, I rattled again. The lights were back, but fainter. But they were colored. On the ridge there were red lights. I felt really frustrated because I thought it should be getting more intense, but it was getting worse!

"By the time I was in my Purpose Circle, the rattling seemed more like a game, a drug-trip thing just to get high." He tried the pipe on his second night. "But I didn't have much connection with it, and I didn't like the taste, and it was hard to get the taste out of my mouth."

He bathed in the river "to wash off my spiritual timidity," found lots of bear scat, and saw many flickers, who seemed fond of the ponderosas at his high, rocky outpost.

And one afternoon, "I looked around, and the air was almost completely still. I looked down-canyon and saw an astonishing thing: the air was filled with bright insects moving around like mists, and long floating silken threads. I have no idea what they were, but they were beautiful. It was magical." I smiled at my memories of the same air, swirling with life.

Every night he had long, complicated dreams, including one with a delightful image: "I was working for a kind of crazy guy. He was an idiot savant or a manic-depressive; I didn't quite know what to make of him. Anyway, he had fits of temper that made no sense. But he had fancy clients like Ted Turner and was a great woodworker. At one point, he took me to the back of his shop where there was a huge table saw with six enormous circular blades. And he had a giant piece of wood, a six-by-six filled with all kinds of bent and rusty nails. It was a real mess. Something you'd never let in the door of a woodworking shop. But he ran the piece of wood through the monster table saw, and out the other end came something with lots of parts, but folded up. When he unfolded it, a perfect dollhouse popped up, kind of Victorian, and with all the details. In the dream I said, 'Oh! Now I see!'"

By the time Vern had gotten to his Purpose Circle on the last night, he knew he needed to reduce his expectations, but he was still going for the big vision. "I kept thinking, 'I've done all this stuff; I've paid my money; something big's supposed to happen. But nothing's happening. This is just meaningless and silly. The vision quest is just silly.' I was trying to follow a recipe and trying to figure out what to do with these changes, but it wasn't working the way I thought it should. I wasn't in a good frame of mind. It was cold. And I thought, 'If I did have a vision, what would I want? That something would come clear in my mind about what I want to do? Teaching? That's tangible. But teaching what?'"

And in the midst of relating his litany of annoyance, he said this, "When I write, a kind of magic happens. I'll keep doing that no matter what."

He went on. "I thought, 'If a big vision happens, I could go back to my sleeping bag!' So I went and got my sleeping bag and brought it into the circle and finally crawled in and fell asleep. I woke up at seven thirty in the morning. And my right arm didn't work at all. I must have slept wrong on it." I thought, I'll bet it was all that rattling. Those rattles are heavy.

He paused.

"Now that I'm back, I'm feeling like I was very arrogant. I'm really a baby in these things and very immature. I feel very small all of a sudden. I think it's a valuable lesson in reduced expectations. But that crazy boss in my dreams—he seems like a kind of guide, maybe."

Sparrow waited a moment, then made a single comment, which seemed his way of closing the story. "I felt your story was in some sense simple and openhearted. You're enjoying the process of looking for answers, and you don't want to be told what the answers are."

Vern looked at him gratefully and said, "You know, those filaments in the air were beautiful, and they were real. That was the most profound visionary experience, and it was *real*."

I smiled again.

"What were they?" Vern asked.

Doug answered, "Haven't you read *Charlotte's Web*? A baby spider was on the end of every thread."

⟩⟩

Silver City. The Celebratory Meal, two hours south of the Mimbres.

Did it start with the salsa and chips? The guacamole? Or the tacos and chile rellenos? I can't remember. We couldn't stop laughing. The trigger didn't matter: we had released into a giddiness beyond laughter, into the silliness of nine-year-olds. As my mother would say, we were slaphappy. Giggles welled up from my gut; I grimaced involuntarily; laughter erupted like sobs. I could vaguely see Vern across from me, trying to stay on his chair. Doug put his face into his hands, shaking and bouncing, as out of control as I was. We couldn't look at each other without making it worse. I couldn't stop. No one else could stop. I wasn't sure what was going on at the other end of the table, but it didn't matter. We'd finally snapped. Tears squeezed out of my eyes. No effort could slow it until it ran its course. We all shook. Slowly I wound down. Doug and Vern wound down. We all finally sighed and turned back to our refried beans.

Someone mentioned Jackson Pollock in the same breath as the painting on the wall: nubile Mexican maidens bringing animals to be blessed by a white-cassocked priest. I said, "My favorite Jackson Pollack story is about when he met Peggy Guggenheim for the first time. He pissed his name on the side of the fireplace."

Dead silence. I leaned back in my chair and moaned slightly through a grin. In a minute, down the table, Sparrow rested on his elbows and said, "That was a conversation stopper." I looked at him sharply, remembering I'd said exactly that sentence to him late the night before. Vern angled across the table toward me. "I'll be your mother: 'That was interesting,'" he said in a flat voice, and we were off again into giggles. They swept over us like waves, washing everything ahead of them, washing out built-up tensions into the brightly lit restaurant, washing us out. Over and over.

By the time Jenny decided she needed coffee for the drive back, the kitchen staff had cleaned the coffeepot. Where to get coffee in Silver City at nine thirty at night? Plus we had four large plastic bags of garbage in our trunks. The Forest Service had removed all the trash cans from the Gila.

Albertsons? Wal-Mart? We hated Wal-Mart. Dunkin' Donuts? No Dunkin' Donuts. Albertsons. Open twenty-four hours, and they had trash cans in the parking lot. Taco Bell? Closed. Wal-Mart? They had trash cans in the parking lot. None of us made any sense, and we couldn't move. We went round and round, happily befuddled. Albertsons? Albertsons for trash cans and to check out how the Red Sox had done in the World Series. We'd keep our eyes open for coffee. But maybe Wal-Mart, after all? No. Albertsons. Was there any place else? No. Albertsons.

At Albertsons we giggled less, but the silliness kept on. Our bonding had carried us into a loose, light bubble of in-jokes and spontaneous affection. We stood close to each other and wisecracked about baseball, chicken fingers, the bizarre brightness of huge grocery stores.

And finally we headed back through the dark to the Mimbres.

🪶

In the white rental car (now caked with mud), I sat in Sparrow's passenger seat and asked, "How was your apprenticeship with Steven Foster and Meredith Little?" Along with another wilderness guide named Joseph Jastrab, they had done more than anyone to thread together the modern framework of this experience, though Sparrow had elaborated it and, like any good director, had made it his own.

"They were the first teachers I found who were the same in their living room as in their books," he started, happily launching into his story. "I'd run into a bunch of folks who sounded one way in their writings but weren't that way at all in person. I'd gotten pretty disillusioned.

"I stayed there for two months, fourteen years ago. I camped on National Forest land about two miles up from where they lived and walked down to their house every morning. I'd usually just spend the day with Steven, doing whatever he had to do—gathering sage or cutting wood—and we'd talk. He's got the biggest heart of anyone I've ever known." He shook his head and smiled at the memory of his friend.

"Did you do a quest with them, too?" I asked.

"Yeah," he said, "it was at the end of my time. I was one of the leaders, but I also went out and fasted. The quest was with a group who had just graduated from the Institute of Transpersonal Psychology. Steven asked me if I was comfortable doing the talk on personal ceremony with them. And he and Meredith didn't even come and watch. I was really nervous. Boy, was that group big on symbolism! Whew!" He laughed.

"And you grew up then?"

He said, "Yeah. Age thirty-seven. Seems old, but better late than never, I figure. I fasted for three days in a narrow canyon, womblike. In the Last Chance Range. But then the old bug hit."

"Old bug?"

"The craving to be melodramatic. Big gestures." He laughed again. "I decided I wanted to do my Purpose Circle on a mountain peak. Pretty nutty; I hadn't eaten for three days—you know how it is."

"Yup," I said.

"And the desert was already hot as hell that time of year. But I packed up the six big stones I'd found for the six directions—big honkers, bigger than grapefruits. Also a jacket and sweater and a couple garbage bags, and took off. No sleeping bag. Well, when I got to the first peak I saw a higher one, and when I got there, I saw another one. I had to run and slide and really push to get up there before sunset. But I made it—just barely. Luckily that was the highest peak.

"All I could think of was the sunrise, the great views in all directions, how tough I was. A big triumph. Well, to make a long story short, once the sun went down it got really cold and windy. No sleeping bag, remember. I pulled on the rest of my clothes, climbed into the garbage bags, and huddled behind my pack. But I still froze half the night, staring at my knees, shivering, really miserable.

"But then the full moon was about to set behind the Inyo Range, and I thought I'd bid her goodnight. So I got up, frozen and stiff, and faced the west and thanked her. I sang her some moon chants, danced a little until she disappeared.

"When I went to sit down again, I realized I wasn't cold anymore. So for the rest of the night, I went around the circle facing each direction in turn, thanking, praising, singing, dancing. Until dawn. Giving instead of inflating myself. As the sun came up, I stopped."

I thought briefly about my own failure to keep awake all night.

"I hiked out," he went on, "taking the rocks with me, of course, feeling chastened but much wiser.

"When I got back to the group at base camp Meredith asked where my Purpose Circle had been. I pointed out the mountain, and she said in this exasperated voice, 'I'm really glad I didn't know where you were.'" He paused. "Then she gave me a hard look and said, 'I hope sometime you get to have a client just like you. Then you'll know!'"

I laughed then. "So," I asked, "when did you start leading quests?"

"That summer I had brochures printed up, and I think I did a quest for two women that fall."

"It stuck then?"

"Yup," he said, "it stuck."

Doug dozed in the backseat. He'd probably already heard this story. Sparrow had surely told it many times.

We bounced down the dirt road again and forded the creeks to our camp. The trip back had passed in a flash, and at eleven thirty, I felt more awake than when we'd left. Not only did a general caffeine buzz hum in the air, but we knew it was our last night. The last night of camp. Jenny and I wandered in the direction of the cold campfire. Out of the darkness, Chuck spoke.

"Where's the action?" We'd aged from giggling nine-year-olds to fifteen-year-olds wanting to hang out. With no strip to cruise in our fathers' Chevys, we settled for standing in a close circle under the shadowy cottonwoods. And singing songs from the sixties. And more songs. And more songs. Mostly I listened, only joining in off-key for my favorites. Unaccountably, Doug had disappeared into his sleeping bag.

With the prodigious memory of a just-released laptop and the voice of an aging Beach Boy, Chuck rolled out tune after tune. Every five songs, Sparrow said, "I wish I could remember how 'Dancing in the Dark' goes." And Chuck was off again.

We sang more songs.

"The tune's almost like 'Here Comes the Sun,'" Sparrow said. "But not quite."

We sang more songs.

My legs started to quiver from tiredness and cold.

"If I could just get a few of the lyrics . . . ," Sparrow said.

We sang more songs.

At one, Doug nosed into the circle. Three of us spoke at once, "Hey!

How could you sleep through all this?" He laughed, his hands deep in his jeans pockets.

"I was sure you all would go to bed after 'Henry the Eighth,' but you just didn't stop! I can't believe you didn't light a fire."

But Jenny and Chuck and I had reached our limits and peeled off in different directions toward our sleeping bags. As I crawled over the huge cottonwood trunk, Vern, Doug, and Sparrow set up a howling from the reduced circle. We all howled together.

⁂

The next morning, I stumbled out of my sleeping bag last and seemed more fuzzed than anyone else. Groggily I lit my stove to make tea. Doug and Sparrow stood on the other side of the cold fire ring. Before my water boiled, Sparrow took off on his serenade, grinning at me as he sang.

"I get up in the evening / And I ain't got nothin' to say / I go to bed in the morning / Feeling the same way." He kept his hands in his fleece-lined flight jacket and hopped back and forth from foot to foot keeping time, his eyebrows scrunched up, his eyes locked on mine.

"You can't start a fire without a spark / This gun's for hire / Even if we're just dancing in the dark." All the verses, all the choruses, without the Boss's E-Street Band, only the oblivious Mimbres, gurgling on.

"You can't start a fire / Worried about your little world falling apart / This gun's for hire / Even if we're just dancing in the dark."

Nothing to do but laugh. Ritual, ceremony, smudging, heroes' journeys, seductions with uncertain endings, pointed Bruce Springsteen before breakfast. Hermes couldn't have done better himself.

⁂

Chuck's story.

Chuck began, "It was painful in many ways and perhaps the most difficult days I've lived through." We were off again on another four-day tour of an externalized psyche. In the circle, attention vibrated like a taut string. A rare gift: a focused audience willing to keep with you for as long as you were willing to speak. We not only told our stories, but knew beyond a doubt our stories were heard.

"Before the fast, I'd had good experiences in my morning walks, and I was surprised at how rough the fast was. But I'll admit the idea of piercing almost got in the way." He took a deep breath. "The night before we went out, I dreamed I was with a baby who was suffocating. I had a respirator but couldn't get it to work. Finally I got it going and just touched the baby with it, but before I could put it on, the baby coughed and breathed. Then it spoke to me with my father's voice." He cleared his throat. He didn't tell us what his father's voice said. A raven laughed up-canyon.

"The hard work began with the leaving ceremony. I'd found a flaked piece of white chert on the ridge and put it on one of the stones in the circle, but when I left, I forgot it. When I remembered, I started berating myself like crazy, and even started to cry. I thought maybe I'd disrupted something or breached some kind of ceremonial etiquette of Sparrow's. I felt really bad." His eyes teared up. "But then I thought: if my daughter had done that, I wouldn't criticize her. I'd be proud of her for being her own person. Maybe I have two children, my daughter and my inner child. Eventually I felt better—if I could be proud of her, I could be proud of myself.

"In the middle of the first day, I did my Death Lodge. But it was about the same as last year, with my daughter, my quasi-wife, my mother, my two sisters, down to my work colleagues. I dispensed with them quickly. Nothing dramatic.

"But on my hike up the canyon I had the first of three unsettling and dangerous things happen.

"I was rock climbing a really steep wall on the northeast side of the canyon. It wasn't very technical, but somehow I dislodged a large boulder—very large." He held his hands two feet apart. "It came crashing down. I just leaned out of the way and it bounced past. But it made me more cautious."

We all sighed.

"Then, after the Death Lodge, I was sitting under some trees writing in my journal, and I looked down and saw a scorpion crawling up my pants leg." Yikes, I thought, scorpion stings can be more deadly than snakebites. "I just watched it. I didn't flinch like I might have done in the past. But those pants have zip-off legs, and the scorpion crawled under the zipper flap. I knew there was a two-inch gap where the zipper stopped, and it could get on my leg, so I carefully folded back the flap and flicked it off."

We all sighed.

"I had real trouble falling asleep and had a hard night. Not much sleep.

"The next day was my Burial Day, which was my cave experience." He glanced at Jenny. "But I could never have stayed in as long as you did. My cave was up the canyon, and I went in about seventy feet, maybe, and I got to some sort of wooden apparatus. I wasn't using my flashlight because a little light came in from the entrance. When I could go no farther, I sat down and thought about death and dying. But only for about twenty minutes. Then I looked over the wooden apparatus and saw a shaft on the other side. I dropped a stone and counted: it was sixty or seventy feet down. To go back out, I turned on my flashlight and could see I'd walked in along a sixteen-inch-wide ledge that dropped off into the shaft."

We all sighed again.

"But my reaction was the same as with the scorpion. I felt taken care of. I wasn't at all freaked out. Just at the entrance, three bats flew in front of me, and the light through their wings made them look luminous. Great feeling. There's a line from some movie I thought of, 'I can't be a ghost; I gotta be a spirit!'

"I walked on up the streambed and found a slanted rock formation covered with bees and hornets, but I got through them OK and returned to my spot."

He had another hard night, very cold.

On his third day, he'd gone on a river journey, a hike downstream. "That day I saw all of you—except Jenny—and two backpackers."

Says writer Susan Griffin, again from *A Chorus of Stones*, "Writing about one's own life, it is only when one writes about the most intimate and seemingly idiosyncratic details that one touches others." Idiosyncratic details didn't belong in the stories science tells about the world, where generalization is the goal. If you do research with lab mice, you can pick any mouse out of the cages, and it will give you what you need, whether it's liver tissue or a functioning immune system. One mouse will act like the next mouse. Or the next thousand mice.

Chuck's trail of six thousand dead rats and ten thousand dead mice had earned him the nickname Dachau Davidson. I'd worked in labs and knew how powerful the urge to black humor, the urge to keep a distance. He was lucky his nightmares had finally nudged him into other work.

Jenny had felt like Mouse on her plane ride west and had seen Mouse and Snake as dark forces where she could go to transform. Chuck identified with Mouse as much as Jenny had, but for different reasons. For Chuck, a mouse had always been a furry machine with the attributes of life: a tool not quite alive, but alive enough to study life. On the first day when Chuck had said, "I'm almost human, but not quite," I'd thought, "Wow. What a thing to say. Of course he's human. What's got into him?" He felt himself and Mouse as equally machines. Science has been skewered for such mechanizing of the animate world, but Chuck offered himself as evidence, with no broader agenda than his personal release.

He didn't tell us in so many words he identified with the many small machine-creatures he'd euthanized, while he'd kept his distance, but used his own images: the leather-encased heart, the shell around his being that needed to be pierced. And he'd never rid himself of his guilt.

Nowhere in any protocols of science could Chuck have found anything remotely like Sparrow's perspective: "The story we tell almost becomes our experience." It reeked of scientific heresy, the non-reproducibility of subjectivity, despite the Heisenberg uncertainty principle.

But he'd embraced the idea of the malleability of experience, despite all scientific method. He clearly relished relating his own idiosyncratic details, and he was comfortable in company where no one blinked at trees speaking in complete sentences, where no one would mock him for focusing on his particular personal, non-reproducible experience. In his real life, he felt dramatically isolated. Chuck knew practically no one he could tell about what he'd been doing out in the Gila Wilderness: fasting, dreaming, encountering scorpions, hanging out in dangerous caves, becoming human.

"So I was a ways down the river and stopped to do the special TM sutra for flying. I've done TM for seventeen years. The flying sutra is like a black belt in karate. It's a big secret. No one's supposed to know what it is without all the initiation hoopla." But he demonstrated it for us anyway.

"You saw it here first!" He grinned. Next to having his bothersome shell pierced, he longed for a dream where he finally could fly. Always in the past, someone had held him down.

"At the very end of the flying sutra, I saw a brief image of one of the cutest animals I ever killed—a tiny monkeylike critter. I was twenty-two and the zoologist on an expedition in South America at the time. The image had its arms raised and was wearing one of those Amazonian feather crowns, which changed to thorns." And he told us the sad details of that trip.

"Then I got into an inner dialogue about guilt. I'm the world champion of guilt. I've kind of thought that by self-punishment, I could be responsible for my actions. But somehow the Christian notion of atonement doesn't work for me. Forgiveness doesn't mean anything unless you have the capacity to feel empathy.

"And just then I saw a pair of backpackers—a father and daughter. So I sprinted away into the woods." On our fasts we treated human encounters like animal encounters. Except: we could talk to animals, but we were supposed to avoid conversations with humans. He'd landed in a sand bank.

"So I thought it might be a good time for a ceremonial piercing. I made a sand angel, like a snow angel, then got up and pierced the heart with a stick. First time the stick broke." He looked at Sparrow. "I swear. But the second time it stuck in the sand. I didn't want to pierce the heart, just the leather membrane around the heart."

Back to camp. "I had another really hard night.

"Day four," he said and took a sip from his water bottle, "I was wasted. And I had terrible heartburn. But I wanted to do a baptism. Every time I'd gone down to the river the other days, Doug was there. The first time he had no clothes on, and the next time he was covered in mud, so I figured he was into his own process." We all laughed. "But about one thirty, I finally took the plunge. As I jumped in, I said over my shoulder, 'Bye, sins!'" We laughed again that someone so wasted with severe heartburn could do something so wiggy.

"Back at camp, I mostly lay down until time to do the Purpose Circle. I named the stones and then spoke to them as a group. I told them I wanted to fly. I wanted to live a life of purpose. And I wanted to rid myself of past guilts.

"I had a really hard time keeping awake, even singing, so in the middle of the night I started doing a stomach clench. Like the flying exercise." He demonstrated again in his Therm-a-Rest chair, rocking and vibrating a little, and bouncing. "First I did it to keep warm, then I was doing it involuntarily."

"How long did you do that?" asked Sparrow.

"Probably about five hours."

We all sighed.

"About six in the morning, I realized I'd been flying all night. When I could see the sun, I finally shuffled out. My threshold was the line between shadow and sunshine."

He paused.

"I was struck by my relationship to a Spirit that for these four days was a cross between a drill sergeant and a teasing older brother, who kept saying, 'You've got a job to do.' And he didn't make it easy. It was like a trial to go through, with love and support, but it was meant to be dangerous. But maybe that's what it took to break that final barrier in my life. In a sense maybe it was a piercing."

Sparrow asked, "Does your gut give you an answer?"

Chuck answered immediately, "It's not a simple answer. It's that and some other stuff. I've worn my guilt all my life like a badge of honor almost. Maybe now I can give it up. Maybe I really want change and atonement now. I'm not sure what else."

Sparrow smiled. "My friend John says, 'Knowing why, that's the booby prize of life.' You chose a hard way, and you loved it. I want to honor it as your way."

We all sighed one last time.

And we all stretched. Then we scattered into the bushes. The sun had moved the shadows around the clearing just the way it had moved them before we'd fasted. We slid our Therm-a-Rests to new shade.

❧

Mirroring Chuck.

Chuck offered us a preface. "I should give you a little background about my father. He was a rather famous engineer and in the field invented things people still use. I always admired him enormously. But he had a hard time expressing emotions. The first time he ever hugged me was when I was in college. My mother was domineering, and I had two sisters, so his influence in the family was small. He was proud of me, I'm sure." He fell silent. He'd finished his intro and the antler began its move around the circle.

Vern said, among other things I've forgotten, "Your guilt is your karma. Give it up as a crutch."

Sparrow said, "You saw more people than anyone on your fast. And I was struck by all the women who came to your Death Lodge. You need more friends. But especially more men friends." He looked at Chuck intently a moment and nodded to emphasize his point. "And you need to treat yourself with the same compassion as you treat your daughter. Usually I mention to people when they head out for their fasts that they might want to leave something at the circle as a token of faith that they'll return from their symbolic deaths. I forgot to say that this time. You were the only one who did it."

Jenny said, "Since you've felt devoured by the feminine—" Chuck interrupted her, "Not devoured, smothered. Big difference." Jenny corrected herself and continued, "I see your strong effort to reclaim an intuitive knowledge that comes from your feminine side."

I finished the last sentence of the notes I'd been writing in Chuck's journal, passed it to Doug, and took the antler from Jenny. I looked up across the circle to Chuck, the morning sun at his back, cottonwood leaves along the Mimbres behind him stirring in the breeze. He wore an uncomfortable, deadly serious expression.

While he'd talked about his nearly endless trail of murdered small rodents, I'd remembered the afternoon my relationship with science had shifted decisively. During the fragrant North Carolina spring of 1969, I stopped by Duke's physiology lab with my lab partner, Nancy. Although protests of new bombing in Vietnam had canceled classes, our grad instructor had modified our experiment for outside the lab. He asked us to observe semipermeable membranes. We needed only a fresh small intestine. Our white rat sniffed around the smooth black counter top while Nancy and I discussed how we'd off her.

"Here," grunted our instructor, eager to be gone, "this is quickest." He gripped the naked pink tail, swung the rat in a wide arc over his head, and whacked her on the counter. Dead rat, and the force of the blow had conveniently popped loose the small intestine at both ends. That afternoon of the rat whack made it clear to me science overlooked a lot. And that incompleteness, particularly when it was denied or ignored, could lead to disturbing consequences. Despite concerted efforts in certain camps, science has never explained war. And it's never explained love.

Back in our circle beside the Mimbres, my inner eye momentarily saw the lab outside Washington where I'd worked the summer after the rat whack, in a much-sought-after job as a microbiology lab assistant. My boss, a dentist turned researcher, remains one of the dearest, gentlest men I've ever known. All the others, from big gun to summer intern, were equally kind and cordial. In their white lab coats, they worked daily at their small pieces of the puzzles of science. I admired their diligence and their careful efforts to be fine craftsmen of the scientific method. And I'd been appalled at the prospect of spending my life that way. That summer I rejected institutional science—though not science as one method of understanding—and skittered off into the unknown.

Chuck's path had been the one I'd run from, smelling certain strangulation. I'd been tempted back several times, most recently by ecology grad school at the University of New Mexico, but I had always sniffed the same dangers.

I began, "I probably understand the world where you spend your days more than anyone in this group." That much I'd thought about beforehand. I had no idea what else would pop out of my mouth.

"I know how nutty this all would seem to most of your colleagues, and I have enormous admiration for the courage it's taken for you to try to sort out your life this way. I was struck by your story this morning about your father's emotional distance and by the obvious pride you feel for his achievements. And your pride in what you are able to do.

Your mind is very strong." I felt myself tearing up, trying to find the right words to express to him what I deeply believed. I identified with his struggles and knew that his work, and probably even his guilt, were only obvious external manifestations of a greater inner turmoil.

I'd known it intimately: disturbing distance, inner cut off from outer by a hard shell, science's culture accentuating an inborn inclination to objectify, needs unmet, isolation, longings. A confusion about how to proceed.

I went on. "Your mind can be a partner in your efforts. You don't need to keep it cordoned off away from this part of your life. But it does need the balance of intuition or Spirit or the unknowable. But they also need the balance of your mind." My sentences came slowly, and I understood I spoke as much to myself, for myself, as to Chuck. The hesitation and emotion that came attached to my words meant they bubbled up from a spot that didn't get much verbal airing. Inner to outer, not to map my own landscape, but to try to be of help to another. I felt more emotion speaking to Chuck than I had when I'd revealed my own most personal details.

"Early on," I continued, "maybe even on the first day, you said, 'I want to become human,' and I thought then, 'He's already human.' You're being unbelievably hard on yourself. You're absolutely human. Take my word for it."

I'd been wholly engrossed in Chuck and what I was saying, but suddenly I caught Sparrow out of the corner of my eye, sitting cross-legged, but leaning forward toward me on his elbows, chin in hands, forehead wrinkled in concentration, staring hard at me as I spoke. And on a track of consciousness parallel to honest expression and focus on Chuck, I had two reactions. The old one: "Oh shit, I'm letting down my camo gear and really exposing myself." And a new one, not entirely admirable: "Oh. I'm putting on a good show here."

And hard on the heels of those thoughts came a surprising synthesis: "I'm probably most useful to Chuck because I'm exposing myself, and no harm's coming from that openness. And I can be honest and put on a good show at the same time. And it feels great. Maybe it's a good show *because* I'm so revealing." I continued mirroring the details of his fasting story, but with less emotion. With my own realization, I'd moved out of the charged territory where our histories overlapped and into a story that belonged completely to him.

I wound up. "I was very impressed by your physical drive and stamina and especially your five-hour stomach clench. Wow. And I loved that your threshold was where shadow became sun."

I nodded I'd finished and sat back. He inclined his head in thanks.

"Do you have any questions or anything you'd like to say to us?" Sparrow asked.

"Some of that was pretty hard to take." He seemed genuinely shaken. "The compliments, I mean. I don't really think I have any questions. Thank you all."

During the break, their words covered by the laughing Mimbres, Chuck and Sparrow stood in the sun talking quietly, Sparrow's hands on his hips, his head tilted back so he could look straight into Chuck's eyes.

🌱

I was next.

After we'd all resettled, Sparrow grinned at me expectantly. We exchanged no freighted glances, spoke no double entendres. Our late conversation around the cold fire ring might not have happened.

"Don't I get a poem?" I asked. He'd read poems for all the others.

He said, "Oh, oh, oh—" and he found his sheaf of poems.

I started, "Mostly I felt like I was in Nirvana for the entire time . . ." and told my story, often pausing to stare up into the trees, searching for words, filling in background.

As I began following my four days, my internal monitor registered the same lack of self-consciousness I'd felt in every circle. And as before, I was relieved and surprised how little of my urge to keep silent remained.

"I love my life, and even when I complain, I know I've been blessed in many ways. And I'm grateful. Every once in a while, I noticed how easy I was with the fast and felt thankful all over again. I did my ceremonies for the elements, not only in words, but in dances for each one." I glanced over to Jenny, who smiled. "But what I hadn't planned hit me harder. Those things still surprise me, and I have no explanations for them at all. It really was like a mythological window opened up for me."

I told them about the embedded barbed wire; the unsettling sexual earthwork; spilling blood from my cut thumb, nearly fainting; the canyon's psychedelic river of blood; the snake's three appearances with her forked red tongue flicking out, fire emerging from fluidity's mouth; the river's energy flowing through me; spilling menstrual blood in the grove on the morning I walked out.

I described the Death Lodge in detail, starting with my mother, continuing with my father. I told them briefly about his life, his first efforts to be a writer before he gave up and became a lawyer, his sadness.

"My only literal case of writer's block happened when I tried to write about him, last fall," I said. "When he died, my mother found a diary he'd kept from college until he retired—more than forty years. She'd never known about it. Nothing too scandalous, but she wasn't much interested. I sure was. Last year I realized he'd grown up just west of the hundredth meridian, where the West begins. I thought I could write a piece about him and central Nebraska and the West. But when I sat down to do it, I couldn't get one word out. A flat standstill. Stunning. And disturbing. I guess I wasn't ready, but that made it clear how charged he still is for me.

"Finally he gave me his blessing. I was wrecked and about to pack it in, but then my first love showed up. He was a writer for years, too, and also finally got beaten down by external difficulties. We split amicably after sixteen years, but we haven't been in touch for five or six years. It was great to talk to him, too."

I went on to describe my elemental ceremonies, then, "On the third morning, I woke up thinking about Hermes." I described Hermes, but skipped over the connection to Sparrow. "Thinking about Hermes convinced me this quest was not only about water but also fire. Not so much personal relationships or physical passion, but about work. Finding gutsier subjects and putting myself more forward. So I switched the order of my last two ceremonies.

"Fire, even the fire of metabolism—which needs water to burn—is a new lens for me."

I went on for more than an hour, uninterrupted. The attention around the circle carried my sentences like the river had carried the polished branches covered with words: buoying them up, conveying them down-stream and out of sight.

﹠

Sparrow read a poem for the transition into the group's responses, the way he had for everyone else. For me he read one from Rilke: "I want to unfold . . . because where I am folded, there I am a lie."

Doug started, quoting me, "'I was in Nirvana almost the whole time.' Your story was rich in images and messages, and your love for the manifest world was clear. The cleft in the riverbank struck a personal note. My wife's a painter, and a few years ago she started doing life-size canvases with long red flowing images. I'd walk into her studio and get almost physically pushed back, they were so powerfully female.

"Your wounded hand suggests you might want to think more about body responses to landscape, working with more intuitive processes in your work. The snake—the kundalini—seems like a powerful omen to integrate spirit into your writing. You're repelled by traditional symbols of femininity, but I don't quite know what that means." He checked his notes.

"I was grateful for your prayers for me while we were fasting," he said with a wavering voice, and I smiled at him.

"In your Death Lodge, I sensed a huge tension around your

mother—her infuriating way of reducing emotions to Hallmark cards and her distrust of passion. You believe she thinks you're unstable? I'd take that as a great compliment coming from her." We all laughed.

"The interaction with your father was healing. His public side and private side didn't match, but somehow finding the diary reconnected them for you, and your conversation in the Death Lodge continued that process.

"The river's water flowing through you seemed like you claiming your authority. More than before. And hand dancing is a great dancing technique for a fast—so little energy. I really liked your writing on the sticks. You took your mental prayers, made them physical, and sent them into the unknown.

"I thought I heard tears once in a while?" He paused to see if I confirmed that. I didn't. "Or at least a catch in your voice. I'd like to suggest you pay attention to that emotion."

He wound up. "It was an honor to hear your story."

Jenny had been taking notes for me while I watched Doug. He'd been so thorough and perceptive, and so good with his eye contact, I sensed he was growing into his role as "ceremonialist." His response mattered as much for the effort he'd put into it as for the insight he'd given me.

Vern cleared his throat and fingered the antler. "Red water seems like passion flowing into your life. The dream of the pottery says to me you've polished your work. That you had time to think about a mythological figure like Hermes suggests to me you have a lack of conflicts." Oh yeah? I thought. Then he said something that had never occurred to me, but it hit home. "Relating to your mother and father, abused children usually are most attached to the parent who doesn't give them enough love." A new take on my father's distance, my mother's overbearing presence. "And I liked it that you weren't bothered by sleeping through your Purpose Circle."

Next, Sparrow grinned across the circle at me. "It's hard to mirror Nirvana. What can I say? 'Next time it'll be better?' I'm not at all surprised you had a great time. It was a confirmation of what's already present." He paused. "You are whole." He could have said nothing more positive, though it wasn't exactly what I wanted to hear. "I especially liked the oak and barbed wire and how you interpreted it. Your wounds are healed.

"But, luckily for me, I did think of two things to say. One's about your mother and father; the other's about menopause. You can be either the Virgin Mary,"—he paused again—"or Bloody Mary. There's no question which you are." We all laughed. I shrugged my shoulders. I couldn't argue.

"I thought your story about yelling at your mother alone in the middle of the night was great. She may flatten emotions, but there's a sense of fire with her, while there's mostly sadness around your father. And your first love. A lack of warrior mode in both men. Your mother in your dream was even upset you'd smoothed out the effects of fire." I nodded. "So I'd like to challenge you to incorporate your mother. I don't know how you'll do that.

"In terms of menopause, one phase of your life is over. Now, well, what's next? Birth is bloody, painful. The blood from your hand, the blood stream, the blood from your womb—the question is, I guess, what's next to be birthed?

"Think about where are things too smooth, too nice, where's the fire, the passion? Your task is to get down and dirty. Snake has her belly on the earth, grows new skin, new life. And you need to discover how the gods will speak through you. Hermes: a great communicator, but a lying scoundrel. Athena, Aphrodite—they're strong characters. Let them run wild in your work." He grinned again and passed the antler to Chuck.

"Oh!" he blurted. "Can I say one more thing?" Chuck nodded. "Put the nerve back in Nirvana!" We all laughed once more. He might have said, "You can't start a fire / worried about your little world falling apart."

🪶

Chuck's turn. He raised one fist and yelled so it echoed off the canyon's walls, "Yo! Get down, mama!"

Now there was a compliment. I blushed.

"Your story was overflowing with primeval energy. The snake represents knowledge to me. The raw, unglazed pottery had an earthiness you rubbed off—maybe you took it on yourself. Lying by the water is being in two worlds at once. Science and spirit, air and water. There's a great lack of support for scientists who are bridging to the world of spirit. I'm mirroring your mirroring to me. And I loved the Battle of the Hallmark Cards, the war against the conventional. But you should remember that by fighting, you're still allowing yourself to be defined by your rebellion, so watch out!" He looked apologetic. "I haven't got a clue about anything to do with menopause. Sorry. But your father was also a symbol: you were imitating him to get away from your mother's influence."

🪶

Jenny took the antler from Chuck and let it rest on the folds of her skirt. "I saw your story as a confirmation of fluidity. Menopause is a time of power when creativity's held within. But you need to think what you're offering to your community. I honor your integration of masculine and feminine. Your identifying with the masculine is a way to wholeness, but perhaps you should ask yourself the question, 'Did I leave something behind?' I'm thinking here of the barbed wire in the tree. Maybe a way to retrieve what you might have left behind is going through the body." She checked her notes.

"Images of interplay between fire and water. Your mother carries a cultural wound, she's a product of history. You might consider taking your rage in a new direction, to compassion. And maybe offering it to others. Maybe to young girls to help them in this culture.

"The snake is the symbol of the goddess." Ah, Snake, I thought, you're a symbol of nearly everything. "Snake's also the one who wounded Eve. When you're thinking of Athena and Aphrodite, remember that later images are encased in patriarchy. Look back to their earlier versions." She smiled. I smiled. And we leaned toward each other and hugged.

"Words?" Sparrow asked me.

"Thanks," I started, "You all have definitely brought up things that hadn't occurred to me." But I didn't want to talk, I wanted to pass out my strange presents.

"What I do all the time is collect things and make things. And I brought back some odd objects for you guys." And I handed them out. Chuck's pierced bird's sternum; Jenny's willow, grass, and spun wool basket with a small clear crystalline stone from beside the river of blood; Doug's very funky box-without-walls tied with wool and dental floss; Vern's four-part bundle; and Sparrow's poem. While I'd waited for Vern, I'd memorized it and now spoke it to Sparrow without consulting my notes. After four lines, he shifted and relaxed, giving up his serious guide look. It took some guts: a public recitation of a poem about the canyon but also about my attraction for Sparrow. I tore out the page from my journal and handed it to him.

Not only didn't I want to talk, I wasn't entirely sure I wanted to mull over their responses, though it had been a great pleasure to hear them. The interchanges—whichever end I'd been on—had not been at all fraught, except in anticipation. They'd been rich and compelling, and, yes, erotic. Yet curiously they were real and not real at once. These weren't people in my life. Real relationships, but only for the moment, except perhaps Sparrow.

Incorporate your mother, Sparrow had said. Now we *did* have a real relationship. I might be able to do that through music. But passion, fire, nerve were ambiguous terms, and I sensed everyone—maybe even including Sparrow—inferred a sexual meaning. I didn't mind; in fact, I agreed. No one had asked me about my love life. Nor did anyone know the crucial role the sexual had played in my life. I'd not mentioned the creativity/sexuality/spirituality framework to anyone. Had I once again been open, but not open enough? The appearance of openness, but not where it mattered? Had anyone? But I had been open with Sparrow around the fire.

Quest. Hunt, pursuit, search, trail, track, trace.

Quest. To seek, to ask. To court.

Quest. Chivalrous enterprise in medieval romance, usually involving an adventurous journey.

Nonrational. Spirit. Muse.

Time would tell.

🍃

We'd made it. Almost.

After a late lunch, our final task. Sparrow had words and warnings for us about returning to our lives. About incorporation.

🍃

Abandon your life for a time, enter a realm of mysteries and dangers, and return. But return with a gift for the community you temporarily left: the head of the monster, the magical wand, the secret of flight, the ability to read minds, the flute that will bring rain to the desert. Bring back the peach twig to start an orchard, potatoes from the Andes, tea from China, the key to the Nazi's secret code, quinine. If you're Walt Whitman, bring back *Song of Myself*; if you're Rilke, bring back *Sonnets to Orpheus*; if you're Allen Ginsberg, bring back *Howl*.

If you've spent ten days in the Gila Wilderness on a vision quest, your personal desire may be to return changed, but your mythological requirement is also to return with a gift.

Sparrow's definition of gift fit less the secret formula for Patagonia fleece and more the compassion of Nelson Mandela or the poems of Neruda. "It's not a thing and it's not martyrdom," he said. "The most powerful gift to your people is most fully embodying yourself. Of course you have to find out who you are first. But after that, the gift you take back is the expansion of your identity and a recognition of interdependence, whether you're a nurse or a poet or a shaman or a chef."

Easy to say, but its value lay not in its comforting apparent achievability but in the way it tilted the prism slightly: from personal transformation, period, to personal transformation that included the well-being of others. And that tilt expanded our focus to include both outer and inner.

We'd all "fully embody ourselves" if we could. But the gap remains between declaring, "I will now walk on my hands up the back stairs," and actually doing it. Not an impossible feat—not like saying "I'll levitate myself up the back stairs without touching them"—but not a snap, either.

I'd spent ten days watching myself and four others alternately struggle and glide through a world rich with nature and rich with human interactions. But this world in the Gila resembled our real lives less than a galloping horse resembles a Ford Mustang.

And the time had come for us to go home. After the realm of the Mysteries where trees and hawks communicated important messages to us, we'd return to a realm where *Obsession* meant a perfume, *Memory* referred to computer hardware, and *Quest* was a consulting firm that ran seminars for middle management. More relevantly, we would return to many of the same conditions that had blocked us from "fully embodying ourselves" in the first place.

Sparrow warned us about the blank stares we'd likely get when we mentioned we'd not eaten for four days on purpose, about the people who would actively ridicule us, and about the depression that would almost inevitably afflict us sometime—in a month, three months. ("Where did that great feeling go?" "Did that make any difference at all?") We'd be afflicted at least for a while. But he also gave us practical suggestions for making the leap to a changed life: return with a strategy, be wily; write a letter of intent about returning and use it as a rudder; ground the changes physically with concrete objects and places.

Kit had used me as a stepping stone: he'd practiced telling his story to me before he flew home. Though I knew I'd been a useful, sympathetic ear, I didn't know how useful until I faced the same transition myself.

In late afternoon light filtering through the cottonwoods, we all took notes for the last time. A pair of light-breasted birds flew over with quick wing beats—peregrines most likely—and a pickup with an empty horse trailer bumped and rattled down the dirt road on the other side of the Mimbres.

"Seeing the world as it is or yourself as you are doesn't necessarily make you happier," Sparrow said. "I got a letter from a woman who'd been on a quest in the Gila last October. She drove to the edge of her hometown and realized her whole life was empty. The return can be hard."

He talked awhile longer, his concern for us clear. Finally he said, "Thank you all for letting me share with you what's been so important to me." And for the first time, his eyes reddened, and he lowered his head, ambushed by his own emotions. Then he said, thickly, "I wish I could think of a joke . . ." And that was a joke. We laughed for the hundredth time. Or the thousandth.

We'd just been warned of multiple dangers, inevitable depression. We'd just been told the quest really lasted a year. But for a short while we still laughed in a communal dreamscape, even though everything in the dream had solid substance, from the sun and shadows to our sparking neural pathways. The real.

Real didn't mean not sentimental, though, and when we stood in a tight circle for some last songs, we squabbled about what to sing. Our arms overlapped, resting on shoulders, on waists. I stood to Sparrow's right, his hand just under my right armpit. Over Vern's mild objections, we finally settled on "Amazing Grace" and "Happy Trails." Group hug, our bill caps bumping into each other. Break.

"That was the hokiest ten minutes I've spent in a long time," said Chuck. "But good," he added quickly, not wanting to offend. My own hokey detector didn't even register a blip.

We took down our tents, stuffed our sleeping bags, packed our kitchen gear, hugged each other good-bye one at a time. Jenny took off first to meet her sister and go soak at the hot springs in Ojo Caliente north of Santa Fe. Everyone else had planes to catch early the next morning. Except me. Chuck and Vern drove out.

Sparrow hugged me and said, "*Vaya con Dios*. Go with God." He kissed my cheek. He said again, "Vaya con Dios. Go with God." Then, insistent, into my ear, "Will you write me?"

I said only, "Yes." Doug already sat in the car. Two minutes later, they drove out, with my pickup close behind.

My white-water rafting friend Stephen says, "Never go straight home after a river trip." No way I'd go straight home.

At the dusty Geronimo Trail, Sparrow and Doug turned left toward the interstate; I turned right heading toward Wall Lake and watched their dust disappear in my rearview mirror. About ten miles up at a high spot, I angled off on a short spur road. At one side, a small meadow tilted east, but mostly ponderosas and junipers surrounded me, silent in the last sunlight. No laughing Mimbres, no laughing friends, not even any laughing ravens. For the first time in years, I couldn't abide the forest's rich silence and slipped on headphones. Hamza El Din's melancholy oud soothed me. In 1964 his Nubian homeland had been flooded by the Aswan Dam, his people exiled from their lives along the River Nile. I felt exiled myself, torn from a place that had been like home, at least for a while. Dark began to gather at the meadow's far side. Shadows lost their edges and flowed into each other.

I split an avocado, dribbled vinegar and soy sauce into the center hollows, and spoonful by spoonful slowly scooped out the soft green flesh. I crawled into my sleeping bag.

Twelve hours later I woke, made tea, then sat in my folding chair staring into the trees. I stared. I got up for more tea. I stared. I got up to pee. I stared for five hours.

No clear thoughts. Just staring. Slowly I began to think again. What had happened?

Had the wind along the Gila torn away any of my distance? Had my neural pathways been loosened and reestablished into new shapes? Had anyone else's life been jolted in a better direction? Had I known the canyon differently for my altered state, for my intentions, for my predisposition to mythological experience? Had the canyon known *me*? Had my deep but brief contacts with the others affected any of us? Had I lessened the effect of the fast by my skepticism? Had I subverted my experience by my unexpected focus on Sparrow? Had I learned anything with my mind? Had I learned anything with my body? *What was my gift?*

Myths include moments that divide past from future like seismic fractures. Before Sparrow had talked about the return to our lives, he'd read us "The Return," another Mary Oliver poem. On his classical hero's journey, Theseus has just killed the Minotaur in the Labyrinth. He's trailed the thread Ariadne had given him in love, a way to return to the world. But in battle with the monster, he'd forgotten it. Coming to himself, limp with exhaustion, he sees the delicate thread and sobs. He follows it back through cold black passageways dense with damp vapors, boulders toppling about him, the ground shuddering.

And the thread held.

The thread. We could find our way back into the world. Perhaps we could also bring the Gila with us.

Seven years have passed since I fasted along the Gila and shared stories with those hopeful folks. I can't be sure what might have been different in my life had I not joined Sparrow's quest, but these things have happened.

- My initial return didn't match Sparrow's warnings. I encountered no "blank stares" from friends. Usually they listened carefully to my story and responded with variations of "Wild. I've always thought those things were a little flaky. If anyone else had told me this, I'm not sure I'd have believed them. But I know who you are, and I believe you. What a thing!" I didn't sink into depression, in a week, or three months, or eighteen months. Not at all.

- My mother surprised me most. When I visited her and my stepfather in Florida for Thanksgiving the month after the quest, I cooked a series of dinners for them in their small apartment. For several nights running, after we'd eaten, I asked my mother some simple questions about her early years. Instead of retreating to her past reticence, she reeled out story after story for many hours with only a few prompts from me. As my stepfather and I sat in rapt attention, my astonishment matched my deep interest. But only after I'd returned home did I see that while I had intended to free my own voice in the Gila, I had inadvertently freed *her* voice. Since then, we've been much easier with each other.

- Eventually other knots began to loosen. For some years, I'd thought of buying a house but perceived a mortgage as a gigantic anchor, a house as a draining responsibility. I now own an old renovated adobe farmhouse along with a big barn for my studio. The house and barn and garden don't feel at all like traps. They feel like home.

- My nervier voice got a chance to test its strength. The house and acre of land I bought is in Albuquerque's South Valley—a semirural area known for its lively population of old New Mexicans, new Hispanic immigrants, and a smattering of Anglos. Soon after I moved in, I found myself deeply embroiled in a fight against a proposed Super Wal-Mart a mile from my house. Eventually, along with another activist, I wrote the appeal to the Environmental Planning Commission's approval of the project. Despite my fearful hesitations, I represented the opposition and presented the appeal to the Albuquerque City Council. By the time I stood at the podium in the council meeting, I felt only exhilaration. Though the Wal-Mart has now been built, the group that formed around the appeal has successfully stopped further inappropriate steamroller development in the neighborhood.

- Just after the quest, I'd rhetorically asked myself, "What is my gift?" I knew two of my "gifts to my people" had long been my skills as an artist and my capacities to find solutions to design problems. I also knew that a more valuable gift—and one that offered me more satisfaction—might be my voice on paper. Although I'd written my effulgences with no thought they'd ever become public, many did find their way into a book and out into the world. That self-exposure surpassed any public openness I'd ever contemplated. And, of course, the most direct gift is this tale of the quest.

- Another kink shook out: with a friend who's a more experienced educator, I've co-taught a seminar at the University of New Mexico, helping students use poetry to track their lives and beliefs. Not a vision quest, but as insistently informed by metaphor.

- Sparrow and I did spend some months in convoluted explorations of a romance between the guide and the guided. Eventually the complexities and our essential mismatch scuttled the affair. But our friendship persists, relaxed and open. He visits whenever he's in New Mexico, several times a year.

- Kit, my old doctor friend who triggered the whole thing, has largely sorted out his life in Massachusetts. After some complicated and unpredicted choreography, four years ago he began living with me in Albuquerque. He's the best "medicine animal" I can imagine. When Kit moved in, so did a small grey schnauzer named Gunther, a guileless, loyal creature who unexpectedly awakened my latent maternal instincts.

"I can tell you the whole story," Kit began his tale to me after his miserable fast along the Chama.

Sparrow urged us on in the Gila, "The story we tell almost becomes our experience."

None of us, of course, can tell another the whole story; and the substitution of story for experience inevitably brings up the limitations of language. Representation with words can never capture the entire physical, emotional, memory-washed reality of a life, even a carefully excised segment of that life. And, as I noted when I first began research into quests, stories can be templates to normalize what seems dangerous. Shoehorn the inexplicable or the subversive into a known framework, and it becomes tolerable. Either one can also lose its power. But despite these caveats, story remains the most effective way we have to order experience and to communicate with each other.

My own attitude about the quest changed from skeptical sophistication to earnest credulity as the experience/story moved along. Some years ago, that whiff of naïveté brought me disbelief and mockery at

Bread Loaf Writers' Conference, where I'd taken a small section of an earlier version of this piece.

"I've seen things like that myself in the backcountry," the workshop leader, a well-known nonfiction writer said, frowning. "Often. And those wilderness guides always have affairs. I could understand it in a twenty-year-old, but not from you. Even twenty-year-olds know the score these days. Did this happen recently?" When I answered yes, she shook her head in mute distaste.

She'd not stopped me. By then I'd grown beyond either denying my own adventures or keeping quiet about them. But she did make me more aware of how dismissive many people would be. I'd once been dismissive myself.

The story we tell almost becomes our experience. The quest, by definition, is a story. But, as Sparrow observed, it's also a dream. And dreams are psychic realities that can leave physical traces that change the dreamer. The story I made of the quest stands as its record, but the physical fallout expanded far beyond my shaping mind. Whether my neural pathways had been reconfigured or something more mysterious had freed my voice, released me from self-protective fear, I still can't say for certain.

More than anything, I learned the usefulness of a childlike open-heartedness. I don't mean the narrow sentimentality often associated with remembered childhood itself, but a belief that what might be labeled fantastic can sometimes offer deeper truths and realer images. These truths and images, given the right conditions, can break open more rigid forms and behaviors. And I reconfirmed that nature always offers a realm free of contrived, deadening tactics, whether it's part of structured time, or simply itself, in all its complexity.

The quest gave me a chance to continue along a path I'd already begun, in a way I couldn't have predicted. But more than that, it enveloped me in transformative good fortune, in innocence regained.

Acknowledgments

Although I often hike alone, I never write alone, even if it looks that way from the outside. I want to thank not only friends who have helped directly with this book but also those who have, in more nonlinear ways, made this journey possible.

Poet and scholar Barrett Price started me on this writing road and helped me find my voice by his attentive listening and careful responses over fifteen years. He's been an open door into many realms, and, more than anyone, he has given me the confidence to keep on my rambling path.

Poet and thinker Craig Watson has hung in over the long haul and has joined me in many concentrated conversations about, among other things, meaning and language, chance and art, wild weather, world music, emergency management, political strategies, and camping gear.

Writer David Guy's intrepid honesty about many matters, his clear mind, his smooth prose, and his long-standing encouragement have been invaluable.

Media scholar Susan Douglas has always inspired me with her coherent understandings of innumerable complicated matters, beginning when we shared an apartment with two others while we were both in school. Her capacity to retain her incredible good humor in the face of almost anything has influenced me more than she knows. I thank her for her friendship and help over many years and changing situations, and for uncountable excellent recipes.

Christine Rack's devotion to finding fair solutions, honest expression, and ways to greater peace persuades me that hope in the future is justified. I'm grateful for her support and loyalty for nearly all my time in New Mexico.

Sculptor Eve Andrée Laramée helpfully opened her New Mexico Rolodex to me long ago, and she continues to hearten me by what she does to act on her belief that words, images, ideas, and the land belong together.

Anne Batterson shared her excitement about Bread Loaf Writers' Conference with me and offered essential feedback at a crucial juncture.

Michael Brondoli was a boon companion on many of my earliest hikes, and he showed me how rich the world could be.

Mark Perry shared many adventures in wet climates and dry and convinced me that if you're flexible enough, you'll always land on your feet.

Sparrow Hart triggered unexpected curiosity and still offers ongoing voyages into territory where the rational and nonrational mingle.

In addition to many of the above friends, others read various versions of these pieces and offered crucial responses: Paul Birkeland, Pamela Westfall-Bochte and Bruce Bochte, Beth Heard Guy, Marianne Spitzform, Douglass Rankin and Will Ruggles, Debbie Weissman and Kayte Blanke, and Martie Zelt.

I owe much to my writing teachers. Reynolds Price whetted my appetite for word projects decades before I finally settled down to serious writing. Garrett Hongo confirmed my belief that writing poetry and writing nonfiction are deeply compatible and suggested a fruitful approach to both. Pat Mora gave me well-considered readings and helpful criticism. Vivian Gornick kept me on my toes by being smart and tough. And I especially thank Richard Nelson for his giving heart and his reverent and practical attitudes toward writing, life, and the natural world.

My two favorite dance teachers, Joy Kellman and Nora Reynolds Daniel, continually reminded me how much my body could learn on its own.

Amy Baker's energetic enthusiasm for art, especially artists' books, enriches the world. I thank her for publishing my artist's book *LAND* just as I was migrating west.

Janet Ross and the Four Corners School of Outdoor Education provided a spectacular trip on the upper Colorado to monitor eagles and peregrine falcons.

The Southern Utah Wilderness Alliance works hard every day to protect Utah wilderness. I'm grateful for the chance they offered me to lobby Congress on behalf of that incomparable land.

I thank Zuni Pueblo, the Zuni Sustainable Agriculture Project (ZSAP), and especially the Zuni men who helped with the corn harvest described in "Zuni Maize." They welcomed me as a fellow worker and paid me the ultimate compliment, "She gets it." Thanks to Carol Brandt who originally opened my eyes to agroecology. Jeff Homburg reviewed an early version of "Zuni Maize." Without Deb Muenchrath and her love of corn, I never would have spent time at Zuni. Beyond the gratitude I owe her for that trip, I owe her special thanks for her example as a thinker who could glimpse the big picture through small details. Her untimely death saddens me and leaves the world much poorer.

Nancy Rutland keeps Bookworks, my favorite independent bookstore, going strong.

Many others have supported me over the years in diverse and indispensable ways. I especially thank Marsha and John Beckelman, Jennifer Hamlin Church, Bruce Daniel, T. R. Durham, Libby Foster, Linnea Gentry, Bennett Hammer, Trica Oshant Hawkins, Barbara Hockfield, Lisa Houck, Dana Howlett, Joanna Hurley, Betsy James, Lisabeth Kirk, Jeff Klas, Brigitte Felix Kludt and Trevor Kludt, Jack Lenor Larsen, Nicky Leach, Colleen Lynch, Lisa Madsen, Stephen Maurer, Baker Morrow, Debra Netkin, Shawn Nordell, Stacy Pearl, Ruth and Lou Perry, Rini Price, Judy Propper, Rod Replogle, Lulu Santamaria, Jeanette Sarbo, Dan Shaffer, Kathleen Shields, Dave Southern, and Deborah Tuck.

Thanks to UNM Press director Luther Wilson for having faith in me, to Mina Yamashita for her elegant sense of design and for her infallible eye for color, and to UNM Press's hardworking staff, especially Maya Allen-Gallegos, Katherine MacGilvray, Glenda Madden, and Amanda

Sutton. A special thanks to Carole Smidt for her helpful attention to grammatical details.

And finally, thanks to my family:

My late father, Paul Robert Beath, always believed in me, and he passed on his progressive politics, his love of books and ideas, and a barely acknowledged urge to head west.

My mother, Phoebe Beath Catlin, has always been on my side, no matter how odd she thought my pursuits. I'm grateful to her for some of my best qualities. It's taken me some years to realize they came from her. Her love has been unwavering.

My grandparents, Ethel and J. P. Carter, created a comforting, down-home nest when I was a child.

My aunt and uncle, Helen and Berry Elliott, stirred my desire for open spaces when they gave me the chance to roam on their Missouri farm, summer after summer.

My stepfather, Glenn Catlin, embraced me as his second daughter from the beginning, and he continues to energize me with his love of all creation.

Atossa and David French have recently welcomed me into their family with a warmth that pleases me enormously and enriches my life.

Gunther, the small grey schnauzer who shares my days, never loses his sense of self and makes it clear that emotional connection doesn't rely on books.

Kit French now often joins me on trails out to familiar or unknown destinations. These days, even when I hike alone, my trails home lead to him. Thanks Kit, for being there.

Designed and typeset by Mina Yamashita
Text composed in Optima Std, a typeface designed by
Herman Zapf for the Stempel Foundry in 1958.
Display composed in Bodoni Std, originally designed by
Giambattista Bodoni at the end of the eighteenth century.
This version of Bodoni was first created by Morris Fuller
Benton for American Type Founders between 1908 and 1915.

Printed by Thomson-Shore, Inc. on 55# Natures Natural.